The New
Dow Jones-Irwin Guide
to Real Estate Investing

The New Dow Jones-Irwin Guide to Real Estate Investing

Gaylon Greer

Fogelman Chair of Excellence in Real Estate
Memphis State University

DOW JONES-IRWIN
Homewood, Illinois 60430

Project editor: Jane Lightell
Production manager: Ann Cassady
Designer: Keith McPherson
Compositor: Publication Services, Inc.
Typeface: 11/13 Century Schoolbook
Printer: R. R. Donnelley & Sons

Library of Congress Cataloging-in-Publication Data

Greer, Gaylon E.
    The new Dow Jones-Irwin guide to real estate
investing.

    Includes index.
    1. Real estate investment.   I. Title.
HD1382.5.G745   1989   332.63'24   88–33450
ISBN 1-55623-085-0

For Maegen, who is just getting started

PREFACE

Is this book really necessary? With book stores already over-burdened, what more can possibly be said about real estate investment? More to the point, why should you bother to read further?

Immersed in the plethora of verbal effluent that passes for bookbound investment wisdom are several legitimate real estate guides. But, because they are intended as university textbooks, they are ponderous and often pedantic. At the other extreme is an epidemic of "easy reader" books that tell you virtually nothing. This book combines the best of both, packaging essential technical information from university texts in an approach and style that won't put you to sleep.

There's more. Textbooks tell you how to do market and property analysis, but skimp on where to get vital data. This book doesn't leave you hanging like that. Interspersed throughout are titles of data compendiums and names and addresses (and, sometimes, telephone numbers) of firms that will generate information for you. Just about any data you can use have already been collected somewhere; this book tells you where to look.

Along the way the book discusses relative performance characteristics of different kinds of real estate assets. It tells you what you must do to consistently clock above average yields and alerts you to investment proposals that offer more froth than substance

After reading this book you will understand what infor mation is vital to intelligent real estate investment decisions, where to get the information, and what to do with it. You will know how to make your money work for you in the real estate market at a risk level you select and with a degree of personal involvement appropriate for you

ACKNOWLEDGMENTS

Special recognition is due to Michael Farrell (recently deceased), my coauthor in numerous other projects, for the time we have spent discussing ideas that form this book's core. Thanks also to the family of Morris S. Fogelman and to Memphis State University for financial support that provided time for writing.

TABLE OF CONTENTS

CHAPTER 1

THE REAL ESTATE INVESTMENT DECISION

Modern investment markets are infected with a product proliferation virus. Faster than facts can be digested, self-anointed savants tout new investment schemes, each promising to cure its predecessor's defects. Yet, instead of the promised panacea, each introduces pitfalls of its own. The motivation for this madness is obvious; there's a lot of money to be made pandering to the public's longing for the big score, the deal that delivers on the promise of sky-high yields with zero risk.

So what if logic tells us that riskless investments can't yield more than a nominal rate of return, that competition for assets drives yields to about the same level on deals that carry nearly equal risk? What has logic to do with it, anyway? Hucksters sell dreams, not logic.

So it goes. Ventures blossom and wither. With garbage-laden portfolios, investors enter a winter of repentance vowing never again to be seduced by the twin sirens of fear and greed. But then comes the financial spring, and winter garments of repentance are cast off in favor of new "once-in-a-lifetime" opportunities.

Yet, amid all the fluff and bluster, there are timeless opportunities that pass in and out of fashion, but whose luster never permanently fades. This book is about the granddaddy of investment perennials. "Invest in land," said Will Rogers, "they're not making any more of it."

THE AWFUL TRUTH ABOUT REAL ESTATE

A plague of books promising fiscal nirvana notwithstanding, real estate is no sure route to riches. The cityscape is littered with schemes gone awry, and every economic downturn spawns splashy stories about defunct developers. Even in the best of times real estate has a way of roughing up people who buy without doing their homework.

Yet, money *is* made in real estate—lots of money. Much of it is made fleecing naïve amateurs who digest the "get rich quick" pabulum dispensed in hotel ballrooms and on cable television channels by pitchmen who, in a different era, would have sold miracle elixirs to cure every ailment. The world-class swaths are cut, however, by daring, imaginative investors and entrepreneurs who learn how to create and exploit opportunities.

Real Estate Investment Alternatives

Don't underestimate the range of real estate investment options. Virtually any investment goal you care to pursue can be accommodated with a real estate–related asset. You can speculate in real estate futures (by buying and selling purchase options), you can hedge your position (with standby loan commitments, for example), you can buy fixed-income assets (mortgage loans, net leased properties); the possibilities are in fact constrained only by your ability to conceive of alternatives. In short, people who think investing means buying stocks, bonds, and related securities should consider real estate a supplement if not an alternative.

Popular mythology has it that recent tax law changes have destroyed real estate's tax shelter role. Don't believe it. New rules have drastically altered how the game is played and have largely accomplished their objective of curbing the most flagrant abuses, but they did not eliminate opportunities to generate untaxed real estate revenue. Thus, even though its benefit has always been overrated, tax shelter still awaits those who seek it.

Real estate is even more promising if you don't approach it

as an investment at all, but as a business opportunity. Enterprises that incorporate a hefty dose of real estate combine the best elements of investment with the advantages of entrepreneurial profit potential.

Figure 1–1 characterizes real estate investment gambits according to the degrees of involvement investors have in operations and by the nature of their claims. Let's move clockwise

Figure 1–1
Real Estate Investment Alternatives

	Passive	Active
Debt	Pass -Through Securities Real Estate Investment Trusts Real Estate Mortgage Investment Conduits	Mortgage Origination Secondary Mortgage Market
Equity	Limited Partnerships Master Limited Partnerships Real Estate Investment Trusts	Direct Real Estate Ownership: Apartment Buildings Shopping Centers Offices Industrial Parks Warehouses Other

around the diagram, starting with the upper left quadrant: Passive positions in real estate–related credit instruments. Your securities broker will be happy to accommodate you if you want to put money in any of a plethora of assets in this box. The common denominator of the alternatives is that you hold a small interest (either directly or indirectly) in a basket of mortgage-secured promissory notes. Pass-through securities, Real Estate Mortgage Investment Conduits (REMICs), or shares of real estate investment trusts that own mortgage notes are the most common examples of indirect investment in mortgage debt. Each is discussed in greater detail in later chapters.

As an active investor in real estate–related debt, you will either originate mortgage-secured loans or will buy mortgage-secured notes on the secondary market. This is a potentially lucrative way of participating in local real estate markets and is discussed in more detail in Chapter Ten.

Active investment in real estate equities implies a direct ownership interest in real property, with operational control, either directly or through hired management. Yields very much depend on how efficiently you operate the property. This book is devoted almost entirely to this approach because, as Willy Sutton explained when asked why he robbed banks, "That's where the money is."

Equity investment without management authority leaves you at the mercy of your investment's sponsor. Common examples include limited partnership shares in real estate syndicates and master limited partnerships (see Chapter Fourteen) or ownership shares in real estate investment trusts that own real estate equities (see Chapter Fifteen).

How Do You Measure Success?

Yield expectations are clouded by, among other things, a lack of uniform definitions. *Yield* is the percentage rate of return on an investment, usually expressed in annual terms. *Annualized yield* would be more descriptive and perhaps less confusing, but we are stuck with the common usage of yield to mean the rate of return expressed on a per-annum basis. Proper use of yield terminology is imperative if you are to avoid a common investment pitfall. Those who would lead you astray often try to muddy the analytical waters by misusing the yield concept. For example, if a venture doubles your money in just eight years, you will have earned 100 percent on your investment; your annualized yield, however, is a relatively modest 9 percent. If you invest $100 for one week and get $108 back, you earned 8 percent. On an annualized basis, however, your yield is about 416 percent.

Yield, in this book at least, means the discount rate that makes the present value of net cash receipts (either before or after adjusting for income taxes) exactly equal to the amount of your initial cash investment. Think of it, if you wish, as the interest rate, had you put your money on deposit, that would net you annual interest income equal to the expected net cash receipts from the investment.

Don't let the arithmetic throw you; the idea is simple. If a property costs $200,000 and generates about $20,000 per year after all operating expenses are paid, the current yield (before income taxes) is about 10 percent. If the $20,000 per year of cash flow is expected to continue indefinitely, the average annual before-tax yield is also about 10 percent; if the cash flow is expected to either grow or decline over time, the annual yield will differ from the current yield.

Most people don't plan to own property forever, and their average annual yield will of course be influenced by net cash receipts from selling. This complicates the math, but not the concept. Average annual yield is still the rate that will enable an initial investment to generate annual cash flows (whether comprised entirely of interest or of a combination of interest income and return of part of your initial investment) and leave on deposit at the end of the investment period an amount equal to the expected net cash flow from selling the property. We will look more closely at the arithmetic in Chapter Six and Appendix A.

How Well Do Real Estate Investments Do?

There is no concrete answer for what sort of average annual yield you should expect. It depends on the type of investment position you take, on when you make your investment, and when you close out your position.

When markets function as economists tell us they should, yield possibilities are directly related to associated risk. From the perspective of classical economics, however, real estate markets are notoriously ill mannered. *Market anomaly* is an overused euphemism that means real estate prices don't always fully reflect the properties' ability to generate income. If you are in a position to exploit anomalies, your yield will be entirely unrelated to any historical trend.

If you elect to be actively involved in property operations, a second imponderable surfaces. How much of your income is a return on the property itself, and how much is compensation for your time and effort? If an allocation of this sort is attempted, average annual yields on the investment will depend in part on the imputed value of your time.

Consider all this a precautionary preface. The market for large commercial properties works reasonably well, and such properties are almost always professionally managed. Historical yields from these types of properties, therefore, are instructive.

Real estate outperformed the stock market so spectacularly during the 1970s that it attracted a large following among institutional investors. One particular relationship that was born of this new era is the Commingled Real Estate Fund (CREF), established to purchase and monitor the operation of real estate on behalf of such institutional investors as pension funds. CREFs have given researchers a trove of new information about real estate's performance. Two recent studies are particularly enlightening.

Data from two of the oldest CREFs were analyzed by William Brueggeman, A. H. Chen, and T. G. Thibodeau, who reported their findings in the Fall 1984 issue of *AREUEA Journal*.[1] These two CREFs, one operated by a bank and the other by an insurance company, accounted at the time for about 25 percent of all CREF assets in the country.

---

[1]*AREUEA Journal*, vol. 12, no. 3 (Fall, 1984), pp 333–54.

One unsurprising discovery was that the relative performance of real estate and other investments depends on the period over which results are measured. Brueggeman and his colleagues measured CREF performance from 1972 through 1983. They broke the data into various subperiods to see whether comparative results varied significantly through time.

Over the entire 12-year period, average quarterly yields were higher for real estate than for widely employed indices of stocks (the Standard & Poor's 500 stock index) and bonds (R. G. Ibbotson Associates). Real estate also substantially outperformed stocks and bonds during the 1972 to 1977 subperiod.

From 1978 through 1983, the researchers found the average yield on the Standard & Poor's 500 stock index exceeded that of the CREF real estate portfolios by a narrow margin. Yet, when risk was introduced into the equation, performance even during this subperiod shifted in favor of real estate. The measure of risk employed in the study, and one that is widely employed and almost universally accepted by academics and investment professionals alike, was standard deviation of returns, a standardized measure of variation from the mean.

To adjust yields for risk differentials the researchers employed the *coefficient of variation*, a simple technique that involves dividing standard deviation of yields by their mean. When adjusted in this manner, the real estate portfolios outperformed the Standard & Poor's 500 by a considerable margin in each subperiod as well as over the entire period. When they used more sophisticated approaches to risk adjustment the researchers found real estate continued to outperform both stocks and bonds.

It is important to note that CREFs do not use borrowed money. If the benefits of borrowing were incorporated into the analysis, the balance would tilt even more decisively in favor of real estate in the Brueggeman, Chen, and Thibodeau study.

A second study, this one by Roger Ibbotson and Laurence Siegel, attempted to compare average annual returns of real estate and stocks from 1947 through 1982.[2] The Ibbotson and

---

[2]Ibid, pp. 219–42.

Siegel study is biased against real estate because it includes farms and residential dwellings yet does not adjust for their rental value. Even so, the study concludes that real estate yields, before incorporating special income tax advantages and without adjusting for the benefits of borrowing, are only slightly below stock yields and are significantly less risky (standard deviation of 17.5 percent for stocks, compared with only 3.7 percent for real estate).

AN ESSAY ON COMMON SENSE

Fundamentally, investing means buying a set of assumptions about the stream of benefits your investment will generate. Ordinarily, the greater the anticipated benefit stream, the more valuable the investment. Expectations, however, have a way of periodically running amuck.

You put money into a deal with the expectation of getting back even more. Where does the "more" come from? Ultimately, the only source of benefits from rental property is net rental income. In that context, it is easy to see that the price you pay is the capitalized value of the property's future income. The larger and longer lasting the expected income stream, and the more certain you can be that the stream will actually materialize, the greater the capitalized value.

Am I forgetting the importance of a property's appreciation potential? No. Remember that value is nothing more than the market's expression of the worth today of anticipated future cash flow from net rental income. If you expect price appreciation, then you must at least implicitly expect that the future net rental income will increase, that the cost of capital will drop significantly, or that future buyers will act irrationally.

Perhaps the best way to visualize this is to review the price behavior of a blue chip nonconvertible preferred stock. Such a security is the closest readily available approximation of a perpetual annuity. Its price will fluctuate basically for two reasons: (1) because of a shift in the market's perception of the firm's ability to continue honoring its dividend obligation or (2) because of a shift in the general consensus about the cost of funds.

When Prices Go Haywire

Rational expectations is an economic theory that says asset prices are determined by investors' expectations about the assets' income potential. If investors act rationally, the theory tells us, prices will change only with altered earnings expectations or with changes in the cost of capital. Disparate income expectations or disagreement about capital cost will cause prices to fluctuate, but, to the extent everyone is operating with essentially the same information, the fluctuations should occur in a narrow range. Only new information about income or capital costs will dictate a substantive shift in the range.

The Wall Street Journal (November 17, 1987) reports research that explains why markets stubbornly refuse to behave the way economists' rational expectations theory tells us they should. In laboratory experiments, traders—novices and veterans alike—regularly drove prices far above and far below what rational expectations dictated.

Acting solely on information about recent income and sales prices, players of a market simulation game factored in not only assets' income streams but also expected sales prices derived by extrapolating trends. In game after game, players gradually drove prices far above what income expectations alone would justify. Then, when prices reached such lofty heights that purchase offers began to dry up, would-be sellers started discounting their properties in an effort to cut losses. They acted like crowds at a theater fire; they all started running for the same exit. A crash ensued, and prices quickly dipped below those justified by expected income streams.

In this manner market "bubbles" occurred repeatedly in the laboratory trading experiments. "We find that inexperienced market participants never trade consistently near fundamental value," a researcher reported. Typically, he said, traders have to go through two cycles of boom and crash before they learn to act rationally. In the third trial of the experiment most traders tended to limit their offers to prices near fundamental value as dictated by assets' earning potential. When all participants in the experiments were permitted to continue for a third round, market bubbles either failed to materialize or were insignificant in size.

The investigators concluded that market bubbles and subsequent crashes can be caused by nothing more substantial than traders' tendency to speculate. By basing their trades on price trends rather than on the relationship between cost of capital and an asset's income potential, they drive prices to unsustainable levels. Then, by trying to bail out when prices begin to stagnate, they ensure the market collapse they are trying to avoid.

Bubbles and subsequent crashes would be far less prevalent in the real world if traders stayed in the game long enough to learn from experience. The problem is that the time from one market bottom to the next is so long that few participants ever go through more than one full cycle. Each generation has to learn by bitter experience what its predecessor already knows but cannot convey convincingly to the upstarts.

Do real estate prices move in cycles reminiscent of the laboratory researchers' boom and bust experiment? The available evidence suggests that they do, but nobody really knows for certain. Research has been hampered by lack of information about real estate prices and earnings over extended periods.

Early work on real estate cycles was limited to observations about the number of transactions, adjusted for the number of families in the metropolitan areas included in statistical tests. These studies revealed an apparent cycle of about 18.5 years from peak to peak. Researchers could only infer that prices followed transactions, reaching a peak when trading was at its briskest.

During the post–World War II period, the United States Council on Life Insurance began collecting data on real estate. They now regularly report the relationship between purchase prices and current operating income for properties on which member firms provide mortgage loans. This ratio, called the *overall capitalization rate*, is determined by dividing a property's operating income by its price. Average capitalization rates ranged from a low of 7.4 percent (in 1951) to a high of 10.8 percent (in 1970 and again in 1975); approximately a 50 percent variation over the base year 1951.

Stock market veterans will find capitalization rates a strange measure. They are accustomed to price/earnings ratios as a performance indicator. Yet the two statistics are essentially the same; they are in fact reciprocals. Inverting the capitalization rate's elements, therefore, we find that price/earnings ratios on real estate financed by life insurance companies ranged from 13.5/1 through 9.3/1.

An index of capitalization rates (or, by inverting the factors, an index of price/earnings ratios) tells us something about current yields and about price behavior. The cyclical movement of capitalization rates suggests that real estate prices do swing, over the years, above and below what can usefully be called a fundamental relationship between price and income—that is, a *fundamental value.*

WHAT MUST I DO TO BE SAVED?

People who consistently outperform the real estate market generally do so by adding value to their property. They do that either by improving management or by converting property to a more appropriate use—they often do both. The common denominator is that they enhance their property's earning capabilities.

To increase annual earnings, clearly you must either increase gross revenue or decrease operating expenses. Applying better management or an entrepreneurial flair toward this end has evident benefits. It also yields less obvious dividends.

We saw earlier that the relationship between operating income and property value is often expressed as a capitalization rate. For a property selling at a capitalization rate of 10 percent and having a net operating income of $10,000 per annum, for example, market price would be $10,000/.10, or $100,000.

Suppose, by astute management, you get the net operating income up to, say, $11,000. Using the same 10 percent capitalization rate, the property is now worth $11,000/.10, or $110,000. You have increased your net worth by $10,000, simply by raising the property's annual income by $1,000.

Investors who improve operations, however, often find to their delight that they also influence capitalization rates. In our example of a $1,000 increase in net operating income, you might discover that the applicable capitalization rate is now, say, 9.5 percent instead of 10 percent. This means the new market value is $11,000/.095, or $115,789. Overall, the $1,000 increase in annual net operating income has increased your net wealth by almost $16,000. Later, we will look at techniques for pursuing exactly this strategy.

Rental real estate is a business, and, like any other business, routine management generates routine profit. The big yields (and, yes, the big risks) go to the innovators, people who exercise their imagination and flex their intellect to make dreams become reality. These are the builders and the rebuilders of America's cities and towns. They are the people who pioneered the shopping mall concept and who are today rebuilding our central business districts. On a smaller scale, they include the person who converts a deserted gasoline station into a prosperous drive-in laundry and cleaners; who converts an old loft-type factory building into a condominium or office complex. Real estate development and redevelopment are discussed at length in Chapter Twelve.

KEY POINTS

• Real estate investors can take an active or a passive market position and can choose between equity or debt-type assets.
• Over extended periods, real estate assets turn in a better average performance than either stocks or bonds, after adjusting for risk differentials. The yield differential is not particularly notable, but it becomes more impressive when you incorporate the advantages of generally greater leverage available to investors in real estate equities.
• The best opportunities for outstanding investment performance come to those who take an equity position as an active investor and treat their rental property as a business. The returns to entrepreneurial effort are not precisely measurable, but anecdotal evidence is impressive.

CHAPTER 2

CHOOSING AN
INVESTMENT STRATEGY

Investors without coherent strategies are like rudderless boats. They go where the current takes them, in directions neither predictable nor purposeful.

"People call me lucky," says Ira Sworthky, who amassed millions in real estate in the Northeast over two decades. "I always agree with them. But, you know, it takes a lot of planning and a passel of work to be consistently lucky." Sworthky started with a detailed business plan. You should too.

WHAT ARE YOU TRYING TO DO?

As with all plans, the starting point of your strategic real estate investment plan is to decide what you want to accomplish. The obvious answer is to make as much money as possible as quickly as you can. But obvious answers are seldom the best.

Real estate investment textbooks usually start with the premise that an investor's objective is either to maximize wealth or to maximize return on investment. Both are laudable goals, but neither corresponds to the reality of most people's needs and aspirations. Real people have complex lives that call for more complex objectives.

If you spend a decent amount of time and psychic energy thinking about it, you will probably conclude that your life cycle will encompass a period of systematic investment followed by a period of disinvestment. You will save part of your income during your peak earning years. Then you will probably decide that, at some point, you will begin systematically liquidating your portfolio and living off the proceeds.

Additionally, you might reasonably expect that occasionally there will be large, one-time demands on your wealth that force you to liquidate some investments. Examples include sending children (or yourself) to college or realizing an ambition to travel, to seek spiritual renewal, or to pursue adventure.

Of course your needs are unique. Precisely what you plan is less important than that you *do* explicitly plan. Whatever course you want your life to take, it will happen only if you incorporate the financial aspects of your dream into your savings and investment plan, of which your real estate investment strategy will be an integral part.

WHAT KIND OF PERSON ARE YOU?

Real estate investment strategies can range from Las Vegas crapshoots to the accumulation of gilt-edged securities that are as secure and unexciting as the federal treasury. The general rule is that profit possibilities and risk travel in tandem. But, like most generalizations, this one masks a plethora of market relationships and anomalies that defy cataloging. In fact, a potentially rewarding strategy is to seek out and exploit exceptions to this rule.

Figure 2–1 illustrates the point. It is intended to represent all possible combinations of rates of return and degrees of risk from real estate. The most desirable asset would be one located in the upper-left corner of the box—very high yields and extremely low risk. The worst strategy is represented by the lower-right quadrant, where risks are at their greatest and yields are exceedingly low.

It is most desirable to invest solely in the upper-left quadrant—in those high-yielding assets that incorporate little or no risk. But of course everyone feels that way, and so that part of the playing field is empty. Competition for assets near the left side of the box (low in risk) will drive their prices up and

Figure 2-1
Risk and Return in Real Estate Investment

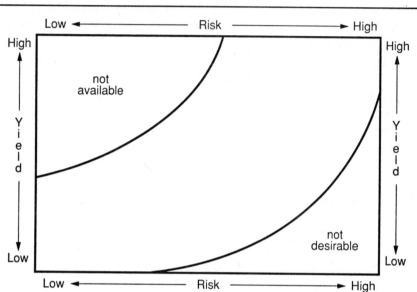

thus their yields down. This moves them toward the bottom
(low-yield area) of the diagram.

In contrast, no rational investor would buy assets in the
lower-right corner. Why buy low-yielding, risky investments
when you can get just as good a yield with less risk by choosing from the lower-left side of the box? Lack of demand for
assets in the lower-right side will cause prices to fall until
these assets become such bargains that their yields increase
dramatically—that is, until they move toward the top of the box.

In reality, then, all investments will reflect combinations
of yields and risk such that they will fit in a corridor through
the box's center. In a highly efficient market, this corridor will
be extremely narrow. Figure 2–1 features a fairly wide corridor, reflecting the real estate market's inefficiency. In any case,
investors choose from an array of assets that range from modest expected yields with little or no risk to high-risk deals with
expected yields sufficient to draw investors.

Before you can develop a coherent strategic investment
plan, you must decide in which part of the corridor you want

to position your portfolio. If you can't afford to take risks, or if dicey propositions keep you awake nights, you will select from the lower-left side of the box. If you are comfortable taking risks, you will move toward the upper right. Most of us will settle in somewhere near the middle.

Only you can decide where on the risk-return spectrum you should put your money. The important point is to consciously make the decision before you start looking at property. Think in terms of selecting an appropriate combination of risk and expected return, and the allure of high yields is less likely to blind you to attendant risk.

HOW MUCH DO YOU HAVE TO INVEST?

Your asset choices as well as your investment strategy will be conditioned in part by the size of your bankroll. Whether you are clinging precariously to the bottom of the middle class or firmly entrenched in the country club set, you have to choose between concentrating resources in a bid for higher yields or spreading your investments to reduce risk. The choice is never easy.

Scale economies is a freshman economics term to express what every investor knows from experience; large unit investments tend to fare better than small ones. Perhaps the most obvious example comes from the stock market, where buying fewer than 100 shares costs a premium over the normal brokerage commission. Shares purchased this way (in *odd-lots*) can never do as well as they would have if purchased in round lots, because of the odd-lot premium. Yields on big-block trades are even better, because the commission is a much smaller part of the stock's value.

Scale economies in real estate work the same way. Transaction costs on small properties are always larger, as a percentage of the property's value. But, beyond transaction costs, large properties are likely to be priced lower relative to their income-generating ability than are smaller parcels.

Offsetting the search for scale economies is the need to manage risk. A basic risk management strategy is diversification; best characterized as not putting all your financial eggs in one basket. Because real estate comes in such expensive packages, diversification is difficult unless you are willing to merge your capital with that of other investors. Stepping down to smaller properties to achieve diverstification may be wise, even if it means sacrificing a small increment of expected profit.

The degree to which you're willing to trade off expected yield for more diversification depends more on your attitude toward risk than on any objective criteria. This is a basic strategic decision that needs to be thought through carefully before you begin your investment program.

TIME REALLY IS MONEY

How much time to devote to your investments is also a basic strategy decision. This question should be approached in much the same way as any other investment issue; what is the expected return on your time, and what is the risk that your expectations will not be realized?

Economists term this idea *opportunity cost* and define it as the benefit forgone by not applying your time to its next best alternative use. For prosperous professionals and highly paid business executives, the opportunity cost of diverting productive time to real estate will probably be prohibitively high. Others may find it time profitably spent.

If time limitations preclude active participation in asset management, you will probably choose passive real estate investment vehicles. In these deals your money buys you an ownership interest and a piece of the profit, but no voice in management. Common examples are limited partnerships, master limited partnerships, and real estate investment trusts. These are explored at length in later chapters.

Investors with the time and inclination will elect varying degrees of involvement with their properties. This might range from simply interviewing and employing a good property management team to actually undertaking development or redevelopment. Between these extremes lies a vast array of alternatives. Let's look briefly at several of the more popular options.

Buy Net Leased Properties

Busy people who want to own real estate but have no time or desire to manage it are often attracted to buildings under long-term net leases to creditworthy tenants. You will hear reference to *net, double net,* and *triple net* leases; don't let the distinction distract you. Since the terms mean different things in various parts of the country, you will want an explicit description of the degree of "netness" from anyone who uses the terms.

Tenants under a net lease agree to pay building operating expenses as well as the contract rent. The degree of netness is an attempt to differentiate between lease terms that have the tenant paying some but perhaps not all expenses. For people whose time constraints or aversion to management attract them to net lease deals, the ideal situation is one in which all expenses, including insurance and property taxes, are paid by tenants. It is the precise terms of the lease, rather than slang used by a broker, that should concern you.

Net leased properties are the nearest thing to a bond that investors in real estate equities are likely to find. Cash flows are predictable as to amount, timing, and duration. Risk depends as much on the tenants' creditworthiness as on property value. Since your tenant will have exclusive use of your property and will usually have the right to make extensive alterations, you might view the property more as security for the tenant's lease obligation.

It is almost as if you had sold the property to the tenant and taken back a long-term, mortgage-secured note; however, there are important differences. If a tenant defaults, eviction—which is your recourse—is much simpler than would be the foreclosure proceedings associated with default on a mortgage note.

In addition to monthly rent, you get benefits from tax savings generated by claiming a deduction for depreciation expense, a topic discussed in detail in Chapter Six. And you also get your property back when the lease expires. This latter benefit is no small matter, particularly during an inflationary period or where a property is ideally situated so that it increases in value over the lease term. As property value grows during the lease period, so does the amount of cash you can pull out of the deal if you decide to sell during the lease term.

Buy Management-Intensive Property

Because the cash flows are so predictable and trouble free, and because risk is low when tenants are highly solvent and have good credit ratings, net leased properties tend to have a comparatively low rate of return—compared, that is, to deals with more risk and those that are more troublesome to manage.

Management, in fact, is a critical factor in most properties' profitability. Key management functions of marketing, tenant relations, and cost containment determine whether a property is a stellar performer or just another entrant in the investment derby. This is particularly true where leases are short term, where high tenant turnover is common, or where property is leased to merchants whose rent is determined by their gross sales.

If you acquire management-intensive property and decide to handle day-to-day management yourself, be prepared to treat it as a full-time job; it will be. More typically, you will hire an on-site manager to handle mundane management chores, engage a leasing agent to show and lease the property, and involve yourself only in personnel matters and contract negotiation. You will be operating a business, and success very much depends on your business acumen.

Many investors who own management-intensive properties elect to turn all responsibility over to a professional property management firm. This generally costs around 5 or 6 percent of gross rent. There is often an additional charge for leasing the property. Keep in mind that this is tantamount to buying a business and hiring a professional business management firm to run it. Outstanding results come only if you engage an unusually adept agent, monitor performance closely, and terminate management contracts whenever performance fails to measure up to objectively determined standards. Chapter Eleven deals with this topic in greater detail.

Exploit Market Anomalies

Markets, a shorthand term for mechanisms that bring buyers and sellers together, serve the additional valuable function of transmitting   information   about   products   and   services.

When a market functions efficiently, all relevant information is reflected in market prices. This often is not the case in real estate markets. If you can afford the time and are willing to make the effort, and if the amount of money you intend to invest is large enough to justify the cost, there are significant opportunities to exploit the imperfect functioning of real estate markets.

Compared to stocks or commodities, real estate transactions are costly and cumbersome. This causes property owners to enter real estate markets with more reluctance than they might stock or commodities markets. With fewer offers to buy or sell, information known by only a few prospective traders is not rapidly reflected in prices. This presents a profit opportunity for those who maintain good information sources.

To consistently exploit market anomalies—situations where important information is not reflected in property prices—you must cultivate information sources assiduously. You need to know more about your chosen market segment than do most other participants. This implies a severely circumscribed market and an iron will to resist moving outside your established market arena.

Using Inside Information

Exploiting inside information in regulated securities markets is considered underhanded at best. At worst, it can land you in the penitentiary. Real estate markets are different. Here, no penalty and no moral opprobrium attaches to trading on inside information. Most real estate fortunes are in fact amassed exactly this way.

The legendary William Zeckendorf, who got his start buying and selling New York properties, claimed to know the detailed ownership history of every major Manhattan office building, including the price and terms of each transaction. Financial difficulties that eventually cost him control of Web and Knapp Corporation were associated with deals in Canada and the western United States; locales far removed from where he could legitimately claim insider status.

Though he makes a less modest claim, it is clear that George Bockl, who made millions as a part-time investor while running a successful real estate brokerage firm, owes much of his success to his intimate knowledge of the Milwaukee real estate market. He has written several books detailing his ownership and redevelopment exploits, in which he discusses debacles as well as triumphs. A frequent characteristic of his flawed forays seems to have been commitments made off his usual market turf.

To exploit insider information you obviously must become an insider. You must either get information sooner or exploit it better than your competitors. An essential first step is to carefully circumscribe your market. This should be done in terms of both geographic area and type of property with which you become involved. Avoid the mistakes of Zeckendorf, Bockl, and anonymous thousands of other investors; stick to the market area you know.

Using Information Better

Even generally available information often finds its way into investment decisions only after considerable delay. This is because so much of the real estate investment market is almost exclusively the terrain of amateurs. Many property owners don't seem to realize that demographic and regional economic trends have a predictable impact on real estate values. Those who systematically track such information and study it to determine its likely import can steal the march on the general public.

Since information search costs are steep, you must be prepared to enter the market with some regularity to make data collection and analysis economical. Some people who start by compiling information for their own and their clients' use, eventually start selling the data to further reduce its effective cost.

A less frequent—but no less effective—scheme for reducing search costs while remaining abreast of relevant information is to pool your collection efforts with other local investors.

Property Development and Redevelopment

Adding value by altering properties' physical nature is another popular route to profitability. Opportunities for entrepreneurial initiative are so significant to real estate success that an entire chapter (Chapter Twelve) is devoted to this issue.

Profit From Other People's Mistakes

Everyone knows that the landscape is littered with real estate deals gone awry; of such disasters are subsequent fortunes made. Buildings that don't generate enough rental income to justify their construction costs are obvious mistakes for the builder; they may be equally disastrous for mortgage lenders. After investors and lenders take their losses, however, these properties often sell at prices (far below construction cost) that make them reasonable deals at their current occupancy levels.

If high vacancy is a temporary phenomenon, such properties eventually become crown jewels in someone's investment portfolio. A building that, after being marked down in a panic sale, just holds its own during the economic cycle's trough may become a high flyer during the subsequent boom.

Other properties are developed in the right place and at the right time but still perform poorly. The culprit in these cases is often incompetent, indifferent management. Such properties are prime candidates for a turnaround artist who can solve the poor performance dilemma. Chapter Eleven considers this in greater detail.

KEY POINTS

- Successful investors start with a strategic investment plan.
- Real estate offers a wide range of investment opportunities that differ drastically in the degree of risk and in yield prospects. An early step in determining where on this spectrum your portfolio should fall is to decide how much risk is acceptable to you.
- The most appropriate real estate investment strategy is conditioned heavily both by the amount of time you have to devote to your investments and by the value of your time. Make this decision before you start looking for investment opportunities.

CHAPTER 3

VALUE AND PRICE

Decision making is never easy. To choose is to foreclose alternatives. Rejected opportunities may be lost forever; at best they can be only partially retrieved. The more important the decision, the more painful the process.

Real estate investments usually take a big bite out of your bankroll; that makes real estate decisions particularly difficult. Too often, the choice is made either to mindlessly shift the responsibility to someone else or to reject real estate as an area for investment.

Real estate investment decisions—indeed all investment decisions—are rendered less agonizing and less haphazard if reduced to a system. Whether good or bad, systems free you from repeating the emotional trauma every time you have to decide. Once your system is in place, you need only compare key elements of an investment proposition with the system's parameters. Decision making is, in effect, put on autopilot.

There is a danger; your automatic pilot may be faulty. If, however, the system incorporates your best thinking—rather than representing surrender to an authority—bad decisions that stem from system faults will be no worse than those you would have made on an ad hoc basis, and you will have avoided the agonizing and time-consuming deliberation attendant to nonsystematic decisions.

The real danger is that a successful decision system will engender complacency. A system that initially incorporates your best thinking and is based on the most recent and appropriate market information can be rapidly outdated by shifts in economic, political, or social factors that influence market relationships. Systems that work well must be constantly updated so that the underlying assumptions always reflect the latest available investment intelligence.

The decision system that we will explore is designed to estimate a property's *investment value*. This is its value to you, as an asset in your portfolio. When facing a purchase or sale decision, simply compare a property's market price with its investment value. Buy when market price is less than investment value. If you're the owner, sell or trade when market value exceeds your investment value.

SOME KEY TERMS

You see a dollar amount quoted on the sticker of an automobile in a car dealer's showroom. Is that really the car's price? An eager dealer shows you her purchase invoice to impress you with her minuscule markup—is that the car's price? After too much haggling you settle on a dollar amount at which you buy the vehicle—is *that* the car's price?

Price obviously has many meanings and requires a modifier. For the auto you just bought there is, as we have seen, an invoice price, a sticker price, an asking price, an offering price, and a transaction price. What about that transaction price? Did you pay too much? Did the dealer accept too little? Is it possible that both of you got a good deal, or must someone have taken a metaphorical skinning?

Let's not tarry in this semantic thicket. The way out is to agree on precise definitions of price and value. Since this is my soap box, I get to provide the definitions. If you don't like them, you can make mental translations every time you see the terms. The important point is that we not let definitional differences dam the communication flow.

Transaction Price

When property changes hands in a market transaction, there is always some consideration involved. The quid pro quo that triggers the deal is the *transaction price*. It is not a matter of opinion, but an historical fact; it is the price at which a transaction actually occurred. The price may be in money or other kinds of consideration, but it can always be expressed in cash-equivalent terms.

Most Probable Price

In contrast to the transaction price, the *most probable price* is the one at which a property is most likely to sell. It is the midpoint in a range of possible transaction prices. Estimates of most probable price presuppose a certain deal structure and market environment. Alter the deal's structure and the most probable price will change. When market conditions shift, most probable prices are likewise altered.

If current market conditions would support a cash price of $200,000, that is the most probable price if the property is exposed to the market for a reasonable period and the seller is not under undue duress. If a quick sale is imperative (perhaps the owner is being transferred or needs cash quickly for other purposes), then the most probable price would be somewhat lower. If current interest rates are 12 percent per annum and the owner is willing to carry a sizeable mortgage-secured note at a much lower rate, the most probable price will be higher.

Market Value

This much-overused phrase is subject to such misunderstanding that it might be better to avoid it altogether. But, because it is widely used, let's make sure there is no confusion. Appraisers use *market value* to mean the most probable price under a strictly circumscribed set of market conditions. Appraisers' limiting conditions are so unrealistic that market value, as they define it, will almost never be the most probable selling price.

Investment Value

We include market value in our lexicon primarily to contrast it with *investment value*, a much more useful term. Investment value is a property's value to a particular individual, either for use in a trade or business or for income-generating purposes. It is unique to each person, and there is no reason to suppose that you and I would impute the same, or even similar, investment values to the same property.

Another way to characterize investment value is as the value today of the expected stream of ownership benefits. Investment value will differ from person to person because:

- We differ in our assessment of a property's ability to generate a stream of benefits.
- We differ in the degree to which we discount future benefits as a consequence of having to wait.
- We differ in the level of confidence we have in our projections of future benefits.
- Even if we agree on all the above, we differ in the extent to which we discount anticipated benefits due to our aversion to uncertainty or risk.

All these individual differences in attitudes, expectations, and opportunities make it purely coincidental if two people agree on a property's investment value If they did agree, they could never put together a deal because transaction costs would then mean that either the seller would net less than her investment value or the buyer would pay more than his.

WHO CARES?

Definitions of no practical significance are an academic exercise of interest only to students who need passing grades and to professors seeking lifetime sinecures. The definitions rehearsed here, however, have immense practicality. Mastering their nuances will make you a more capable real estate negotiator, able to put together agreements that offer something for all parties.

To begin, let's diagram a typical real estate transaction. Figure 3–1 compares a current owner's estimate of investment value with her estimate of the most probable selling price.

Before an owner will be willing to offer a property for sale, the owner's estimate of most probable selling price (here, $310,000) must exceed the investment value (in this case,

Figure 3–1
Seller's Investment Value

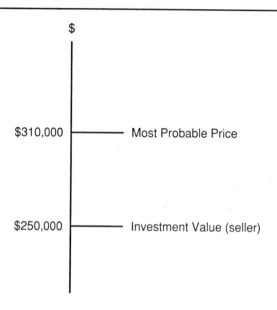

$250,000) by at least the amount of the seller's expected trans-
action costs, including taxes. If this is not the case, the owner
will be better off continuing to own the property rather than
offering it for sale.

An owner's investment value, therefore, adjusted to include
transaction costs, represents a floor below which a transaction
will leave the owner worse off and below which he or she simply
will not agree to a sale. From the owner's point of view, investment value plus expected transaction costs is the lower bound
of a range of possible transaction prices, any one of which would
leave the seller either equally well off or better off than before
the transaction.

A putative buyer approaches a property from a similar
perspective. The buyer's investment value is the value today
of the benefits that are expected to accrue if the property is
purchased. Unless the prospective buyer's investment value
exceeds his or her estimated probable price by at least the
amount of expected transaction costs, it is better not to own
the property

Figure 3–2
Buyer's Investment Value

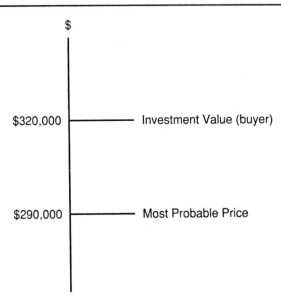

A prospective buyer's view is shown in Figure 3–2. Note that the owner's and the prospective buyer's estimates of most probable price are not the same in our illustration ($310,000— from Figure 3–1—for the owner; $290,000 for the buyer). This is a common situation, and there is no reason that buyers' and sellers' estimates should be even close. Nor is it particularly important. The really crucial variable is that the difference between the parties' investment values at least equal aggregate transaction costs. Only then can a transaction occur at a price that will leave both parties at least as well off as before the transaction.

Assumptions from Figure 3–1 and Figure 3–2 are consolidated in Figure 3–3. The distance between the buyer's and the seller's investment values, after adjusting for aggregate transaction costs, comprises a range of possible transaction prices, any of which will leave both parties better off than they are now. Exactly where within this range an actual transaction price will fall depends on the buyer's and seller's relative bargaining skills and strengths.

FIGURE 3–3
Range of Possible Transaction Prices

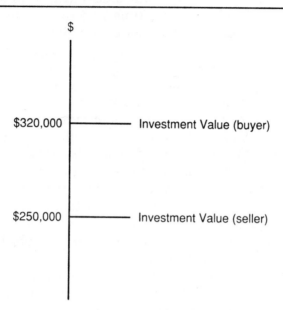

A buyer who is unduly influenced by a competent broker, for example, might accept a price very close to his investment value, thinking that is the best deal he can hope to negotiate. An anxious seller might accept a price very close to her investment value, perhaps in fear that the prospective buyer will move on to another property and a second buyer will not materialize.

ESTIMATING MOST PROBABLE PRICE

Earlier, we saw that most probable price is a first cousin to the real estate appraiser's concept of market value. If actual market conditions and terms coincide with restrictions embedded in the definition, then the two concepts will be identical. This is about as likely as November sunshine in Nome.

Yet, the procedure involved in estimating market value and most probable price are essentially the same. By getting a firm grip on this concept, you will be able to assess more accurately the reasonableness of an asking price. By comparing your investment value with your assessment of most probable price, you can avoid wasting time negotiating for properties that you almost certainly will not eventually own.

Appraisers estimate value in three different ways and reconcile the results into a single point estimate of what a property will most likely sell for under the restrictive conditions set forth in the appraisers' definition of market value.

1. They note the selling prices of similar properties that sold recently, make adjustments for differences that would affect the price, and draw an inference about the price the subject property would command if placed on the market.

2. They estimate the cost to replace the property with a new building, and make an adjustment to allow for the age of the subject property. This adjusted cost, plus the value of the land, represents an estimate of the price the subject property would command on the open market.

3. They note the relationship between the selling prices of similar properties that recently changed hands and the net operating income the properties generate. The most frequently employed relationship is the capitalization rate—net operating income divided by price. From these observations they infer an appropriate capitalization rate for the subject property. They multiply the subject property's net operating income by this rate to derive an estimate of the price it would bring on the market.

Of these three techniques, the most useful for you is the third: the income capitalization technique. By noting the capitalization rate for several recently sold properties of the type in which you are interested (you can get this information from a local real estate appraiser for a pittance), you can readily estimate the most probable selling price under typically prevailing market conditions.

A similar and perhaps even more useful technique is called the *gross income multiplier* or *gross rent multiplier* technique. Since similar properties usually require about the same percentage of the gross income to cover operating expenses, the relationship between gross income and price will be almost as stable as the capitalization rate

The virtue of the gross multiplier technique is that you need less information about a target property to estimate its most probable price. By noting the gross rent and applying the locally prevailing multiplier, you can quickly evaluate the seller's posted price to determine if it is reasonable enough to justify further exploration. This is important because some people test the market by listing their property for sale at an unreasonably high price, with no expectation that it will actually sell.

STRENGTH THROUGH KNOWLEDGE

There are scores of books and many traveling road shows on the subject of becoming a winning negotiator. All the techniques and style in the world will avail you little, however, if you enter negotiations with substantially less knowledge than the other party. Besides the knowledge and understanding of human nature and the interactive processes that form the core of negotiating books and seminars, you need to have confidence about the property's most probable selling price and its investment value under a variety of possible deal structures.

Altering Terms

If you thoroughly master the idea of investment value, the value of the property as an asset in your portfolio, then you know the price below which you will not go as a seller or above which you will not go as a buyer. Only you are privy to this valuable information, and for you it is a nonnegotiable, bedrock position.

A substantial part of this book is devoted to estimating investment value. But investment value always presupposes a specific deal structure. It depends in part, for example, on the amount of borrowed money (financial leverage) involved in the deal, and on interest rates and repayment provisions. If these factors are altered, investment value changes. It is entirely possible, therefore, to alter both the buyer's and the seller's investment value by changing the structure of the deal.

Suppose you have made an offer on a property, for example,

which the owner indicates is far too low. The owner may be fencing to get information about your investment value or may feel that was the purpose of your initial offer. You might choose to resubmit your original offer with only slight modifications, to indicate that it is a serious offer that is not substantially below your investment value. But suppose the owner also stands pat?

At this point you are far apart on bid and asked prices. How do you narrow the range? If you simply increase the bid price, you signal the owner that indeed your prior bid was artificially low and offer encouragement for additional fencing to more nearly determine just how high you will go. Yet, if you are adamant, the deal may be needlessly killed. Often, the solution is to alter the terms instead of the price.

William Zeckendorf, of whom legends are told wherever real estate veterans congregate, had a favorite phrase that neatly sums up the idea, "You can name the price if I can name the terms." You might offer a price very near the owner's demands but couple it with seller financing under favorable terms. The value (to you) of these favorable terms should equal the increase in your offering price, so that you are indifferent between the old offer and the new. You will often find sellers that are more sensitive to price than to terms.

A little study will make you a master at trading off between price and terms. Perhaps a property needs a new roof; you might offer the owner the asking price but stipulate that an amount will be withheld from the sale's proceeds and placed in escrow to cover all or a portion of the cost of roof repairs. Or, you might incorporate an offsetting provision that the other party pay your transaction costs. There are myriad ways to alter investment values so that both parties get what they want from a transaction. Experiment!

ESTIMATING INVESTMENT VALUE

Before you can wring all these benefits from the concept, however, you must be able to determine investment value. It will then serve as an anchor to reality when descriptions of the wonders of creative financing and of imaginative deal structures threaten to cast you adrift. The final test is this: Will the proposed deal yield a purchase price that is less than a property's investment value to you, or a sales price that exceeds your investment value, when the consequences of the structure are incorporated into the analysis?

Let's start by borrowing a concept from accounting. Accountants typically develop balance sheets with asset values in one column and claims against assets in the other. Since all assets must be owned by someone, it follows that the dollar amounts in the two columns must be equal. This is usually referred to as the *balance sheet equation*. It can be stated as follows:

$$\text{Assets} = \text{Liabilities} + \text{Equity}$$

Investment value is alien to an accountant's characteristic way of looking at the universe because it involves prospective prices rather than transaction prices. Even so, we can make the balance sheet equation work for us. No matter how the numbers are derived—transaction price or investment value—claims against an asset still must account for the asset's total dollar amount.

With this idea in mind, we can restate investment value as the value of the debt position plus the value of the equity position. But, instead of the accountant's approach of listing everything at transaction prices, we list both the debt and the equity positions in terms of the value today (to whomever holds the claim against assets) of anticipated future benefits from the claim.

Stated this way, the value of the equity position is the *value today* (to the equity investor) of expected after-tax cash flows from operations and from disposal. The value of the debt position is the value today (to the mortgage lender) of the expected future debt service payments. These relationships are diagramed in Figure 3–4.

If you estimate the value of the two positions separately and sum them, you will have arrived at the property's investment value. The value of the *debt position* for a prospective investment can be estimated by determining the maximum amount of borrowed funds that will be employed. Let's reserve further

FIGURE 3–4
Cash Flows and Investment Value

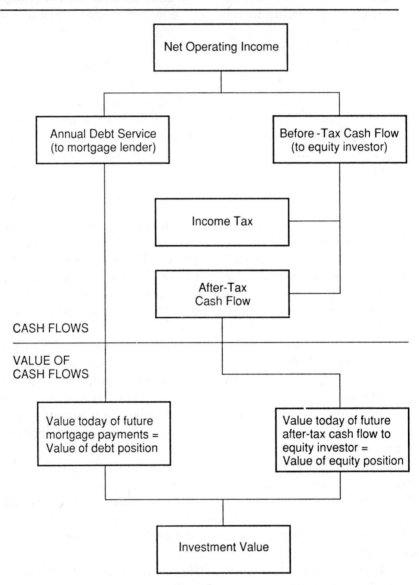

consideration of that until Chapter Nine. Estimating the value of the equity position is a two-step procedure. First, estimate the after-tax cash flows the equity investor will get from the property. Then determine the value to the investor of these anticipated cash flows. Cash flow estimation is the subject of Chapters Four through Six.

MAPPING A PATH THROUGH THE DATA THICKET

Real estate investment decisions are not fundamentally different from other investment decisions. Whatever the asset involved, whether it is real estate, stocks, bonds, collectibles, or pogo sticks, rational decision making involves the same fundamental process:

1. Set goals based on value judgments. Goals are unique to individual investors and need not conform to any objectively defined criteria. Goal setting must precede rational investment analysis because the analysis draws on the goals for decision criteria.

2. Develop a method for identifying opportunities consistent with goals. Investment opportunities are virtually limitless, and you can't possibly consider every alternative. Yet, the greater the number of possibilities that you filter through your decision system, the more likely you are to achieve your predetermined goals. Thus, you need a system that incorporates an economical way to search through a large number of alternatives, to quickly filter out the obvious junk, and to subject survivors to progressively more intense analytical scrutiny.

3. Construct a decision system for selecting specific investments from the alternatives that survive your preliminary screening. The system should represent a compromise among the needs to preserve capital, to generate an acceptable return, and to expedite the decision process and economize on analytical and information-gathering costs.

Goal setting is addressed in Chapter Two. Observations made there bear reviewing because your decision model's nature will depend in part on what you are trying to accomplish. Certain properties that are ideal for one set of goals may be anathema for another. You have to have a precise destination before you can map an efficient route.

Once you have decided what you hope to accomplish and the general property characteristics that will make the greatest contribution to your goals, you are positioned to develop a decision model. You want to incorporate a set of characteristics that you have identified as being crucial to success and whose absence will make a property unacceptable. You also need a model that will enable you to put a price (an investment value) on the degree of "fit" between the property and your goals.

Use Investment Screens

A complete catalogue of desirable and essential characteristics, and the contribution to investment value of each, would be lengthy. The resulting decision model would be cumbersome and costly to employ. Research and analytical economies demand that you construct a scaled-down version, one that incorporates essential features in a form that enables you to identify obviously unacceptable properties without investing much time.

Such a "reduced-form" model involves identifying relationships that reflect the underlying causal variables. For example, you might use average per capita income as a simplified measure of the socioeconomic caliber of tenants you want in your residential property. We will return to this idea in later chapters with additional suggestions for reduced-form indicators.

Be Your Own Person

Having determined the kinds of properties most likely to contribute to your goals, stick to your convictions. During your search you will be besieged with advice, both well meaning and self-serving. Don't be swayed. People who bring you "once-in-a-lifetime" opportunities are not really concerned with your best interests. Such "never-to-be-repeated" offers occur almost daily. Moreover, missing a bona fide super deal isn't catastrophic; putting your limited resources into a dud may be.

This doesn't mean you can't or shouldn't change your goals

and revise your investment plan accordingly. But keep your priorities straight. As a real estate investor you are a self-employed business person. And a common failing of the self-employed is a tendency to move into areas where superior knowledge gives their competitors a distinct advantage.

In *The Corporate Steeplechase* (Facts on File, 1984), psychologist Srully Blotnick does a masterful job of reporting on characteristics of successful and relatively unsuccessful business people. A substantial portion of his research subjects were self-employed, and he concluded that among these individuals the tendency to shift from their primary activity into related areas was the most important cause of failure. A key characteristic of the most successful subjects, in contrast, was their ability to stick with a specific activity long enough to become outstandingly competent. These people, he found, invariably decide on a course of action and stick with it until it has had a solid chance to pay off. Regardless of the field, he reported, persistence turned out to be crucial for success.

KEY POINTS

• *Investment value*, the most you are justified in paying for a property and the least you are justified in accepting when you sell, is the value at the time you must make the decision, of the anticipated stream of benefits flowing from all ownership claims.

• Investment value is the value of the debtor position plus the value of the equity position. On a property you are buying, the debtor position is the amount you will borrow; on a property you are selling, it is the remaining balance on existing mortgage loans. The value of the equity position is the present worth of the expected after-tax cash flows to the equity investor.

• Since investment value is unique to each individual, it will differ from investor to investor. It would be purely coincidental, therefore, if you placed the same investment value on a property as does the other party to a prospective transaction.

• When the most probable sales price of your property exceeds its investment value to you by more than the amount of anticipated transaction costs, put the property on the market. When the most probable price of a property you do not own is less than its investment value to you, consider making an offer.

• The most probable price, the midpoint of a probability distribution of possible prices, is affected by current market conditions as well as by the terms of a possible sale. If you alter the terms of the transaction, you change the most probable price as well as the investment value to both parties.

• When you are about to enter into contract negotations, compute the investment value to you under a variety of possible price and credit term combinations. This will position you to make immediate counteroffers should the other party make an offer that is unacceptable to you, or to make a revised offer if your first proposal is rejected.

CHAPTER 4

RECONSTRUCTING
THE OPERATING HISTORY

Don't forget the basic reason for investing in real estate. Neophytes are almost universally afflicted with a "sticks and bricks" fixation, yet the physical assets, the land and the buildings, are purely coincidental. It's the cash flow that is coveted; real estate is a mere means.

Since cash flow, either annually from operations, eventually from sale, or perhaps from both, is the only reason to hold a property from which you anticipate no personal enjoyment, this is really a self-evident proposition. Even so, it's easy to forget. Investors too frequently get caught up in the romance of a property's history, are seduced by its ambience, or are entrapped by pride of prospective ownership.

Remember the earlier admonition that investment involves buying a set of assumptions about an asset's ability to generate cash flows. But whose assumptions are to be bought?

Sellers have a vested interest in overstating a property's operating potential. The only safe assumption is that information they provide is biased. Data presented by real estate brokers are also suspect because brokers have a personal interest in closing a transaction at the highest possible price; brokerage commissions are almost always a percentage of the gross sales price. In short, the only prudent approach is to carefully estimate a property's operating potential, using data that are either gathered independently or that can be verified from disinterested sources.

THE PRIMACY OF THE PAST

As a general rule the single most reliable indicator of what a property can do is what it has done. Of course, history is not an infallible guide. It should, however, be taken as the upper limit of what you are willing to pay for. To quote one successful investor and developer, "I only pay real money for real performance, prospective performance is worth only prospective money."

A property's operating record is always the starting point for estimating potential; it is never the final product. Incorporate the past into your forecast by adjusting the history to reflect the expected consequences of shifts in the economic, political, and social environment that might alter operating results.

In any case, begin your analysis by reconstructing a reasonably reliable operating history. Without this information you will be hard pressed to develop rational expectations.

Let's be careful about this. The property's actual history stems from an amalgam of causes, including physical property characteristics, geographic location, and the skill (or lack of skill) of those responsible for marketing and management. Unusual marketing or management competence can radically alter operating results. Yet a buyer will usually not inherit the old management team. What you really want to know is what the operating history would have been with typically competent management.

OVERVIEW OF THE OPERATING STATEMENT

A property's history is reported on statements that show cash flow from operations. The statements are usually prepared on an annual basis, though management firms will prepare interim statements more frequently for their client's use.

The financial statement conventionally used in real estate investment analysis first presents cash inflows and outflows from operations and then extends the presentation to include certain nonoperating cash flows. Figure 4–1 illustrates a typical operating statement.

Figure 4–1
Income Property Operating Statement

XYZ Apartment Building

Reconstructed Operating Statement

Potential gross rent		$XXX,XXX
Less: Allowance for vacancy and rent loss		XXX
		$XXX,XXX
Plus: Other income:		
Parking Fees	$ X,XXX	
Concession income	X,XXX	$ XX,XXX
Effective gross income		$XXX,XXX
Less: Operating expenses:		
Property tax	$ X,XXX	
Insurance	X,XXX	
Maintenance	X,XXX	
Etc.	X,XXX	XXX,XXX
Net operating income		$XXX,XXX
Less: Debt service:		
Interest	$XX,XXX	
Principal	X,XXX	XX,XXX
Cash flow before income taxes		$ XX,XXX
Less: Income tax obligation (Plus: saving)		XXX
Net cash flow		$ XX,XXX

There are important differences between this and the income statement typically prepared by accountants, who concentrate on income and expenses rather than on cash receipts and disbursements. An appreciation of this distinction is critical. Accountants' income statements are concerned with recording income "when earned" and expenses "when incurred," whether or not there have been corresponding cash flows. As an investor, though, your focus should be on cash receipts and disbursements. Ultimately, only cash matters.

Effective Gross Income

Potential gross rent is the starting point for an operating statement. This is the amount of rental revenue a property would generate if there were no vacancies or rent losses and if all units were rented at currently prevailing market rents. Potential gross rent is not actually realized, of course, because virtually all properties experience some vacancies and some bad debt losses.

Subtracting vacancy and rent losses from potential gross rent and adding income from sources other than rent (vending machine income, for example) yields *effective gross income*. On an historic basis, this would be the gross income the property actually generated (or would have generated with typically competent management); on a forecast basis, it is the revenue the property is expected to generate.

Operating Expenses

Operating expenses are subtracted from effective gross income to determine *net operating income*. Operating expenses are the cash expenditures required to maintain a property in sufficient condition to generate the effective gross income. Here are some representative operating expenses:

Management fees
Painting and redecorating
Maintenance and repairs
Trash removal
Supplies
Services
Insurance
Real estate and other taxes
Payroll and payroll taxes
Advertising
Utilities
Rental commissions
Heat

Expenditures that are *not* included in operating expenses include capital improvements, debt service (payments made incident to mortgage indebtedness), and income taxes.

Capital expenditures are designed to increase a property's market value or useful life and are more in the nature of an investment than an operating expense. Such expenditures do, of course, affect net cash flow from the property and must be included elsewhere on the statement. They reflect a management decision not incident to actual property operation, however, and should be omitted from the net operating income calculation.

Payments on a promissory note secured by a mortgage on the property are called *debt service*. They result from a decision to utilize financial leverage (that is, to use borrowed money to supplement personal funds). Leverage affects the rate of return on the personal funds you invest, but it does not have an impact on the property's actual operating results. Therefore, debt-service payments on mortgage indebtedness are not considered operating expenses.

Income taxes are levied against the owner rather than the property. The amount of your income tax obligation is more a function of your personal tax position than of the revenue generated by a particular property. Consequently, the income tax liability arising from property ownership and operation is excluded from the operating section of the financial statement. (We shall see, however, that income tax consequences are included in the nonoperating section and thereby deducted from net operating income to arrive at net cash flow.)

Replacement Reserves

Some maintenance expenditures occur only episodically. Examples include the cost to repair or replace mechanical equipment such as furnaces, air conditioners, refrigerators, and garbage disposals, which last several years but are very costly when they finally do malfunction. No funds may be needed for these items during the first few years of a building's useful life. Then everything seems to fall apart at the same time.

To make sure there will be cash available for such contin

gencies, landlords sometimes set aside a *replacement reserve* of relatively liquid investments. These funds can be drawn upon as needed without precipitating a liquidity crisis. To ensure their availability, replacement reserves must be invested in securities that are readily marketable and that do not fluctuate widely in market value.

Whether deposits to a reserve account should be included as an expenditure depends on whether these funds that, in the absence of the real estate venture, would be used more profitably elsewhere. Since the idea is to track projected cash flows stemming from the venture, you should include the replacement reserve deposits as nonoperating outlays and earnings on the fund as nonoperating cash receipts.

The alternative is to attempt to estimate actual periodic outlays required for repairs and replacements and to include them in cash expenditure projections for the appropriate years. Because they tend to be a perennially optimistic breed, most real estate investors spurn the suggestion that liquid reserves be set aside. They are confident that additional funds can always be raised when needed.

Net Operating Income

The actual cash-flow consequences of owning and operating a property, as opposed to the manner of financing its acquisition, is called *net operating income*. It is simply effective gross income less the operating expenses that require cash outlays. The forecast of net operating income is the net cash flow you expect to get from operating the property before making payments on the mortgage note and before accounting for income taxes.

Cash Flow before Income Taxes

If you don't borrow money to finance a part of your purchase commitment (that is, if you choose to own on a free-and-clear basis), net operating income will generally be the same as cash flow before provision for income taxes. Rarely, however, will an individual investor find it advantageous to buy real estate wholly with equity funds. And, of course, when you do borrow on a property, a portion of net operating income will go to service the debt. Only the residual after debt service accrues to you as an equity investor.

Cash flow before income taxes, then, is the net operating income minus the annual debt-service requirement. It is sometimes called *cash throw-off, equity dividend*, or simply *cash flow*. By whatever name, it represents the cash flow accruing to an equity investor before provision for state and federal income taxes.

Income Tax Consequences

Unless you incorporate yourself as a church, real estate investments will always affect your income tax position. If, as is often the case, your tax bill is reduced as a consequence of the real estate, the tax saving represents additional cash inflow attributable to the venture.

Net Cash Flow

The bottom line of an operating statement is the amount of "bankable cash" from the project. This is the balance remaining after satisfying *all* prior claims, which most emphatically *do* include any obligation for state and federal income taxes. It is this after-tax cash flow, net of all debt service, that investors generally refer to as *net cash flow*.

Filling in the Blanks

The preceding summarizes the cash-flow statement most commonly used in real estate investment analysis. Figure 4–1 illustrates the format for such a statement, variously called an *operating statement*, an *income statement*, or a *cash-flow statement*. Nomenclature aside, it presents the net cash flow from property ownership and operation, either as a statement of historical fact or as an estimate for the future.

The past may be interesting in its own right, but its significance to investment decisions is limited to what it suggests about the most probable course of future events. Investors buy only the right to *future* cash flows, and only sheer coincidence will make these correspond exactly with past experience.

Nevertheless, the property's immediate past history is usually the starting point for a forecast. The recent trend is modified and projected according to what is known or suspected about the future environment in which the property will be operated.

If the property's recent history is to be used as a basis for estimating current gross income, you need several years' information in order to determine the trend. Unfortunately, multiple-year operating information is almost never available. When it is provided, it is seldom reliable.

If you can reconstruct last year with reasonable confidence, however, a trend can usually be established using other sources. We will talk about trend estimation after reviewing sources for the other information you will need.

In order to estimate market rental value by reference to comparable properties you need information on properties that provide the same services and amenities as the property under analysis. Locational influences and other major market factors must be approximately equal. Unit rental rates of comparable properties may then provide a guide for estimating the current market rental for this type of property.

Time and budget constraints place practical limits on the number of comparable properties about which you gather information. The greater the number of properties in a sample, and the more truly comparable they are, the more reliable will be the resultant estimate of market rental rates.

Because the properties included in a sample of comparable rental units will seldom correspond exactly in size and amenities with those under analysis, some common unit of measurement must be employed to make rental rates more directly applicable. This can be done by expressing rents in a common denominator, such as dollars per room, per apartment, or per square foot.

Example 4–1 (see page 53) shows how you might use a small sample of comparable properties to estimate market rental rates. To facilitate comparison and analysis, gross rental

TABLE 4–1
Derivation of Market Rental Rates on Properties Comparable to
48-Unit Apartment Building

	Comparable Property			
	A	B	C	D
Two-bedroom units				
Monthly rental	$240	$260	$235	$245
Square feet	890	925	870	895
Rental per square foot per month	$.27	$.28	$.27	$.27
One-bedroom units				
Monthly rental	$180	$200	$190	$200
Square feet	625	650	630	655
Rental per square foot per month	$.29	$.31	$.30	$.31
Studio units				
Monthly rental	$155	$160	$150	$165
Square feet	500	510	495	550
Rental per square foot per month	$.31	$.31	$.30	$.30

and vacancy data on the comparable apartment buildings are arrayed according to type of rental unit, and the results are shown in Tables 4–1 and 4–2.

Based on data from the comparable properties, potential gross rent and estimated vacancy rates for the 48-unit apartment building are estimated as indicated in Table 4–3. Since the estimates are from a very small sample, they contain a large margin of error. Ideally, you would use a much larger sample, which would permit you to apply statistical sampling tools. But that's usually not possible, either because more usable information simply does not exist, or because collecting it would cost more than it is worth.

Where vacancy loss estimates are drawn from such a small sample, though, they cannot be unquestioningly applied. An unusually high rate in one of the comparable properties will

TABLE 4–2

Derivation of Vacancy Factors on Properties Comparable to 48-Unit Apartment Building

	Comparable Property				
	A	B	C	D	Market
Two-bedroom units					
Number	35	15	45	20	115
Vacancies	1	0	1	0	2
Percent vacant	2.9%	0	2.2%	0	1.7%
One-bedroom units					
Number	10	15	15	25	65
Vacancies	0	2	0	2	4
Percent vacant	0	13.3%	0	8.0%	6.2%
Studio units					
Number	5	7	12	15	39
Vacancies	3	3	3	2	11
Percent vacant	60%	42.9%	25%	13.3%	28.2%

have a disproportionate impact on the average for the entire sample. The vacancy rate in the nonconforming comparable, however, may be an aberration caused by some temporary problem with the property, by incompetent management, or by some other unusual influence not expected to be present in the property being analyzed.

If a larger sample of comparable vacancy records can be collected, it will give you a much more reliable estimate of the market. Such data are often available from local property-management firms, brokers, appraisers, and property owners. In larger metropolitan areas, the results of reasonably current market surveys by lenders or professional research groups are occasionally available.

For large properties, and for those of a specialized nature, such as major hotels, resort properties, and large office buildings, professional trade associations often publish standards that are helpful in judging the reported experience of the subject properties.

As with gross income, the most appropriate starting point for estimating operating expenses is the experience of the prop-

TABLE 4–3
Estimated Potential Rent and Vacancy Rates for 48-Unit Apartment Building

	Estimated Potential Gross Rent		
	Market Value per Square Foot ×	Square Feet per Unit =	Rent Value per Unit
Monthly potential gross rent:			
Two-bedroom units	$.27	× 900 =	$243
One-bedroom units	.30	× 650 =	195
Studio units	.30	× 500 =	150
Annual potential gross rent:			
Two-bedroom units	(20 units × $243 × 12)		$ 58,320
One-bedroom units	(20 units × $195 × 12)		46,800
Studio units	(8 units × $150 × 12)		14,400
Total potential gross rental revenue			$119,520

	Estimated Vacancy Factor		
	Potential Gross Rent	"Market" Vacancy Rate	Vacancy Loss Estimate
Two-bedroom units	$58,320	× 1.7% =	$ 991
One-bedroom units	46,800	× 6.2% =	2,901
Studio units	14,400	× 28.2% =	4,061
Total rental loss estimate			$7,953
Vacancy loss as percent of potential gross			6.7%

erty in question. But any information from the property owner has to be considered suspect unless it can be verified from a reasonably disinterested source.

Revising the Owner's Operating Statement

An early step in evaluating reported operating results is to convert the owner's or manager's statement into a more useful format. Table 4–4 presents a statement typical of what might be received from existing owners or managers. Such statements are often prepared for accounting purposes, with an eye to satisfying the Internal Revenue Service's record-keeping

TABLE 4–4

Statement of Most Recent Annual Operating Results for 48-Unit Apartment Building

Apartment Owner's Income Statement
For Year Ended June 30, 19＿

Total receipts:		
Rent Receipts		$118,260
Parking and concession income		1,800
Total receipts		$120,060
Expenses:		
Management fee (at 5 percent)	$ 5,913	
Salary expenses	9,500	
Utilities	4,500	
Insurance	9,600	
Supplies	750	
Advertising	195	
Maintenance and repairs	12,300	
Mortgage payments	38,780	
Depreciation expense	12,200	$ 93,738
Net income for the year		$ 26,322

requirements. They are thus likely to be based on different concepts of revenue and expenses from those used in investment analysis.

The owner's statement includes only the rent actually received, with no reference to potential gross rental income and offsetting allowances for vacancy and income losses. To form a basis for forecasting, these additional data must be included in the current statement. Revising the statement to reflect the potential gross from Example 4–1, with attendant provision for vacancy and rent losses, yields the effective gross income reflected in Table 4–5.

Questioning the owner about the maintenance and repair charge in his statement reveals that it includes $8,580 spent to replace several old refrigerators. The remaining $3,720 seems rather low for a building of this size and age. Further inquiry reveals that the owner keeps costs down by doing much of the repair and maintenance work himself. Comparing the building with others in the area suggests that a proper maintenance and

TABLE 4–5
Reconstructed Operating Statement for 48-Unit Apartment Building

Potential gross income		$119,520
Less: Allowance for vacancy and rent		
(at 6.7 percent)		7,953
		$111,567
Plus: Other income		1,800
Effective gross income		$113,367
Less: Operating Expenses		
Management fee	$ 5,580	
Salary expenses	9,500	
Utilities	4,500	
Insurance	9,600	
Supplies	750	
Advertising	195	
Maintenance and repairs	10,000	
Replacement reserve	2,220	$ 42,345
Net operating income (annual)		$ 71,022

repair charge, including all routine costs but excluding replacements and major repair items, is about $10,000.

Investigating the need for a replacement reserve, you might determine that the only major appliances provided by the landlord are refrigerators and ranges. These cost approximately $250 (for refrigerators) and $180 (for tabletop ranges). An appropriate replacement reserve, assuming an average life of 8 years for refrigerators and 12 years for ranges, is:

Refrigerators ($250 × 48/8)	$1,500
Stoves ($180 × 48/12)	720
Annual reserve deposit	$2,220

The other operating expense items appear reasonable for the building when compared with information from comparable properties. Revised operating expenses total $42,345. These items, along with resultant revised net operating income, are illustrated in Table 4–5.

An alternative approach to estimating operating expenses, and one frequently employed when adequate reliable data are not otherwise available, it to use a "typical" operating expense ratio. For many smaller properties, particularly those which are owner-operated, there simply are no reliable records of actual expenses. In such cases, you might assume expenses to have the same relationship to potential gross as have expenses of similar properties in the locality. If the ratio is derived from a substantial sample of comparable properties, the resulting estimate is more useful than one drawn from the actual experience of the property, since it includes a measure of variance that can be used for risk analysis.

A major advantage of the typical ratio approach is that it eliminates the effect of current management as a variable in projected operating results. Since actual experience reflects the relative effectiveness of management as well as market factors and the physical condition of the building, using actual historical cost data requires that you adjust for management influence. In most cases, you will not inherit the old management team. I have a distinct preference for using typical ratios, carefully constructed to reflect market conditions, stratified for type, size, and property age, and modified to reflect any nonconforming aspects of the property under analysis.

WHERE TO GET THE INFORMATION

Before we leave this investigation of reconstructed operating history, let's consider where information for the statement might come from. You have two basic choices. You can collect data yourself (or, of course, pay someone to collect it for you), or you can search out data that have been previously collected and are suitable for your purpose.

When it is available, the latter approach is almost always less expensive. It will also usually get you the information in a more timely fashion. It's smart to exhaust readily available information from existing data banks before starting your own collection efforts.

The price you pay for the ease and economy of using other people's information is that the data are almost never in exactly the form you would like. In many cases that shortcoming is easily rectified by simply rearranging the format. In other cases you might find it necessary to draw inferences after examining information that, while similar, is not quite what you need.

Example 4–1. The property to be analyzed is a 48-unit apartment building containing 20 two-bedroom units, each having 900 square feet of living area; 20 one-bedroom units, each containing 650 square feet of living area; and 8 studio units, each with 500 square feet of living space. Management permits you to inspect the rent role for the past year, which reveals the following:

	Rental Rates and Vacancies		
	Two Bedroom	One Bedroom	Studio
Latest 12-month period:			
Monthly rent	$250	$205	$160
Vacant units	None	1	2
Previous 12-month period:			
Monthly rent	$235	$200	$160
Vacant units	1	2	2
Earliest 12-month period:			
Monthly rent	$215	$190	$150
Vacant units	1	2	3

Inspecting the rent role also reveals that some tenants are on 24-month leases, some on 12-month leases, and that some rent on a month-to-month basis. Most month-to-month tenants are in studio apartments. As a further complication, tenants have been offered a variety of terms. Some received special decorating allowances as an inducement to sign a lease. Others received special parking concessions. The concessions seem to be related to periods when vacancy rates were particularly high, but this is impossible to verify because management refuses to confirm the concessions reported by tenants.

There are in the neighborhood several apartment complexes offering comparable accommodations. Services provided there are essentially the same as at the property being analyzed. Data on comparable units have been obtained from a property-management firm that has no interest in the property under analysis and is judged to be reliable. The data are as follows:

- *Comparable A* has a total of 50 units. Thirty-five two-bedroom units, each with 890 square feet of living area, rent for $240 per month. Ten single-bedroom units with 625 square feet each rent for $180 per month. Five studios with 500 square feet rent for $155 per month. Currently, one two-bedroom unit and three studios are vacant. All the one-bedroom units are under lease.
- *Comparable B* has 15 two-bedroom units, 15 one-bedroom units, and 7 studio units. The two-bedroom apartments have 925 square feet of living area and rent for $260. The one-bedroom units have 650 square feet of living area and rent for $200. The studios have 510 square feet and rent for $160. There are currently two vacant one-bedroom units and three vacant studios. All the two-bedroom units are currently occupied.
- *Comparable C* consists of 72 units, of which 45 are two-bedroom units and 15 are one-bedroom units. The remaining 12 units are studios. The two-bedroom units have 870 square feet of living area and rent for $235. The one-bedroom units have 630 square feet of living area and rent for $190. The studios, which have 495 square feet of living area, rent for $150. The complex currently has one vacant two-bedroom unit and three vacant studios. All the single-bedroom units are rented.
- *Comparable D* has 20 two-bedroom units, 25 one-bedroom units, and 15 studios. The two-bedroom units have 895 square feet of living area and rent for $245. The one-bedroom units have 655 square feet of living area and rent for $200. The studios rent for $165 and have 550 square feet of living area. There are two vacant one-bedroom and two vacant studio apartments.

All the units in the comparable properties have only one bath, and all have a kitchen-dining room combination rather than a formal dining room. This conforms to the observed facilities in the property being analyzed.

KEY POINTS

• The only reason for putting your assets at risk in any investment venture is the expectation that you will eventually be able to take some cash out of the deal. After-tax cash flow, therefore, is the only outcome that really matters. Other investment performance measures are at best proxies for after-tax cash flow.

• The single best indicator of how any rental property is likely to perform in the near future is how well it would have performed in the recent past had it been operated by reasonably competent management. The starting point for estimating future cash flows, therefore, is to reconstruct recent operating history.

• All information from anyone who stands to benefit from your investment decision is suspect. Look at the recent performance of comparable properties, make adjustments for size differences and other elements of noncomparability, and make inferences about how the target property performed.

• Collect raw information about properties only as a last resort. There will almost always be a cache of information, gathered for some other purpose, from which you can draw most of the data you need. This is a much quicker and less expensive approach.

CHAPTER 5

FORECASTING CASH FLOWS
IN AN UNCERTAIN FUTURE

Your only interest in the operating history discussed in Chapter Four will be what it tells you about a property's future prospects. You are, after all, buying assumptions about future operations, not about the past. The reconstructed operating statement described in that chapter is the starting point for developing information critical to all investment decisions: a property's ability to generate net cash flows over the prospective holding period.

CONVENTIONS AND INNOVATIONS

In primitive form, real estate investment analysis has been around for a long time. Certain conventions have been adopted over the years, some of which facilitate analysis, and some of which have outlived their usefulness.

Cash-flow projections are traditionally made on an annual basis. Semiannual, quarterly, monthly, or even daily forecasts could just as well be used, but that would contribute little if anything to the analysis and would greatly complicate interpretation and communication.

A less benign convention is something called *stabilizing* the forecast. This is a process of adjusting, or smoothing, projections so that cash-flow figures represent a "typical" year's operating results. The motivation is to facilitate mathematical manipulation. There was perhaps some justification for this before the advent of high-speed, inexpensive personal computers and hand-held calculators. No more. The additional precision gained in estimating anticipated annual variations in cash flows certainly justifies the slight additional calculational effort involved. Wide general ownership of computers renders the question moot.

All receipts and disbursements are conventionally treated as having been made at the end of each period. This facilitates analysis by making it possible to use standard present-value tables that incorporate the same assumption. Alternative assumptions about the pattern of receipts and disbursements, while more realistic, do not substantially alter the analysis. They do complicate the arithmetic.

THE PAST AS PROLOGUE

Most of the time, the single most reliable clue to the immediate future is the recent past. Unless key political, economic, or environmental influences shift, a property's operating history will be a reliable guide to its prospects.

Some of these influences are outside your control; others you can alter to a greater or lesser degree. Those you can control, you will change to enhance your property's cash flow. Those over which you have no control, but which nevertheless influence profits, you should analyze in an effort to estimate possible change and the likely impact on your property.

An early step in forecasting, therefore, might be a simple-minded extrapolation of past results into the future. If you have reconstructed at least one year's operating history, and you also know the average rate of change in rent and operating expenses for similar properties, simply apply that rate to the reconstructed data, and you have a naïve forecast.

This, however, is only a rough approximation. Past rates of change will not continue indefinitely. A great many investment mistakes are exactly this; we act as if trends never change. To avoid this common error, use informed opinion about impending changes in the economic, political, and social environment to alter your naïve forecast.

Forecasting Gross Income

Estimating gross income for the projection period is the first step in forecasting net cash flows. There are actually two gross incomes to be projected. The first, *potential* gross, is adjusted for vacancies and bad-debt losses, and for expected income from other sources, to arrive at *effective* gross income.

As explained in Chapter Four, potential gross income is that which would result from 100 percent occupancy at market rental rates. If, however, the property is currently under a long-term lease, contract rent should be used rather than market rent. *Market rent* is defined as that which the real estate would most probably command if placed on the market during the period for which the forecast is being made. *Contract rent*, in contrast, is the rent actually being paid by current tenants.

Forecasting Operating Expenses

Once you have estimated operating expenses for a single year, you can roughly calculate them for a number of additional years by including an inflation factor and "guessing" whether management will face some extraordinary expense such as major salary increases.

Were generating an accurate inflation factor as simple as the previous paragraph implies, many well-paid economists would become unemployed overnight. Indeed, the most often demonstrated characterisitic of inflation is its unpredictability.

Two factors act to mitigate the seriousness of this problem The first is that you need not be exactly right. If you estimate an inflation factor of 6 percent and the appropriate factor proves to be 7, for example, this will seldom be fatal to the usefulness of your analysis. The second mitigating factor is that any misstatement of the inflation rate with respect to expenses is likely to be offest by an equally great misstatement with respect to rental revenue and the property's terminal market value. In practice, analysts generally rely on published estimates from sources recognized as authoritative.

Estimating Nonoperating Cash Flows

Nonoperating cash flows generally consist entirely of debt-service payments and income tax consequences. However, on occasion there will be other nonoperating receipts or disbursements. Examples include additional expenditures for capital improvements, to cure problems arising from deferred maintenance, and for back property taxes. They might also include cash inflows from projected partial dispositions.

The annual cash expenditure for debt service depends on the availability and cost of borrowed money and on your inclination to use such funds. Applying standard mortgage amortization tables to determine the projected debt-service obligation is a simple mechanical process, explained in Chapter Nine.

Estimating income tax consequences requries extensive information about your expected taxable income and your other investments, as well as additional data too extensive for inclusion at this point Income tax factors are explored more fully in Chapter Six

THE UNCERTAIN NATURE OF FUTURE CASH FLOWS

Forecasting problems are multiplied many times over as you push the forecast further into the future. Without some systematic procedure, the uncertainty of future events would create an impenetrable haze in which the most astute analyst would become lost.

Reliable long-range forecasts require knowledge of trends already established in the market and of their likely influence on the property's relative desirability. They require, also, an estimate of future additions and subtractions in the number of competing rental units and of changes in the population making up the market segment.

What Is the Product?

As every student of basic economics knows, changes in revenue from the sale of any product or service are caused by altered demand for and supply of the product. But before we look at supply and demand relationships we have to do something even more fundamental; we must identify the product itself.

Remember that the product is a service; the right to occupy three-dimensional space for a specified time period. The demand for this right is a function of benefits from occupancy. The benefits can usefully be characterized as amenities and locational advantages.

Amenities are the physical improvements that make occupancy more desirable. They determine how well a property does the job for which it was designed. Amenities include basic protection from the elements plus the extras that make one's environment pleasant. The more nearly a property contains all the amenities generally desired by prospective tenants, the greater will be its marketability and its ability to compete with similar properties in the same market.

Locational advantage is a more subtle concept. Advantages are not inherent in the property but, rather, are unique to the user. Thus, a supermarket and a major department store would probably not wring the same benefit from a particular location. Locational factors include the economic and social status of the immediate neighborhood, ease of access to closely linked activities, and the prestige of the specific site. Gross rent forecasts must include an estimate of the direction and rate of change in these key locational variables.

Property location is a prime factor in the property's ability to command rent. Because location is fixed, neighborhood economic and social trends have a strong impact on a property's marketability as rental space. A gross rent forecast, therefore, must incorporate an estimate of the likelihood that the neighborhood will retain its attractiveness over the projection period.

DEVELOPING THE FORECAST

We have noted that factors influencing a property's ability to command rent include both the desirability of the space being offered (locational advantages and amenities) and the desirability and price of competing space. Future changes in these same factors determine the property's ability to continue generating rental income. Hence, gross rent forecasting starts with an estimate of how these causal factors will change over the projection period.

Some physical features (amenities) can be altered at management's discretion; others would be prohibitively costly to change and so must be considered fixed. Locational elements are even less amenable to manipulation and control. Yet location and amenities are major factors in a property's ability to command rent.

Because availability and cost of substitutes are strong influences on rental space's marketability, the nature of the competition, both present and potential, must be thoroughly analyzed. This requires that you consider not only existing properties that cater to the same clientele, but also potential additons to the existing stock during the projection period. Relevant factors include the amount of properly zoned building sites that are available now, the likelihood of significant zoning changes that would add more sites, and the probable cost and availability of construction loans.

Forecasting Functional Efficiency

How well a structure does its intended job is the acid test of its *functional efficiency*. Because the very concept of functional efficiency is related to use, it can be judged only in that context. Houses are tested against the requirements of modern family lifestyles, factories against the demands of contemporary manufacturing technology, and so on.

As structures become less able to meet current standards of acceptability and less able to render intended services, they generally experience a corresponding diminution in their ability to command rent, and they may experience increased vacancy rates. This decline in acceptability resulting from defective or dated design or engineering characteristics is called *functional obsolescence*. At the extreme, it may result in a succession of uses or abandonment.

Functional obsolescence is an inherent characteristic of structures. It is a consequence of continual evolution of social, business, and industrial life and concomitant changes in the desired functional form of buildings. It reflects the perception of potential users regarding actual versus ideal layout, space, structural specifications, and amenities that contribute to productive capacity.

Examples are readily available. Recent trends in family lifestyles have resulted in a preference for residences with large, well-equipped family rooms and the capacity to accommodate complex, power-absorbing mechanical equipment such as air conditioners, washers, and dryers. This renders many older, differently equipped residences functionally obsolete.

In the industrial and commercial area, obsolescence has resulted from changes in manufacturing procedures, storage and shipping technology, and sales methods. Modern industrial technology favors single-story manufacturing plants, thus rendering older, multistory facilities obsolete. Other common items of functional inadequacy include ceilings with insufficient clearance, floors with inadequate load-bearing capacity, and unacceptably narrow spans between load-bearing walls.

Some buildings can be modifed to accommodate rather drastic changes in style and technology; other structures or other changes in use might require prohibitively expensive modifications. This places a premium on ability to foresee the rate and direction of change in the nature of activities for which a structure is designed. Always evaluate the ease and cost of altering the structure to accommodate potential changes required during the projection period.

Forecasting Locational Desirability

Urban growth both creates and destroys locational advantage. Because immobility is an inherent characteristic of real property, locational factors have a pervasive influence on value. Urban complexes exist in response to the economic and social needs of inhabitants. The city's internal organization reflects these needs as they originally were and as they evolved over time. As inhabitants' needs change, the consequent alterations in the structure of urban space alters the relative value of urban locations.

Our concern is with the contribution locational factors make to real estate productivity. Location itself is a geographic phenomenon, but it has social, economic, and institutional dimensions as well.

Linkages

We live in a society characterized by economic specialization and interdependence. Activity at one site often initiates a complex set of economic and social interactions generating movement of goods or people between that and other sites. This requires transportation between the sites and is called *linkage*.

The costs of moving people or goods between linked sites are called *transfer costs*. If two properties were the same in all other respects, the one that results in lower transfer costs would be more desirable and would command higher rents.

Transfer cost is a complicated idea, and the costs can be difficult to estimate. Those representing direct outlays for vehicle operation or commercial fares can, of course, be measured directly. But transfer costs also include the value of time lost traveling between sites, as well as the personal aggravation and bother. Total transfer costs per unit of time are the product of the cost per trip (measured to include both explicit and implicit costs) and the frequency of such trips.

Examples of implicit costs that are difficult to quantify include the risk of children having to cross a busy highway to travel to and from school or of a housewife having to traverse a disreputable neighborhood to reach the most convenient shopping center.

A worker who commutes between home and employment creates a linkage between residence and workplace. Goods moving from warehouse to store or a person going from work to a restaurant for lunch are examples of important linkages. Other significant examples include movement of food products from farm to market and movement of manufactured goods from factory to consumer via retail outlets.

Were this the only consideration, the optimal location for any social or economic activity would be that which minimizes total transfer cost. Locational choice is constrained, however, by physical characteristics of potential sites, by desirable or undersirable neighborhood influences, and by institutional arrangements. Moreover, firms compete for the more desirable sites, and those firms for which transfer costs are most significant generally can outbid other firms for the better locations.

Neighborhood Influences
Site usages that are not linked may nonetheless be attracted to proximate locations, while linked establishments may be mutually repelled so that tenants will incur substantial transfer costs in order to avoid proximity. Locational arrangements unrelated to linkage considerations may result from a number of causal factors, or they may be simple historical accidents.

Two major sources of locational decisions not directly related to transfer cost minimization are institutional constraints and neighborhood influences. The first of these represents attempts by individuals or political units to restrict certain types of activity to specified locations for reasons which are not necessarily economic (though they often are motivated in part, at least, by economic considerations). Such institutional factors are considered in a subsequent section of this chapter. The latter factor, neighborhood influences, includes a number of elements that are all related in some manner to what urban economists term *externalities*.

Externalities may be favorable and thus attract people or businesses, or they may be unfavorable and so act as a repelling influence. The influence of externalities, or neighborhood factors, stems from real estate's long life and physical immobility. Since a firm, once established, cannot easily move to escape undesirable external factors or to capture desirable ones, the nature of neighborhood influences is a powerful factor in locational choice.

Special value often attaches to sites in a neighborhood considered to reflect favorably on the resident's character, for example. For many residential tenants, and for certain types of businesses, prestige is an important locational issue. Thus, in Chicago a Gold Coast residential address implies a certain socioeconomic status, as does a Park Avenue address in Manhattan. For similar reasons, legal firms often desire to locate near other law firms that have achieved a high level of professional recognition, financial firms tend to seek the favorable aura of location in established financial districts, and so forth.

Favorable externalities include aesthetic considerations. For residential users, and for many commercial purposes, a pleasing view is particularly important. Locations adjacent to golf courses, near attractive parks, or with an impressive view of a large body of water or of the cityscape often command a premium price unrelated to the issue of transfer costs.

Just as residents and business establishments are attracted by desirable neighborhood factors, so are they repelled by undesirable or incompatible conditions or activities. These objectionable influences include noise, smoke, odors, and unsavory neighbors. A favorable location shields one from these objectionable influences, whether by physical barriers, by distance, or by law.

Destroying or creating physical barriers can drastically alter neighborhood influences. Removing a railroad bed or public building complex that previously separated a highly desirable residential area from an area of decay or slum housing, for example, might foster decline in a previously stable area. Altering a barrier that is more psychological than physical might have the same effect. A small park or neighborhood shopping area, for example, might be a symbol of neighborhood solidarity and uniqueness, setting the residents apart from those in surrounding areas.

Moving or discontinuing ancillary services such as schools or churches usually alters neighborhood influences. Consolidating school districts or simply destroying the traditional linkage between place of residence and location of school attendance can cause massive and often unforeseen shifts in residential neighborhood's relative desirability.

Without protective zoning and building codes, inharmonious or incompatible land usage can quickly destroy a neighborhood's locational value. Recent successful court challenges to existing zoning laws deemed to be unfairly exclusionary serve to emphasize the danger of relying on these institutional arrangements as a major element in preserving locational value.

Institutional Factors

Protection from unfavorable influences may be ensured by the existence of physical barriers such as a river, unbuildable terrain, or the existence of intervening compatible structures and uses. Frequently, in urban places reliance is placed on private or public land-use-control provisions for such protection.

Private land utilization restrictions are created by including special provisions in a deed of conveyance. A subdivision developer might, for example, include in all deeds a restriction against usage thought to be incompatible with the subdivision's intended purpose. Generally, these restrictions enhance site values because potential purchasers feel protected from objectionable neighborhood influences.

Increasingly, residents have come to place reliance on special public land-use restrictions and other land-use-control ordinances to protect them from inharmonious or incompatible usages. These ordinances include zoning regulations, subdivision controls, and building codes, all of which are designed and intended to regulate the nature and quality of structures erected at a locality or the nature of the activities therein, or both. Public control over land use, which constitutes the exercise of the state's police power, exerts a pervasive influence on the type and intensity of property use, and thus on its power to command rents.

A Program of Locational Analysis

Site value can be destroyed as well as created by social and economic events beyond an owner's control. Therefore, you must carefully assess present and projected locational factors and their probable impact on a site's productivity.

The first step is to identify linkages that characterize existing or planned land uses. Judge the relative importance of each linkage and locate linked establishements in terms of their geographic relationship to the target site. This permits you to assess transfer costs and the contribution linkages make to potential profitability of the planned use.

Futurity in Locational and Physical Analysis

Locational analysis is meaningless without reference to a time element. Those factors that affect a site's desirability must be considered in the context of a specific use, a particular geographic location, and a specified time period. All the elements except geography are in a constant state of flux. Analysis of locational desirability must therefore consider probable future changes in locational factors.

Because locational factors dominate a site's ability to produce income, you should pay particular attention to this issue. The analysis must be done in the present, but the focus is on the future. Not only are locational factors themselves subject to change, but even the importance of given factors vary through time.

An important but often overlooked aspect of properties embodying questionable physical or locational characteristics is the contribution these characteristics make to the property's vulnerability to marginal changes in demand. The aggregate vacancy factor might change only minutely during a projection period, yet the impact of the change is felt disproportionately by properties on the fringe of a market classification.

Social, technological, and economic changes often create new, or destroy old, site values. Because causal elements are diverse and interrelated, analysis of probable change in locational benefits must take into account probable future changes, not only in the factors themselves, but also in their interrelationships.

Changes in Linkages

Lifestyle alterations, business pattern shifts, or technological change can sever existing linkages and create new ones. For example, the shift from urban to suburban living, combined with the popularity of automobiles as a transportation mode, created linkages between communities and regional shopping centers while severing the old linkage between residential neighborhoods and the central business district.

Other examples abound. The declining importance of public transport facilities has reduced the locational value of housing and retail stores along such public transportation arteries as commuter railways and major bus routes. Concomitantly, mass automobilie ownership has greatly increased the locational value of residential sites convenient to major highways. Shifting transportation patterns have diminished the locational significance of industrial sites adjacent to rail sidings, while the increased congestion of urbanization has magnified the value of industrial sites outside of, yet convenient to, the central urban area.

Changes within Linked Establishments

Old linkages grow less important as locational decision factors, lifestyles, or production modes reduce the value of ready access to the linked locations. Televison, for example, has decreased the importance of existing linkages to community entertainment centers. Widespread ownership of refrigerators and deep freezers has reduced the frequency of shopping trips and weakened the need for quick and convenient access to grocery stores and restaurants.

Changes in Transportation Arteries

Modification of existing transport systems, such as the rerouting of major highways, the closing of railway spurs, or alterations in the cost and availablity of parking facilities, can render an existing linkage insignificant. Constructing a bridge over a previously impassable river or building a new limited-access highway can destroy a site's locational advantage by providing ready access to the linked locations from competing sites.

In recent years, freeway construction has provided many graphic examples of unanticipated alterations in traffic patterns that have destroyed existing linkages and created new ones. The locational value of proximity to a desirable envirnomental factor, such as a park or beach, can be completely destroyed by having ready access severed by a controlled-access highway or an intervening railway or canal.

THE SUPPLY FACTOR IN RENTAL VALUE

Both desirability and the relative scarcity and price of close substitutes affect the value of any good or service, including rental space. Therefore, analysis of future ability to command rents must include a forecast of changes in the supply of comparable space during the projection period.

Demonstrably, the supply of land is far in excess of current needs. Census data indicate that about three-quarters of the population occupies less than 15 percent of the country's space. Moreover, more than 65 percent of exurban space is uncultivated and available for uses other than agriculture. Clearly, there is abundant room for urban expansion.

Moreover, there is adequate room for expansion at the fringes of most cities. As outer fringes expand arithmetically, the space within city boundaries expands geometrically. It is therefore true that the total supply of developable land is virtually unlimited.

What is limited is land well-suited for specific uses. Most available undeveloped land lies on the urban fringe, but that is not the optimum location for many activites. Since only one parcel of land can occupy any particular location on the urban landscape, the supply of land with specific site characteristics is necessarily limited to one unique parcel.

Of course, while it may be true that there is "one best" location for many activities (because of the location of other urban economic and social activities and the unique physical characteristics of a particular site), it is equally true that there are almost always several alternative sites that are nearly as good. These substitute sites may yield slightly less total utility, but several may adequately fulfill the basic requirements for most urban economic activities.

To summarize the question of supply, sites are what economists call a *differentiated product*. That is, they have some characteristics that differentiate them from all others, but the differences are generally not so great that several slightly different sites will not serve *almost* as well. The choice between the ideal site and a close substitute will be based on their relative costs and the relative present values of the anticipated future flow of benefits from their use.

Futurity in Supply Analysis

Were it possible to actually plot demand and supply relations as depicted by economists' graphs, analysts would live a less stressful, if also less interesting, life. Even though that is not possible, the bare bones of supply and demand tell us much about likely future developments.

There must be some level of vacancies to provide an inventory of rentable space. Imperfect information makes it impossible for all space to be rented at all times at market-clearing prices. Orderly functioning of markets in the face of imperfect information requires an inventory to compensate.

When vacancy rates drop significantly below the historical average (that which experience has demonstrated generally prevails in the market), it is safe to infer that there is "excess demand" at currently prevailing prices. Rents can then be expected to move upward toward a new equilibrium over the short run. Conversely, when vacancy rates are running significantly above normal, there is insufficient demand for available space. This suggests a moderation in rents until demand shifts sufficiently to absorb the available supply.

As a temporary analyst your task is to forecast changes in the current demand and supply relationship over the period you expect to be holding a property. This requires estimating the possible impact additional rental units will have on market rental rates and how this will interact with shifts in the demand for rental space over time.

The starting point in estimating long-term supply is to observe that additional rental units will continue to be produced as long as building costs are less than the present value of the expected stream of future rental property net operating income. Supply changes, therefore, are dependent on future rates of change in construction costs, on the cost and availability of appropriately zoned land, and on developers' perceptions of the direction and rate of changes in demand.

Monopoly Element in Supply Analysis

Beyond the question of availability of competing space, future rental rates depend on the relative degree of prestige associated with a property. The physical amenities and locational convenience of New York's Rockefeller Center are not appreciably greater than those of surrounding properties, yet the center commands premium rents. The distinction lies solely in the perception of tenants who desire identification with this specific address. Economists refer to this as a *monopoly element.* Marketing specialists prefer the more neutral term *product differentiation.*

As with other products, rental space that has a prestige image can command a premium price. In market terms, product differences—whether real or spurious—desensitize buyers to price differentials. The distinction may lie in unique architecture, quality construction, luxurious appointments, or any other element that creates a compelling image for potential tenants.

Product differences that exist only in the buyer's mind are even more valuable than physical differences. Styling, quality, and functional features can often be duplicated by competitors, but reputation is unique to individual properties and is often generated consciously to appeal to a specific class of tenants. Depending on the image assocated with an address, rental units may consistently command a premium price or rent at discount from prevailing rates for properties similarly located and outfitted.

Owners who successfully cultivate and protect a particular property image capture some of the monopoly advantages associated with unique location. The power of such an image to command rent is far less vulnerable to future supply variations.

REDUCING INFORMATIONAL CLUTTER

Investors intent on making decisions based on hard facts rather than hot tips often find themselves the victims of information overload. They encounter so much data and so many conflicting opinions as to what it all means that they are less well-equipped to make rational decisions than they would have been with only a minimal amount of information. A surfeit of data clogs their intellectual sensors; they need a filter to block out misleading or irrelevant opinions and data bits.

Information Filters

An early step is to bypass the distorting influence of pseudoinformation. This may represent a deliberate effort to mislead; more likely, it stems from a distorted frame of reference or from unmitigated incompetence. Your best defense is to avoid having pseudoinformation injected into the decision process at all. Everyone has an opinion, but most are either worthless or downright damaging.

Brokers are a valuable source of relevant information. Unfortunately, they are also a prime source of pseudoinformation. In evaluating what a broker tells you, or in deciding whether to even let one express an opinion, ask yourself (and the broker) two vital questions: (1) what are the broker's qualifications, and (2) what are the broker's biases?

A really old inside joke has a grocery store customer trying to cash a check and being asked to show her real estate broker's license. "Why not my drivers license?" she asks. The response: "Some of our customers don't drive." Sometimes it does seem that, at one time or another, virtually every adult has held a license to sell real estate.

Therein lies a serious problem. The average experience level is low because of the high turnover among licensed real estate people. Very little specialized education is required, and most practitioners have little more than the required minimum. Nothing in the entrance or practitioner requirements qualifies a salesperson to render a valid opinion as to real estate's investment quality, yet I have never seen a salesperson at all reticent in this regard. The shock would be overwhelming should a broker or salesperson ever say:

> Gee, I don't really know about that. You see, I'm not an analyst or real estate economist. My specialty is convincing people to buy and tying them as tightly as possible to the commitment with a binding offer and nonrefundable deposit. You should look elsewhere for advice.

Not to worry. I'm not likely to be subjected to such a shock unless an answer of that sort is mandated somewhere by law. The point is that the typical broker's opinion is probably no more useful than that of a randomly chosen person on the street. Don't ask for it; try to avoid it; if it is given, try to ignore it.

I must digress. This is not intended as a condemnation of brokers, or in any way as a denigration of their competence or their loyalty to their principal. They (usually) are working for the seller and conscientiously try to get you to buy—which is what they are paid for. Moreover, not all brokers are inexperienced in investment analysis or lacking in training. A special cadre have been superbly trained, and many of them earn a substantial income as consultants. You can recognize them by the letters *CCIM* (a copyrighted abbreviation for Certified Commercial and Investment Member, a designation conferred by the Realtors National Marketing Institutute) following their names on business cards and letterheads. They have completed a rigorous training program and have demonstrated their understanding of the issues by making passing grades on a formidable battery of examinations. They are a breed apart.

Here are simple rules that have served me well in working with brokers:

• Ask only for relevant information that the broker is likely to have collected as a by-product of listing and selling property. The cooperative listing services that have been established in most metropolitan areas, for example, are gold mines of important information, all at the fingertips of participating brokers.

• Qualify all information with the broker's answer to the question "How do you know?" Completely discount mere opinions, no matter how fervently they seem to be held. Those facts that everybody knows are often most likely to be wrong.

• Avoid, wherever possible, allowing a broker to express an opinion regarding the property's investment quality or the appropriateness of its price. Don't let the broker influence the price you offer. You don't have to be rude, just adamant.

• Remember that, unless sellers have placed express instructions to the contrary, the broker is obligated to deliver all offers, no matter what the broker thinks about the price or terms.

KEY POINTS

• The single most reliable indicator of what will happen in the near future is usually what has happened recently. Unless there are major shifts in political, social, or economic forces affecting an area, you can expect a continuation of established trends in property income and operating expenses.

• Long-term forecasts are inherently unreliable. This fact is mitigated by a reduced need for accuracy as the forecast is pushed further into the future. To make a rational investment decision, you need only an approximate feel for a property's long-term prospects.

• Locational advantages are the key determinant of your property's ability to continue generating income. Physical features and property amenities can often be altered to conform to modern competitive standards, but there is little you can do about most of the forces that alter the desirability of your property's location.

• To forecast a property's rent-generating ability, note the relationships that require your tenants to make frequent trips to other locations (to home, to work, to school, to shopping, and so forth). Other factors being equal, people will elect a location that minimizes aggregate transfer costs, the cost of moving between sites.

• Neighborhood influences are a common reason that tenants opt for a location that actually increases their aggregate transfer costs. They may pay premium rents and incur the cost and discomfort of long commutes to benefit from a particularly desir able neighborhood or to escape an undesirable one.

• Supply, the number of competing properties, is a major factor determining future rental income. Since it is a factor over which you will have little control, it makes sense to select a site that gives you some monopoly benefits. You may be able to create a monopoly element by differentiating your buildings from others. You can sometimes do this by promoting a desirable location (pleasant view, good access, etc.) or even by generating a particulary prestigious reputation for your building

• Information is the key to making good decisions. But you need an efficient and economical way to filter out extraneous or mis' leading information. Real estate brokers are a major source of both good information and bad. To minimize the bad information, insist that brokers give you only well supported data, devoid of editorial comments. Always expect that what is presented as a broker's informed opinion is really a polished sales pitch

CHAPTER 6

PUTTING IT
ALL TOGETHER

What do you do after you have all the data you can digest? You could, of course, spend your productive years collecting information and never do anything with it. That's exactly what will happen if you defer your investment decision until you've learned everything you need to know. We never have all relevant information until it's too late to act.

At some point, the research must stop. You have to look at what you have and either ante or fold. In this chapter we see how a rational and informed investor might set about making such a decision.

Let's assume that you have found a structurally sound and reasonably well-maintained five-year-old apartment building that you believe has attractive prospects. Your preliminary estimate is that the property will sell for about $3.6 million and that your transaction costs (not including the cost of acquiring mortgage money) will run about $100,000

THE FORECAST

Your first step will be to get information on the property's operating history. Starting with the owner's operating statement and making adjustments as discussed in Chapter Four, you derive the adjusted statement shown in Table 6–1

TABLE 6–1
Adjusted Operating Statement for Altamese Villa Apartments

Potential gross revenue		$768,000
Less: Vacancy and rent loss		20,000
Effective gross income		$748,000
Less: Operating expenses:		
Real estate taxes	$146,000	
Insurance	15,000	
Wages	80,000	
Fuel	58,000	
Water	12,000	
Electricity	9,000	
Scavenger	8,500	
Painting & redecorating	5,000	
Repairs & maintenance	8,000	
Supplies	4,000	
Management	30,000	
Miscellaneous	7,000	
Reserves for replacement	10,000	
Total expenses		$392,500
Net operating income		$355,500

Estimating the Debt Service

Inquiring of several mortgage brokers, you discover that lenders will probably insist on a minimum debt-coverage ratio of 1.2, based on a conservative estimate of the first year's operating results. Expressed differently, they will lend an amount such that the property will generate at least $1.20 of first-year net operating income for every dollar of annual debt service. This assures the lender that the income can fall about 17 percent below projections before the property fails to generate enough income to meet the mortgage payments.

Adjusting last year's operating results (Table 6–1) by the expected 3 percent growth rate, you conclude that you can justify a first-year net operating income projection of 1.03 times $355,500, or $366,165. To determine the amount of debt service this implies (remembering the lender's requirement that you have $1.20 of income for every dollar of debt service), divide the expected income by 1.20. This reveals that the property will support annual debt service of $366,165/1.20, or $305,138.

/

Each lender cites slightly different loan terms, but you conclude that the most attractive package is one featuring a 10 percent interest rate with a 3 percent origination fee and a 20-year amortization period. To determine the monthly payment per dollar borrowed on such a loan, look at the 10 percent column and the 20 year row of the amortization table in Appendix B. Multiply that amount ($0.00965) by 12 to determine the annual debt service per dollar borrowed:

$$12 \times \$0.00965 = \$0.11580$$

Since you have determined that the property will support annual debt service of no more than $305,138 and that the annual debt service per dollar borrowed will be about $0.11580, you can estimate the amount you will be able to borrow by dividing $305,138 by that number. The quotient, $2,635,043, is the maximum loan that will meet the lender's criteria. As a practical matter this will round to $2,635,000, an amount that will bring the annual debt service to $305,136.

Table 6–2 shows the annual debt service broken into interest and principal portions for each year of the expected ownership period. You can construct your own table, called an *amorti-*

TABLE 6–2
Amortization Schedule

Loan amount:	$2,635,000
Interest rate:	10 percent
Loan period:	20 Years
Payment:	$25,428

Year	Debt Service	Interest	Principal	Balance
1	$305,136	$261,536	$43,600	$2,591,400
2	305,136	256,973	48,163	2,543,237
3	305,136	251,928	53,208	2,490,029
4	305,136	246,354	58,782	2,431,247
5	305,136	240,201	64,935	2,366,312
6	305,136	233,403	71,733	2,294,579
7	305,136	225,892	79,244	2,215,335
8	305,136	217,593	87,543	2,127,792

zation schedule, for any interest rate and any loan terms, using
the technique explained in Appendix A. You can do it even more
simply by cranking the numbers through an inexpensive (about
$25.00) financial calculator. Table 6–2 was constructed with a
calculator, by the way, and rounding error will give you slightly
different numbers if you use the table.

Estimating After-tax Cash Flows

Investigating local economic and demographic trends, you conclude that the property is in a stable neighborhood where operating results and market values will continue to closely track
changes in the metropolitan area's consumer price index. The
index has been rising at about 4 percent per annum, and a
nearby university's economic research bureau has estimated
that it will accelerate only slightly to about a 4. 5 percent average over the next five years. You conclude that the property's
net operating income should grow at least 3 percent per annum,
and this is the rate you decide to incorporate in your analysis.

With this information in hand, we can construct a multiple-year cash-flow forecast. The precise number of years is not
really important, as we will soon see. But let's use an eight-
year forecast.

The operating forecast is summarized in Table 6–3. Since
our reconstructed net operating income for the year before purchase was $355,500, the expected income for the first year in the
forecast is this amount plus 3 percent, or $366,165. To derive
the forecast for subsequent years simply increase each year by
3 percent over the previous year. These amounts are shown on
line one of Table 6–3.

To move from net operating income to taxable gain or tax
deductible loss for each year, subtract any tax deductible item
that is not considered an operating expense and thus was not
deducted in developing the net operating income forecast. For
our project these items are interest expense (line two of Table 6–
3) and depreciation allowance (line three). The interest expense
estimate can be pulled directly from the amortization schedule
(Table 6–2). Estimating depreciation allowances is a slightly
more involved process.

TABLE 6–3
Eight-Year Cash-Flow Forecast

	Year of Operations							
	1	2	3	4	5	6	7	8
01 Net operating income	$366,165	$377,150	$388,464	$400,118	$412,122	$424,486	$437,220	$450,337
02 Less: Interest	261,536	256,973	251,928	246,354	240,201	233,403	225,892	217,593
03 Depreciation	103,155	107,640	107,640	107,640	107,640	107,640	107,640	103,155
04 Taxable gain	$ 1,474	$ 12,537	$ 28,896	$ 46,124	$ 64,281	$ 83,443	$103,688	$129,589
05 Times tax rate	.28	.28	.28	.28	.28	.28	.28	.28
06 Tax (Saving)	$ 413	$ 3,510	$ 8,091	$ 12,915	$ 17,999	$ 23,364	$ 29,033	$ 36,285
07 Net operating income	$366,165	$377,150	$388,464	$400,118	$412,122	$424,486	$437,220	$450,337
08 Less: Debt service	305,136	305,136	305,136	305,136	305,136	305,136	305,136	305,136
09 Income tax	413	3,510	8,091	12,915	17,999	23,364	29,033	36,285
10 After-tax cash flow	$ 60,616	$ 68,504	$ 75,237	$ 82,067	$ 88,987	$ 95,986	$103,051	$108,916

The portion of the purchase price (including transaction costs other than those encountered in getting a mortgage loan) that is attributable to buildings and other man-made items will be written off as a depreciation or cost recovery allowance over a period mandated by law. The portion of the cost attributable to the land is not recovered until the property is sold. Your first task, therefore, is to apportion the purchase between land and structures.

Earlier we estimated that the property will cost $3.6 million. Adding the estimated $100,000 of transaction costs gives you an initial tax basis of $3.7 million. Tax law specifies that the basis must be allocated between land and buildings in a ratio that reflects their relative market values. You look at the tax assessor's records for this property and note that 20 percent of the assessed value has been attributed to the land and the balance to the structures. Since tax assessors' records are generally acceptable to the Internal Revenue Service as an indicator of relative market values, you conclude that 80 percent of the initial tax basis, or $2.96 million, will be properly attributable to the structure, and this becomes the basis for depreciation deductions.

Current tax law provides that residential income property will be written off on a straight line basis over 27.5 years. Dividing the depreciable amount by 27.5, you determine that the annual depreciation deduction will be $107,636. This comes to $8,970 per month. You need the monthly figure because you can only claim the deduction for the number of months each year that you actually own the property, including half a month's allowance in the month of acquisition and again in the month of disposition. If the acquisition occurs in the first month and disposition during the last month of your taxable year, annual depreciation deductions will be 11.5 times $8,970, or $103,155, in the first and last year of the expected eight-year holding period, and 12 times $8,970, or $107,640, during the intervening years.

Subtracting interest expense and depreciation allowances from net operating income brings us to the taxable income line (line four) of Table 6–3. Multiplying this amount by your marginal income tax bracket yields the forecast annual income tax consequences of owning the property. Let's assume that the first year's income forecast will put you in the 28 percent incremental tax bracket and that, lacking any good information to the contrary, you conclude that you will likely pay at this rate throughout the expected holding period. That brings us to line six, anticipated annual income tax consequences.

Line seven starts again with expected net operating income, which is simply brought down from line one. On the top half of the table we were concerned with income tax consequences, which are needed in order to move to the cash-flow projection. Cash flows are the focus of lines seven through ten.

Net operating income would be the net cash flow from operations if there were no nonoperating receipts or expenditures. But, there almost always are. In our example, debt service (line eight) and income taxes (line nine) are nonoperating items. Debt service, which we determined earlier to be $305,136, is based on a loan of $2,635,000, with interest of 10 percent per annum and a 20-year amortization period. Income taxes are brought down from line six. Subtracting the debt service and income taxes (or adding back tax savings where you anticipate a deductible loss) yields expected after-tax cash flow, which is the table's bottom line.

Cash Flow from Disposal

At some point you will probably decide to dispose of your new asset. Let's adopt the initial assumption that you expect to sell after eight years; later, we will see that the precise assumption is not really crucial to the investment decision. What is crucial is a rough estimate of after-tax cash flow from disposal.

Looking at prices and operating records of similar properties that have sold in recent years, you note that capitalization rates (the relationship between net operating income and market value), when based on current values and past operating results, have ranged from 8 to 13 percent, but that they tend to fluctuate around a central value of 10.5 percent. You adopt the convenient—and altogether reasonable—assumption that the typical relationship is most likely to prevail when you are ready to sell.

Applying a 10.5 percent capitalization rate to the expected eighth year net operating income gives us an expected sales price of $4,288,924. From this amount subtract transaction costs (which you estimate to be about 8 percent of the sales price) and the adjusted tax basis just prior to selling to derive the estimated gain on disposal. The adjusted tax basis is the initial basis (what you paid for the property, including transaction costs) minus all depreciation deductions claimed over the holding period. Multiply the expected gain by your anticipated incremental income tax rate to derive a forecast of the tax liability from selling. Here are the numbers:

Selling price		$4,288,924
Less: Tax basis	$2,847,850	
Selling costs	343,114	3,190,964
Gain on disposal		$1,097,960
Times incremental tax rate		.28
Tax on sale		$ 307,429

Cash flow from disposal will be the sales price minus all related cash disbursements. Outlays will be for selling costs, income taxes, and the remaining mortgage balance. We have just estimated taxes and selling costs; the mortgage balance will be the initial $2,635,000 loan minus all principal payments during the holding period, and is shown on the amortization schedule (Table 6–2). Anticipated after-tax cash flow from selling after eight years is $1,510,589, determined as follows:

Selling price		$4,288,924
Less: Transaction costs	$ 343,114	
Income taxes	307,429	
Mortgage balance	2,127,792	2,778,335
After-tax cash flow		$1,510,589

THE ANALYSIS

You now have a "best estimate" of the after-tax cash flow that will result from buying this property at its most likely transaction price. To decide whether the deal looks worthwhile, adjust anticipated cash flows to convert them to present worth equivalents. But first, you must decide on a minimum acceptable rate of return.

The Opportunity Cost of Capital

The question you have to answer is: Where else can you invest your money without exposing yourself to appreciably greater risks, and what rate of return could you expect from those investments? The highest rate you could reasonably expect from such alternative ventures is your target rate of return, and is the rate you should use to convert expected cash flows into present value equivalents.

Using this rate, called the *opportunity cost of capital*, as a common discount rate applied to all prospective ventures that involve roughly the same degree of risk will permit you to make direct comparisons between proposals, even when they involve significantly different amounts of your cash.

Look at appraisal reports on several recently sold income properties. Note the after-tax cash flow those properties will probably generate, and you can infer the yield rates that equate the cash flows with the purchase prices. Or, estimate what average rate of return you can get in the stock or bond markets. These are both ways to determine the minimum expected rate of return that will induce you to buy real estate. This becomes your hurdle rate; the rate you use to discount expected cash flows.

Table 6–4 illustrates that, with a 12 percent discount rate, the present value of the expected cash flows for your project is $1,014,264. Expressed differently, this is the largest down payment you can make and still expect to earn 12 percent per annum on your equity investment. In the terminology of Chapter Three, it is the value of the equity position. Since our forecast was predicated on borrowing $2,635,000 on a first mortgage loan, the value of the debt position is that amount minus the 3 percent loan origination fee, or $2,555,950. Therefore, the most you would be justified in paying for the property is $3,570,214:

Value of equity cash flows(at 12 percent)	$1,014,264
Value of debt position(at 10 percent)	$2,555,950
Investment value	$3,570,214

TABLE 6–4
Present Value of Cash Flows

Year	Cash Flow	Present Value Factor	Present Value @ 12%
1	$ 60,616	.89286	$ 54,122
2	68,504	.79719	54,611
3	75,237	.71178	53,552
4	82,067	.63552	52,155
5	88,987	.56743	50,494
6	95,986	.50663	48,629
7	103,051	.45235	46,615
8	108,916	.40388	43,989
Sale	1,510,589	.40388	610,097
Present value of equity cash flows			$1,014,264

Our analysis reveals a problem. As the deal is currently structured, the most likely price ($3.7 million, including transaction costs) exceeds your investment value. Remember that investment value is the most a buyer would be justified in paying for a property. Expressed simply, you cannot anticipate earning your 12 percent per annum after-tax target rate of return.

Does this mean you should scratch the deal? Not necessarily. You may be able to salvage it by restructuring the terms. Suppose you propose that the seller take back a $360,000 note with interest at 10 percent per annum to be paid monthly and the principal amount due in 10 years or when you sell the property, whichever comes first? This will reduce your annual cash flow and your cash flow from disposal, but it will also radically cut the amount you have to put into the deal.

Table 6–5 shows the revised after-tax cash-flow forecast

TABLE 6–5
Eight-Year Cash-Flow Forecast

	Year of Operations							
	1	2	3	4	5	6	7	8
01 Net operating income	$366,165	$377,150	$388,464	$400,118	$412,122	$424,486	$437,220	$450,337
02 Less: Interest[1]	297,536	292,973	287,928	282,354	276,201	269,403	261,892	253,593
03 Depreciation	103,155	107,640	107,640	107,640	107,640	107,640	107,640	103,155
04 Gain (Loss)	($ 34,526)	($ 23,463)	($ 7,104)	$ 10,124	$ 28,281	$ 47,443	$ 67,688	$ 93,589
05 Times tax rate	.28	.28	.28	.28	.28	.28	.28	.28
06 Tax (Saving)	($ 9,667)	($ 6,570)	($ 1,989)	$ 2,835	$ 7,919	$ 13,284	$ 18,953	$ 26,205
07 Net operating income	$366,165	$377,150	$388,464	$400,118	$412,122	$424,486	$437,220	$450,337
08 Less: Debt service	341,136	341,136	341,136	341,136	341,136	341,136	341,136	341,136
09 Income tax	(9,667)	(6,570)	(1,989)	2,835	7,919	13,284	18,953	26,205
10 After-tax cash flow	$ 34,696	$ 42,584	$ 49,317	$ 56,147	$ 63,067	$ 70,066	$ 77,131	$ 82,996

[1]Includes first mortgage interest from Table 6–2 and $36,000 per annum interest on second mortgage note.

with the additional $36,000 per year interest expense. After-tax cash flow from disposal will be reduced by the $360,000 principal amount of the second mortgage note. These revised cash flows are converted to present value equivalents (again using a 12 percent discount rate) in Table 6–6. The net result is that your investment value is increased to $3,656,057:

Revised value of equity cash flow(at 12 percent)	$ 740,107
Value of debt: 1st mortgage note	2,555,950
2nd mortgage note	360,000
Investment value	$3,656,057

TABLE 6–6
Present Value of Revised Cash Flows

Year	Cash Flow	Present Value Factor	Present Value @ 12%
1	$ 34,696	.89286	$ 30,979
2	42,584	.79719	33,948
3	49,317	.71178	35,103
4	56,147	.63552	35,683
5	63,067	.56743	35,786
6	70,066	.50663	35,498
7	77,131	.45235	34,890
8	82,996	.40388	33,520
Sale	1,150,589	.40388	464,700
Present value of equity cash flows			$740,107

Revising the financing arrangements has added almost $86,000 to the investment value. But we are still approximately $44,000 short. You might ask the seller to pick up half of your $100,000 closing costs. Or, what is effectively the same thing, you could lower your offering price by $50,000 from your esti-mated market price. You will find many sellers more resistant to straightforward price reductions, however, than to indirect ones.

THE HOLDING PERIOD ASSUMPTION

Our analysis has assumed an eight-year holding period, but the assumption is not critical to the analysis. If we assume a constant growth rate for net operating income, value, and transactions as a percentage of sales price, altering the holding period assumption by one year changes the investment value by an amount ranging from 1.2 percent (when the holding period is extended from seven to eight years) to 0.6 percent (when the holding period is extended from eleven to twelve years).

Variation in the anticipated yield rates with different holding period assumptions is attributable to the number of years over which transaction costs and loan origination fees are amortized. The longer the holding period, the smaller the annual cost of these items, and thus the higher the expected annual yield. But, after seven or eight years the additional yield boost from amortizing them over another year or two is almost inconsequential.

KEY POINTS

• You should never pay more for a property than its investment value to you. This is the present value of the expected after-tax cash flows, net of debt service, plus the amount of the mortgage loan incorporated in the cash-flow forecast.
• Investment value is estimated by discounting expected after-tax cash flows at the opportunity cost of capital; the rate you could earn on the next best investment alternative that incorporates about the same level of risk.
• If the investment value is less than your estimate of the property's most likely sales price, you can often increase investment value by altering the terms of your purchase offer.
• When you are developing your cash-flow estimate, incorporate a holding period of eight to ten years unless you have specific alternative holding period plans. Varying the holding period assumption by a few years on either side of 10 will usually make little difference in the investment value computation.

CHAPTER 7

INFORMATION: THE KEY TO INVESTMENT SUCCESS

If everyone had the same level of knowledge and were privy to the same information, real estate investment would be like playing the lottery; success would be randomly distributed. The pattern of yields would be what investment analysts call a random walk.

Even casual observers know that real estate doesn't behave like that. What, then, makes the difference between mediocre investment success and hitting the jackpot, between merely riding the carousel and grabbing the brass ring? Years of research and participation have convinced me that success has three essential ingredients: luck, daring, and information.

Luck we can't do much about. But let's not impute too much to this element. Luck is just another name for chance, and chance tends to be randomly distributed. Furthermore, what appears to be chance often has a substantial causal element. Getting struck by a bolt of lightning might seem to make you a victim of chance, but standing on a hill during a thunderstorm, under the only tree in the area, isn't bad luck; it's stupidity. Let's accept that, stripped of the contributing elements of stupidity or prudence, chance is randomly distributed. That leaves daring and information.

Daring is certainly a key element. If luck is truly random, then your chances of being influenced by it depend in large part on the extent to which you put yourself in its path. You can't win a game of chance if you don't play (of course, you can't lose either). Analysis of the careers of very successful real estate investors reveals that they systematically put themselves in the path of luck; when they estimate the odds are in their favor, they play the game.

That brings us to information. For people with modest resources, access to information seems to weigh heavily in investment success. Simply put, you need accurate data to make good decisions. Investing without reliable information is like venturing into alien territory without a map.

Real estate markets tend to be inefficient—a phrase that means, among other things, that you can get above-average returns without taking above-average risks. A key element in this situation is that most people don't know how to get, at affordable prices, the information they need. This causes them to make uninformed investment decisions, thereby providing the opportunity for people with good information to out-perform the market.

This need not be. Most of the information you need to make rational, informed real estate decisions is readily available at modest cost, if only you know where to look.

WHAT YOU NEED TO KNOW

Real estate investors need two kinds of information. They need to know about the specific property in which they have an interest; its structural characteristics, physical condition, age, functional efficacy, operating costs, rent-generating capacity, market value, and so on. They also need general information about the geographical area in which the property is located—population growth rates, demographic and economic trends, political and social change, and so forth—and about the broader investment environment.

Site-Specific Information

To make rational decisions about a particular building or land parcel you need to know about building costs, operating expenses, and income. Numerous reports and information services generate data from which these can be estimated. Most of the information is available free at major public or university libraries. Here are the most widely employed sources.

Boeckh Building Valuation Manuals

(American Appraisal Associates, 525 East Michigan Street, P.O. Box 664, Milwaukee, WI 53201, updated bimonthly). The Boeckh manuals are widely used by real estate appraisers and are generally considered to be a reliable way to estimate building costs. Adjustments for cost differentials between major U.S. cities are included. Using data from these manuals you can estimate building costs in three different ways:

1. Component Cost; useful if you have access to building plans.
2. Model Method; used in consort with a walk-through inspection of the building.
3. Comparative Cost Multipliers; a general estimate based on using comparative cost multipliers to adjust for annual cost increases for different classes of construction.

Building Construction Cost Data

(R.S. Means Company, Inc., Construction Consultants and Publishers, 100 Construction Plaza, P.O. Box 800, Kingston, MA 02364-0800, annually). Aimed primarily at industrial and commercial projects costing $500,000 and up, or large multifamily or custom single-family housing, this service gives material, labor, and equipment costs for each stage of a construction job.

Dodge Cost Systems Publications

(Dodge Cost Systems, P.O. Box 28, Princeton, NJ 08540, annually). These publications comprise a series dealing with various types and stages of construction costs. Included in the series are:

1. *Dodge Assemblies Cost Data.* A guide to the cost consequences of design decisions made at an early stage. A reference tool for measuring the cost impact of each system included in building. Figures include the usual contractor's markup and are based on national averages.

2. *Dodge Heavy Construction Cost Data.* Material costs based on research of cost information from many sources and analysis of current economic trends. Labor and equipment costs are calculated using the listed production rates, wage rates, and

equipment operating costs and are based on observed current practices of many contractors. There is an adjustment index for cost differentials in various cities.

3. *Dodge Square Foot Cost Data.* Designed to help make preliminary budgets, bids, or estimates of building cost. Permits you to compare their figures with costs of similar buildings that have been recently constructed. The contract costs are obtained from the architect/engineer in charge of each job as soon after the award as possible. To ensure that all listings are on as uniform a base as possible, data sources are requested to follow procedures for computation of area and volume described by the American Institute of Architects. The bid prices are reported by major components of the projects—structure, plumbing, heating and ventilation, air conditioning, electricity—as well as for the total project. Codes are provided that enable you to translate listings for any project from the bid time to the current time and from one location to another.

4. *Dodge Unit Cost Data.* Contains current construction cost information printed directly from the computerized construction cost data base. Files are updated almost daily with data from actual job sites throughout the country and from frequent cost surveys. Provides material and labor adjustment indices for cities and follows the established Uniform Construction Index format for rapid reference. The productivity information represents an average for work that has actually been performed throughout the country within the recent past. Gives output and unit costs for each job at each stage.

Marshall Valuation Service
(Marshall & Swift, 1617 Beverly Blvd., P.O. Box 26307, Los Angeles, CA 90026-0307, updated monthly). This provides information on construction cost and housing characteristics within the United States, which enables users to develop reproduction or replacement cost estimates for more than 1,000 different building types. Information is divided into five major cost groups based on classification of construction quality. Includes cost multipliers used to adjust for cost differentials between local areas and between construction quality classes, as well as to reflect changes in the general price level. Data are available in loose-leaf format, on computer diskettes, or on-line

General Information

We have seen that information about a property's current status isn't enough. You also need to estimate what will happen over the next few years, since benefits from your current expenditures are expected to be received in the future. Here are several sources from which forecasts can be generated without recourse to original research.

American Housing Survey

(Bureau of the Census, U.S. Department of Commerce; Superintendent of Documents, U.S. Government Printing Office, Washington, D.C. 20402, published quadrennially). At irregular intervals the Census Bureau surveys 12 to 15 of the 60 Metropolitan Statistical Areas that are included in the housing survey program. Housing units included in the survey are divided between the central city and the remainder of the Metropolitan Statistical Area (MSA) according to the relative distribution of total housing units in the area. Key information reported in the American Housing Survey includes:

- Housing characteristics for selected metropolitan areas.
- Quarterly and annual vacancy rates, and characteristics of vacant units.
- Quarterly and annual absorption rates for rental units by size, rental price, and nature of facilities, and for condominium units by size and asking price.
- Size, rental rates, and asking prices for newly completed apartments.

American Profile

(Donnelley Marketing Information Service, 1901 South Meyers Road, Oakbrook Terrace, IL 60148). This report includes information specified by clients and covers political divisions and areas defined by zip code or census tract. You can also order data for areas within a user-defined polygon or circle. Data that may be incorporated in reports include:

- population
- age

- number of households
- household income
- household mobility
- household vehicles
- race and sex
- education
- marital status
- employment, by economic sector
- employment, by trade/profession
- travel time to work
- school enrollment
- home value
- monthly rent
- housing characteristics
- housing tenure
- financial institution deposits
- neighborhood socioeconomic ranking

Building Stock Database and Forecast

(Dodge/DRI, F.W. Dodge Division, McGraw-Hill Information Systems Company, Two Ravina Drive, Suite 1210, Atlanta, GA 30346, annually). These reports, which can be ordered in print format or transmitted on-line via a direct computer link-up with the publisher, summarize construction activity and space inventory by county for 35 structural types aggregated into 15 structural groups:

- retail stores and restaurants
- auto service and parking garages
- offices
- manufacturing plants
- warehouses
- educational buildings
- single-family residential
- hotel/motel
- government buildings
- religious buildings
- hospitals and health care
- amusement, social, and recreational
- miscellaneous

- multifamily residential
- dormitories

Bureau of the Census Guide to Programs and Publications, Subjects and Areas

(Bureau of the Census, U.S. Department of Commerce; Superintendent of Documents, U.S. Government Printing Office, Washington, D.C. 20402). This guide contains charts that describe the statistical information available in Census Bureau publications since 1968, defines geographic areas covered, and outlines programs and activites. It is fully indexed.

CACI's Siteline Service

(CACI, 8260 Willow Oaks Corporate Drive, Fairfax, VA 22031). This company sells customized reports (available in printed format or via electronic transmission through a direct computer link-up) for the user's marketing area defined by zip code, metropolitan area, county, city, census tracts, or any user-defined market area of any size or shape throughout the United States. Available data include:

- demographic and income forecast
- census profile
- sales potential
- market segmentation
- housing value by age

Census Catalogue and Guide

(Bureau of the Census, U.S. Department of Commerce; Superintendent of Documents, U.S. Government Printing Office, Washington, D.C. 20402, annually with monthly updates). This catalogue contains abstracts of all products issued by the Bureau of the Census since 1980. Included in the listing are available data files, special tabulations, and other unpublished census materials. Includes a Monthly Product Announcement that reports on new publications available from the Bureau.

Census Data by Zip Code

(Bureau of the Census, U.S. Department of Commerce; Superintendent of Documents, U.S. Government Printing Office, Washington, D.C. 20402). This is a computer print-out of selected census data by zip code. Data, gleaned from that collected in the decennial census, include:

- number of persons
- education completed
- location of work place
- occupied units
- number of single persons
- labor force
- rent information
- number of persons over age 3 in school, by race
- number of households
- income ranges
- housing information
- number of families
- households by type
- class worker
- units in structure
- number of persons over age 25, by education and race

Census of Housing
(Bureau of the Census, U.S. Department of Commerce; Superintendent of Documents, U.S. Government Printing Office, Washington, D.C. 20402, decennially, published about three years after census is taken). This is a tabulation of housing characteristics for the entire population, presented in 53 tables and cross-referenced for householders by race. It includes such details as age, sex, race, and marital status of householders.

Census of Population
(Bureau of the Census, U.S. Department of Commerce; Superintendent of Documents, U.S. Government Printing Office, Washington, D.C. 20402, decennially, published about three years after census is taken). This is a tabulation of population data for states, MSAs with population of 250,000 or more, counties, urbanized areas, and minor civil subdivisions. It contains 229 tables presenting such population characteristics as:

- place of birth
- school enrollment

- marital status
- occupation
- place of work
- travel time to work
- place of residence five years earlier
- citizenship
- years of school completed
- family size
- year last worked
- income (amount and source)
- mode of transportation to work

Census of Population and Housing

(Bureau of the Census, U.S. Department of Commerce; Superintendent of Documents, U.S. Government Printing Office, Washington, D.C. 20402, decennially, published about three years after census is taken). This publication includes descriptive population and housing data for each MSA.

Census of Retail Trade—Metropolitan Statistical Areas

(Bureau of the Census, U.S. Department of Commerce; Superintendent of Documents, U.S. Government Printing Office, Washington, D.C. 20402, every five years). This includes separate data for each state, MSA, county, and city with at least 500 retail establishments. Data include:

- number of retail establishments
- retail employment
- retail sales
- kinds of retail businesses
- retail payroll

Additionally, for cities of 2,500 or more population and for all counties, the number of retail establishments and retail sales are given for 10 major retail business classifications.

Construction Review

(U.S. Department of Commerce, International Trade Administration; Superintendent of Documents, U.S. Government Printing Office, Washington, D.C. 20402, bimonthly). This reports monthly construction activity for the United States, regions, and selected MSAs. Information is based on sample data collected by public and private agencies. The information's validity is suspect because most of the data are from building permits, which do not reflect construction activity outside areas subject to local permit requirements. Moreover, some construction activity in permit areas may fail to be recorded, and some may be reported in the wrong period. As a consequence, information from the *Construction Review* is useful primarily for estimating trends. Construction data are reported in eight sections:

1. Feature article.
2. New construction put in place (private and public).
3. Housing units (private and public).
4. Construction authorized by building permits.
5. Value of construction contract awards (public and private).
6. Cost and price indices, interest rates, and housing payment factors (principal, interest, and rents).
7. Construction materials cost indices, shipments, imports, exports, and sales.
8. Contract construction employment.

Consumer Expenditure Survey: Diary Survey
(Bureau of Labor Statistics, U.S. Department of Labor; Superintendent of Documents, U.S. Government Printing Office, Washington, D.C. 20402, biennially). The *Diary Survey* gives regional (multistate) data on consumer expenditures, which are categorized and then cross-tabulated to consumer characteristics. Consumers who participate in the survey keep a detailed record of all expenditures for two consecutive one-week periods.

Consumer Expenditure Survey: Interview Survey
(Bureau of Labor Statistics, U.S. Department of Labor; Superintendent of Documents, U.S. Government Printing Office, Washington, D.C. 20402, biennially). The *Interview Survey* presents information similar to that in the *Diary Survey,* but it is based

on quarterly data generated by interviewers who visit sample households every three months for a twelve-month period.

County Business Patterns
(Bureau of the Census, U.S. Department of Commerce; Superintendent of Documents, U.S. Government Printing Office, Washington, D.C. 20402, annually). This gives data about each county's economic base, employment, income, earnings, and labor force. Data are tabulated by county and by industry within each state, and cross-tabulated by Standard Industrial Classification (SIC) numbers. Reports are based on information provided by business firms to the Bureau of the Census. Data for non-census years are drawn from annual reports made to the Internal Revenue Service and other government agencies.

County and City Data Book
(Bureau of the Census, U.S. Department of Commerce; Superintendent of Documents, U.S. Government Printing Office, Washington, D.C., 20402, periodically). This book presents statistical data for states, counties, and cities of 25,000 or more population. It includes 216 different data items for counties and states and 170 items for cities. It includes tables of:

- population
- vital statistics
- social security income
- housing
- education levels
- personal income
- manufacturers
- service industries
- elections
- number of households
- health
- crime
- journey to work
- labor force composition
- income
- wholesale and retail trade
- banking

- agriculture
- government employment and spending

Current Construction Survey Series
(Bureau of the Census, U.S. Department of Commerce; Superintendent of Documents, U.S. Government Printing Office, Washington, D.C. 20402, monthly, quarterly, annually). This series reports information on construction activity and cost, incorporating data from approximately 17,000 places that issue construction permits.

Department and Specialty Store Merchandising and Operating Results
(Financial Executives Division, National Retail Merchants Association, 100 West 31st Street, New York, NY 10001, annually). This gives comparative data on income, expenses, and other financial characteristics of department and speciality stores. Data are reported on a per-square-foot basis and as a percentage of various operating measures of importance to retail management. Percentage measures are used to indicate year-to-year changes and to show the contribution of each merchandise group to total store sales. Data are included for approximately 175 merchandise groups. Department stores are reported separately in seven groups, and specialty stores in three groups, according to gross sales. Information is from survey data reported by cooperating companies who report at the end of each fiscal year.

Department Stores
(Chain Store Guide Publications, 425 Park Ave., New York, NY 10022, annually). This publication lists the addresses of headquarters and the branch locations of independent and chain department stores. It gives telephone numbers, number of stores, resident buying office, and names of executives and buyers.

Directory of Federal Statistics for Local Areas: A Guide to Sources
(Superintendent of Documents, U.S. Government Printing Office, Washington, D.C. 20402, irregularly). This guide to local

area socioeconomic data contained in 182 publications from 33 different federal agencies is published as a supplement to the *U.S. Statistical Abstract.*

Directory of Federal Statistics of States: A Guide to Sources

(Superintendent of Documents, U.S. Government Printing Office, Washington, D.C. 20402, irregularly). The directory gives references to state socioeconomic data contained in more than 750 publications from federal agencies and is published as a supplement to the *U.S. Statistical Abstract.*

Directory of Non-Federal Statistics for State and Local Areas

(Superintendent of Documents, U.S. Government Printing Office, Washington, D.C. 20402, irregularly). This supplement to the *U.S. Statistical Abstract* is a guide to non-federal sources of current statistics on social, political, and economic subjects for all 50 states, the District of Columbia, Guam, Puerto Rico, and the Virgin Islands.

Discount Department Stores

(Chain Store Guide Publications, 425 Park Ave., New York, NY 10022, annually). This lists headquarters' addresses; telephone number, location, and square footage of each store; lines carried; leased operators; and names of executives and buyers. It includes a special section on leased department operators.

Dodge Local Construction Potentials

(F.W. Dodge Division, McGraw-Hill Information Systems Company, 1221 Avenue of the Americas, New York, NY 10020, monthly and annual summary). This reports construction activity and cost by MSA and by county as valued in current dollars and square footage classified by type of construction.

Donnelley Demographics — Dialog Information Retrieval Service

(Donnelley Marketing Information Service, 1901 South Meyers Road, Oakbrook Terrace, IL 60148). The Report covers states,

MSAs, counties, and selected towns, by zip code. Data include current census, current year estimate, five-year projections, and, in some instances, percent change from current census to current year. Areas reported are:

- population
- households
- household income
- household vehicles
- education
- employment
- home value
- housing tenure
- age
- household size
- household mobility
- race and sex
- marital status
- travel time to work
- monthly rent

It also includes Donnelley's Socioeconomic Status Indicator, used to rank neighborhoods and to estimate private sector employment. Organizations that define their markets by Arbitron's Area of Dominant Influence, A.C. Nielsen's Designated Market Area, or Selling Areas Marketing Code may search these areas.

Dun & Bradstreet Million Dollar Directory

(Dun's Marketing Services, Dun & Bradstreet, Inc., 3 Century Drive, Parisippany, NJ 07054, annually). The directory lists approximately 160,000 businesses, each of which has a net worth of $500,000 or more. Separate sections list firms alphabetically, geographically, and by line of business. Another section lists each firm's officers and directors. For each firm, the directory gives business name, state of incorporation, address, telephone number, SIC code number, function, sales volume, number of employees, and name of officers and directors. A separate volume, *Top 50,000 Companies,* gives details on the largest of the 160,000 and lists those that have an indicated net worth exceeding $1,850,000. Data from the directory are also available via direct computer link-up.

Editor and Publisher Market Guide

(Editor and Publisher, 11 West 19th Street, New York, NY 10011, annually). This guide gives income, earnings, population, retail sales, and sales potential data for all cities where a daily newspaper is published. Data are based on latest Census of Business, which is conducted every five years, and current year estimates generated by Marketing Economics Institute, Ltd.

Employment and Earnings

(Bureau of Labor Statistics, U.S. Department of Labor; Superintendent of Documents, U.S. Government Printing Office, Washington, D.C. 20402, monthly). This reports labor force information categorized by state and by MSA. It also reports on employment by broad industrial categories for each state and MSA. Data include:

- labor force status
- average number of hours worked
- worker earnings

A Guide to Consumer Markets

(The Conference Board Inc., Information Services, 845 Third Ave., New York, NY 10022, annually). This guide contains a detailed statistical profile of U.S. consumer markets and includes data on population growth and mobility, employment, income, and spending patterns.

Home Sales: Existing and New Single-Family, Apartment Condos and Co-ops

(National Association of Realtors, Economics and Research Division, 777 Fourteenth Street, N.W., Washington, D.C. 20005, monthly). This reports monthly data on the single-family home market for the previous year and annual statistics for the last six years. Sales data are from more than 400 Boards of Realtors and multiple listing systems.

The National Association of Realtors uses a regional weighting system based on data from the most recent Census of

Housing. Seasonal adjustments are based on the Bureau of the Census adjustment program. Comparison of sales reports from Boards of Realtors with data from the Annual Housing Survey indicate that these data are highly representative of prices and sales activity within each region. The report includes:

- sales of new and existing homes (monthly data are seasonally adjusted).
- number of homes on the market at the end of the reporting period.
- median sales prices of existing homes.
- unit sales volume, dollar volume, and median and mean sales price for four regions and for the entire United States.

Industrial Real Estate Market Survey
(Society of Industrial and Office Realtors (SIOR), 777 Fourteenth Street, N.W., Washington, D.C. 20005, annually). This survey provides recent data and a one-year outlook on prime industrial space for central cities and suburbs in 90 metropolitan markets, based on sales transactions reported by members of the Society of Industrial and Office Realtors and other sources. It includes comparative statistics and trends on:

- industrial property sales
- property prices
- rental rates
- construction activity
- interest rates
- mortgage loans

Local Area Personal Income
(Bureau of Economic Analysis, U.S. Department of Commerce; Superintendent of Documents, U.S. Government Printing Office, Washington, D.C. 20402, annually). This provides information on personal income on a per capita basis and by income source. Data are gleaned from various federal and state government administrative records, such as state unemployment insurance programs, federal income tax records, and Census Bureau records.

Local Population Estimates

(Bureau of the Census, U.S. Department of Commerce; Superintendent of Documents, U.S. Government Printing Office, Washington, D.C. 20402, annually). This gives population and per capita income estimates for states, counties, metropolitan areas, and incorporated places. Estimates are a joint effort of state agencies and the Bureau of the Census. County estimates are derived from sources such as birth and death certificates, property tax records, and school enrollments. Two independent approaches are employed, and the results are averaged.

Marketing Economics Guide

(Marketing Economics Institute, Inc., 186-26 Avon Road, Jamaica, NY 11432, annually). Prepared from a data base containing demographic, economic, retail sales, industrial, and environmental information collected by government and private agencies, the *Guide* gives the following information for regions, states, MSAs, counties and cities:

- population
- percent urban population
- household gross income
- disposable personal income
- total retail sales
- retail sales by category (nine categories)
- ratio of retail sales to disposable personal income
- number of households
- population density

Measuring Markets: A Guide to the Use of Federal and State Statistical Data

(Bureau of Domestic and International Business Administration, U.S. Department of Commerce; Superintendent of Documents, U.S. Government Printing Office, Washington, D.C. 20402, periodically). The guide describes federal and state government publications useful for measuring markets and demonstrates the use of federal statistics in market measurement.

The Metropolitan Area Forecasting Service
(Data Resources, Inc., Two Ravina Drive, Atlanta, GA 30346, semiannually). The service provides economic and demographic forecasts for 313 MSAs. Based on a proprietary model that analyzes each MSA's economic base relative to national, regional, and state economic conditions, it draws information from several data bases, including the Bureau of Labor Statistics, to generate 10-year forecasts. Two basic types of custom reports can be produced: a report for one or more concepts for a given geographical area and a rank report by concept across MSAs or other geographical areas. Data are provided for:

- industry employment
- income
- total resident population
- housing permits issued
- labor market indicators

Money Income of Households, Families, and Persons in the United States
(Bureau of the Census, U.S. Department of Commerce; Superintendent of Documents, U.S. Government Printing Office, Washington, D.C. 20402, annually). This is a report of income and earnings in the United States, regions, and divisions. Total income is reported in both current and constant (that is, inflation-adjusted) dollars, and the median income is provided for households, families, and unrelated individuals.

Monthly Retail Trade: Sales and Inventories
(Bureau of the Census, U.S. Department of Commerce; Superintendent of Documents, U.S. Government Printing Office, Washington, D.C. 20402, monthly and annually). For selected MSAs, cities, and states, it gives estimates of retail sales, inventory, and employment, by major business category. Estimates are based on sample data collected by the Bureau of the Census from retail employers. Samples are drawn from those retailers who made social security payments for their employees. Estimates are made for nonrespondents.

National Decision Systems Reports

(National Decision Systems, 539 Encinitas Blvd., Box 9007, Encinitas, CA 92024-9007, updated annually). Based on data from the Bureau of the Census and other public records, it provides information on housing, employment, labor force participation, population, and demographics for the United States and individual states, cities, and counties, zip codes, and census tracts. Several separate reports cover aspects of:

- households
- housing tenure
- race
- travel time to work
- consumer expenditures
- school attendance
- retail competition
- household income
- urban and rural population
- gender
- marital status

Report titles include:

- *Demographic Reports.*
- *Business and Employment Report.*
- *Consumer Expenditure, Shopping Center & Target Marketing.*
- *Consumer Demand Reports.*

In addition to the written reports these data are available on diskette, magnetic tape, 12-inch laser disk, or CD-ROM.

National Travel Survey

(United States Travel Data Center, 1899 L Street, N.W., Washington, D.C. 20036, monthly, with an annual summary) The survey provides estimates of projected travel activity, tabulations of major travel indicators and comparisons with the preceding month, and an outline of major travel trends. It contains summary information about travelers and trips.

1. Data on Travelers:

- age
- credit card ownership
- education
- employment
- household size and structure
- home ownership (own or rent)
- residence (city, state, region)
- marital status
- number of wage earners per household
- income
- gender
- occupation

2. Trip Information·

- destinations
- origin
- distance traveled
- trip duration
- travel mode
- trip purpose
- number in party
- type of lodging
- whether a weekend or longer term traveler

For a specified city, it lists visitor expenditures and jobs and payroll generated by visitor spending.

R.L. Polk Reports
(R.L. Polk, Marketing Services Division, 6400 Monroe Blvd., Taylor, MI 48180, on request). City directories from R.L. Polk contain delivery addresses for nearly 95 percent of U.S. households, with more than 85 percent by name. Polk's *Carrier Route Marketing Report* gives demographic data by postal carrier routes

The Rand McNally Commercial Atlas and Marketing Guide
(Rand McNally & Company, Fulfillment Center, 5535 North Long, Chicago, IL 60630, annually) This contains population

trends and characteristics for counties, MSAs, and cities, and gives summary data by county for:

- business
- manufacturing
- income
- buying power

It summarizes data by MSA and zip code for:

- business
- population
- retail sales

Real Estate Analysis and Planning Service
(Dodge/DRI, F.W. Dodge Information Systems, Two Ravina Drive, Suite 1210, Atlanta, GA 30346, semiannually). This gives economic, demographic, construction, and real estate activity data for 50 U.S. cities. It includes six years of historic data and five years of projection data for six types of construction with vacancy rate data for four types of nonresidential real estate for 50 major cities. For 150 additional cities, it gives an assessment of overall investment attractiveness, with an historical analysis focusing on supply, demand, market balance, market size, and potential.

Real Estate Index—Subject
(National Association of Realtors, 430 North Michigan Avenue, Chicago, IL 60611-4087). This is a 10-year index of 20,000 titles and 500 journals. All references pertain to the real estate industry and related fields. Publications indexed appeared between January 1975 and June 1985.

The Regional Economic Projection Series
(National Planning Association Data Services, Inc., 1616 P Street, N.W., Suite 400, Washington, D.C. 20036, annually). For regions, states, counties, and MSAs, it provides historic and projection data on

- population
- employment and earnings

- gender
- age
- race
- personal income, by source

Data are also available on diskette or tape and in computer print-out form.

Sheldon's Retail
(Phelon, Sheldon & Marsar, Inc., 15 Industrial Avenue, Fairview, NJ 07022, annually). Section I is a Retail Directory, which lists chain and independent department, junior department, and specialty stores arranged by states and cities. It lists the department buyers and managers. Section II lists resident buyers and merchandise brokers arranged alphabetically by buying office. Section III is an index of all the retailers in the directory and the names of their buying offices. The publisher will provide mailing lists for a variety of parameters.

Shopping Center Directory
(National Research Bureau, Inc., 310 South Michigan Avenue, Suite 1150, Chicago, IL 60604, annually). The directory gives detailed listing and summary data for shopping centers (strip, neighborhood, community, and regional) throughout the United States. Data include:

- fact sheet for each center
- center type
- planned expansion
- leasing agent
- architect
- developer
- size
- leased area of each anchor tenant
- address
- location
- physical characteristics
- construction activity
- current owner
- cost

- leasable area
- statistical summaries

Sourcebook of Demographics and Buying Power of Every Zip Code in the U.S.A.

(CACI, 8260 Willow Oaks Corporate Drive, Fairfax, VA 22031, annually). This gives demographic compostion and income distribution data by zip code and provides current estimates and five-year projections for total population, population distribution, race, age, and number of households. It includes a socioeconomic profile, income, education, and employment profile, plus an income and buying power profile, and gives a household-distribution-by-income and purchasing-power-potential index for 13 broad areas.

There is a separate section for demographic data on businesses. It provides the number of firms, gives estimates of employment, and ranks the top five employers in each zip code area.

The sourcebook is also available as an on-line service by subscription.

State and Metropolitan Area Data Book

(Bureau of the Census, U.S. Department of Commerce; Superintendent of Documents, U.S. Government Printing Office, Washington, D.C. 20402, annual). This publication summarizes data from census and current surveys. It presents extensive trend data for states, metropolitan areas, and central cities. Data are from the most recent U.S. census, surveys of private sources, and government administrative records. Source reference is given for each item included in the book.

Statistical Abstract of the United States

(Bureau of the Census, U.S. Department of Commerce; Superintendent of Documents, U.S. Government Printing Office, Washington, D.C. 20402). This summarizes social, political, and economic statistics for states, MSAs, counties, and cities and consolidates data from diverse government and private publications. Data that may be useful for market analysis include:

- population
- employment and earnings
- construction and housing
- manufacturing
- services
- number of businesses
- expenditures and wealth
- labor force size
- income

Statistics Sources: A Subject Guide to Data on Industrial, Business, Social, Educational, Financial, and Other Topics for the United States and Selected Foreign Countries
(Gale Research Co., Book Tower, Detroit, MI 48226). This cites thousands of statistical sources on voluminous subjects.

The Survey of Buying Power Data Service
(Sales and Marketing Management Magazine, 633 Third Avenue, New York, NY 10017, annually). This is an annual survey of consumer buying power, presenting detailed market, population, household, and retail sales data by location. It includes market data projections for five years ahead and comparisons to five years back and contains 21 sections including:

- Maps and selected Metropolitan Statistical Area (MSA) data
- MSA rankings by market and household data
- Retail sales by kind of business and merchandise line, census division, and state
- MSA rankings by retail sales and merchandise

Survey of Current Business
(Bureau of Economic Analysis, U.S. Department of Commerce; Superintendent of Documents, U.S. Government Printing Office, Washington, D.C. 20402, monthly). This survey of U.S. economic activity estimates county and metropolitan area total and per capita personal income and also provides metropolitan projections of total personal income, per capita

personal income, employment, and population. Tables provide major economic series obtained from public and private sources.

The Bureau of Labor Statistics contributes data related to wages and salaries of covered employees, while the Internal Revenue Service provides information pertaining to business income. The *Statistical Abstract of the United States* provides information pertaining to the reliability of data appearing in this publication.

United States Postal Services Address Information Center

Metropolitan mail delivery areas by zip code are provided in two forms:

- Delivery Stats—provides the carrier identification number and the number of residential, commercial, and P.O. Box deliveries on each route within the zip code.
- Carrier Route Information—names the streets within the zip code area and gives the carrier identification number for that street. The highest and lowest house number on the street are also given.

This is a complete count of the addresses for each post office, categorized as residential or commercial. Postmasters send monthly updates to the Address Information Center (AIC). The AIC main file is updated twice yearly—February 15 and July 15.

Urban Decision Systems Report Series

(Urban Decision Systems, Inc., P.O. Box 551, Westport, CT 06881, updated frequently). These reports cover the United States, states, counties, and census tracts and are issued in a series:

- Income and Demographic Trends
- Retail Potential: General Information
- Business Reports
- Population Benchmark Reports
- Shopping Center Reports
- Colorsite Grid Images
- Other Data Reports—designed to customer specifications

These reports are available in a printed format or on magnetic tape or diskette.

The reports and services reviewed here range widely in cost. Most of them are available, either free or at modest cost, at university libraries or public libraries in major metropolitan areas. Many libraries also provide access to on-line computer services for a very modest user fee. Take time to talk with the reference librarian at your library about their availabilty.

KEY POINTS

• Most of the information you will need has already been collected for other purposes and can be easily revised to fit your needs.

• Vast pools of data are on file with the government and private data collection agencies. You only need to know where to look.

• University and public libraries maintain files of many major data banks. Others are available via direct computer hookup between the library and the collection agency.

CHAPTER 8

WHERE TO FIND PROPERTY

It has been said, with excessive simplicity, that real estate investors make their profit when they buy. Like most maxims, this overstates a valid underlying precept. If you overpay for a property, only an outstanding operating and appreciation record can bail you out. Conversely, if you buy in at an attractive price, even mediocre productivity will make you look like a genius.

Suppose, for example, that market forces dictate a reasonable price of $100,000 for a property that is generating net operating income of $10,000 per year and whose operating income and market value are growing at 2 percent per annum. Let's assume you will sell after five years, and—to keep the example uncluttered—let's ignore transaction costs. Our final assumption is that you will finance $70,000 of the purchase price with a 30-year, 10.5 percent mortgage loan. This results in an annual loan constant of approximately 11 percent (remember, the constant is the annual mortgage payments expressed as a portion of the amount borrowed) and a remaining balance after five years of 97 percent of the initial loan amount.

If you buy at the reasonable $100,000 price, which represents an overall capitalization rate of $10,000/$100,000, or 10 percent, and sell after five years at the same overall capitalization rate, your before-tax cash flows will have been as follows:

Before-tax Cash Flow

Year		Receipts	less	Mortgage Payments	=	Cash Flow
1	from NOI	$ 10,000		$ 7,700		$ 2,300
2	" "	10,200		7,700		2,500
3	" "	10,404		7,700		2,704
4	" "	10,612		7,700		2,912
5	" "	10,824		7,700		3,124
5	from sale	110,405		67,900		42,505

Don't get bogged down with the numbers. The annual receipts are simply the net operating income, which we are assuming will start at $10,000 and grow at 2 percent per annum. The mortgage payments are the annual debt service on the presumed $70,000 mortgage, computed by multiplying the loan amount by the 11 percent annual constant. After five years the receipts from sale (assuming, for simplicity's sake, no transaction costs) are the sixth year's expected net operating income (the fifth year's net plus 2 percent) divided by the market-determined 10 percent overall capitalization rate.

Now comes the tricky part. If you look for a discount rate that will make the present value of all the future cash flows exactly equal the initial $30,000 equity investment, you will find the compound annual rate of return to have been about 15 percent per annum, before tax. (If you want to see how it's done, study Appendix A. Otherwise, just take my word for it.)

But suppose you paid, say, 10 percent too much for the property. With the same $70,000 mortgage loan, your initial cash outlay will be $110,000 minus $70,000 or $40,000. If the eventual sales price is unaffected (your buyer can't be expected to be as imprudent as you were), we must look for a discount rate that makes the present value of the same cash flows equal to your $40,000 initial equity investment. That figure turns out to be about 7.8 percent, before tax. A 10 percent overpayment has cut your yield rate almost in half!

So you bargain hard. This means you will decline many deals for every one that you ultimately close. Looking again at our example, we can see the wisdom of this approach. If you can get the property for 10 percent less than the $100,000 that we have taken as a reasonable price, you will be paying only $90,000. Subtracting the $70,000 mortgage loan, we find your equity investment will have been only $20,000.

What is the yield rate that gives the expected future cash flows a present value equivalent of $20,000? If you repeat the laborious arithmetic (or, if you have access to an inexpensive financial calculator) you will discover that the before-tax yield is better than 25 percent per annum—about a two-thirds increase from driving a hard bargain.

Is this an unrealistic example? I think not. A 10 percent variation in purchase price is not unreasonable because property valuation is at best an inexact science. At worst, it is hit-or-miss artistry. Moreover, an owner who really wants out will see the wisdom in selling now for a somewhat lower price rather than holding for an additional six to twelve months in hopes of a better deal that might not materialize.

FINDING MOTIVATED SELLERS

You will be frustrated regularly by property owners who don't really have a strong urge to sell. They find it interesting to "test the water" occasionally, to offer their property with no serious expectation that anyone will buy. For them, showing the property to prospective buyers is low-cost sport. And, who knows, someone might even buy the overpriced dog.

Your challenge is to develop an efficient method of sifting through the market chaff in search of the occasional kernel that has been overlooked; to get the good deals before others have a chance to bid.

Stake Out a "Farm"

Brokers know the value of becoming intimately familiar with a limited geographic area or a specialized type of property. Toward this end, many brokers will define geographic boundaries within which they seek to become known by property owners as the best person to deal with when it's time to sell. You can adopt this same strategy for finding good buys.

Regularly drive through the area you have chosen as your farm. Look for buildings that show signs of neglect, such as untended grounds, peeling paint, deteriorating drives and walks, and so forth. Such are often indicative of landlords who are in financial difficulty, who have found they have no time to devote to the property, or who have simply lost interest. Contact these owners and ask whether they will consider selling. They can usually be identified from records in the tax assessor's office. If you don't want to spend time researching the records, ask a broker to look into it for you. A good broker will be responsive and becomes your unpaid researcher.

Those Intriguing Newspaper Ads

If we believe the ads concocted by eager real estate brokers, every seller must be a pushover. "Make an offer," the ads urge. "Seller anxious." We know, of course, that this is harmless trade puffery. Yet, under the hype there occasionally lurks a real note of desperation. Many prospective sellers do have compelling reasons to dump their properties.

Human nature being what it is, people under pressure to sell will be more than a little apprehensive about their property's market prospects. The less experienced they are in the market, the more uncertain they are likely to be. You will want to play on their greed for a quick sale and their fear that the property might not sell at all.

So, don't dismiss the real estate ads out of hand. Puffery aside, you can sometimes locate good buys that have just come on the market. But you have to follow the ads regularly, and that can be time-consuming. The ad writers make every property sound like the opportunity of a lifetime, but most of them aren't worth following up. If you limit your search to a specific area and become familiar with properties there, you will become adept at spotting advertisements for new market entrants.

Working with Brokers

A better approach is to cultivate good relationships with brokers in your market area. They can be the advance guard in your campaign to find good prospects. Don't agree to work exclusively with one broker, but assure all of them that you will diligently protect their interests with respect to properties they bring to your attention.

When you find a broker with whom your interpersonal chemistry clicks, explain your investment screens and let the broker do the preliminary work for you. If a broker insists on wasting your time by bringing you data on property that obviously doesn't satisfy your screens, break off the relationship—you have better uses for your time.

DEFAULT AND FORECLOSURE

The plague of "get-rich-quick" real estate seminars and books that have blighted the environment in recent years has a bright side for investors who know there is no free lunch. People who play the real estate "musical chairs" game these promoters advocate, and who hold highly leveraged real estate when the music stops, provide an enticing opportunity for prudent investors.

Dancing in the Financial Graveyard

Picking up real estate at bargain basement prices from hapless believers in the financial free lunch is sometimes called "grave dancing," the implication being that we dance in glee at the death of someone's dream of building a real estate empire. Yet, we can sympathize with the financially unfortunate without standing idly by while unharvested opportunities wither.

Acquiring property that is subject to foreclosure has long been a lucrative strategy for specialists who have mastered the relatively arcane laws associated with foreclosure proceedings. They have had this market to themselves because the general

investing public either has been unaware of the opportunity or
has not understood how to locate and tap the supply of such
properties.

Opportunities Are Cyclical

Foreclosure is a regularly occurring process. There is always
someone who makes imprudent investment decisions that lead
to foreclosure, in all phases of the business cycle. Yet the pick-
ings are not uniformly bounteous. The supply of foreclosure
properties varies with general economic conditions and also
goes through local cycles.

During the middle and final phases of inflationary cycles,
such as we experienced during the late 1970s, the fervid shift
into real estate drives prices far above fundamental values. Only
the expectation that they can eventually sell to someone who is
even more zealous for inflation-driven profit offers any prospect
for ultimate profit for buyers during this phase of the cycle.
Transactions are like a game of musical chairs; whoever holds
title when the music—in this game, buying—stops is the loser.

Investor sentiment is subject to sudden, wild swings. When
the consensus shifts to a belief that the market has peaked,
there are no buyers to bail out those who recently bought at
outlandish prices. With no prospect that they will ever profit
from their injudicious acquisitions, many investors will simply
abandon their properties.

Thus it is that the supply of properties subject to foreclosure
increases dramatically during the leveling of the price spiral
that trails each inflationary spurt. When recession begins to
erode earnings, even those who hope to salvage something from
their investments may find themselves unable to meet their
mortgage obligations. In many cases they find their loan balance
actually exceeds their property's value, net of selling costs.

You Don't Have to Wait

Does this mean profits from distressed properties are available
only during the early stages of cyclical economic downturns?

Not at all. During good times and bad, some properties are subject to foreclosure action. In many cases the problem stems from an investor having paid too much; in other cases the underlying problem is not directly related to the property itself.

People sometimes invest in real estate without understanding just how management-intensive it is. They soon tire of the detail involved in running a rental operation and begin to neglect management fundamentals. Failure to aggressively market space or to carefully maintain a property will quickly erode profit margins of even the best-located rental units. Soon, declining cash flows become inadequate to meet mortgage payments, and the investor defaults.

Negligent owners are not the only source of default and foreclosure of well-located, quality properties. Far too many people who bill themselves as professional property managers do not deserve the title. Those who are more adept at selling their services than in delivering on management promises can ruin a property's profitability every bit as quickly as can a negligent or inept owner-manager. The pernicious combination of incompetence and outright fraud by self-proclaimed management specialists has dashed many investors' hopes.

Personal or family distress often precipitates default and foreclosure. Investors whose careers are cut short by corporate mergers, acquisitions, or bankruptcy, whose health deteriorates, or who experience major family disruptions (divorce, death, or other misfortune) often simply lose interest in their rental property.

Phases of Foreclosure

Grave dancers find opportunities in each of three distinct phases through which foreclosure proceeds. Phase one starts with the default; debtors fail to live up to their contractual obligations. Many defaults are "cured" by the debtors; others lead to foreclosure petitions filed by lenders. Following this action there is a period of time (specified in state statutes) during which borrowers have the right to pay off loan balances and redeem property. If they don't do so, phase two is initiated, in which the property is sold at a public auction. During phase three, which follows the sale, borrowers have one final opportunity to redeem their property—by compensating successful bidders in the amount of the winning bids plus interest and expenses as provided by state law.

A Brief History

Arcane foreclosure procedures stem from centuries of legal wrangling between borrowers and lenders, with the advantage going first to one side then the other. Early English law, from which our system evolved, provided a swift and sure default remedy; the hapless borrower was evicted and stripped of all claim to the property. Free-and-clear title thereafter vested in the lender.

This harsh remedy was eventually modified by the King's Chancellor, whose job it was to balance legal principles with fairness and equity. Soon, defaulting borrowers who petitioned the Chancellor were routinely permitted to redeem their property by paying off the delinquent loan. This eventually became a principal embedded in the common law, called the *equitable right of redemption*. The right has been codified and exists today in one form or another in every state in the Union.

Now it was the lender's turn to squirm. With the ever present possibility that defaulting borrowers would some day redeem their property, lenders who had gained conditional title were loath to make any property improvements, and they found no willing buyers for property that could be reclaimed at will by previous owners. Distressed lenders petitioned the Chancellor to foreclose the borrowers' right to redeem. This was done by setting a date after which the defaulter's rights were extinquished. The petition, which exists today, came to be known as a *foreclosure suit*. State law dictates the period following a foreclosure suit after which the equitable right of redemption is foreclosed.

Though we Americans inherited much of our law and customs from the Old World, we have never been comfortable with the status quo. Our penchant for tinkering with established institutions has led, in many states (about 27), to a law that extends to defaulting borrowers one last chance to redeem property even after the foreclosure sale. This right, called a *statutory right of redemption*, varies from state to state, and in many states it can be waived on any property other than the borrower's personal residence.

Fifty Different Codes

Each of the fifty United States cherishes its sovereignty. This independent spirit is reflected in interstate variation in laws governing commerce, and even more so in foreclosure rules. Even so, certain general principles are evident in those states whose legal principles are derived primarily from the English model. Figure 8–1 illustrates the general procedure.

Multiple Opportunities

Your first opportunity comes after the default point, which is triggered when a borrower violates some mortgage loan provision—usually by missing several payments. Letters from the lender will have become increasingly threatening, and a sense of impending doom may be growing. Once a foreclosure suit is handed down, although the borrower usually (but not always) continues in possession, a precise Armageddon date is looming. After the foreclosure sale the borrower no longer controls the property, but may have a residual interest through the statutory right of redemption, which is a property interest and therefore can be sold or otherwise conveyed.

Buying before the Foreclosure Sale

A defaulting borrower knows that foreclosure is just around the corner, but might deny reality. Many people have a knack for pretending that the inevitable is imaginary until it hits them squarely where it hurts the most.

At this point there is no formal notice of default, but phys ical signs will be abundant. At first, owners usually skimp on upkeep in order to make mortgage payments. By the time they start missing payments the property will have a distinctly dog-eared look. Poor maintenance will have taken its toll on the

Figure 8–1
Phases of Foreclosures

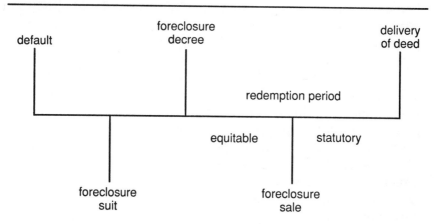

property's competitive position, and there will be a high vacancy rate—evidenced by unlit apartments during the early evening hours or by stores and office buildings with empty windows (what wags call "see-through buildings").

This is a good time to approach an owner with a suggestion that you might be interested in buying or leasing. But first, check the public records to see what liens and other actions have been filed against the property. This will alert you to additional problems and may give you a better feel for the current owner's negotiating position.

If a suit is pending on the property, the plaintiff will have filed a notice of action (*lis pendens*). This gives constructive notice to all interested parties that legal action is imminent and that anyone acquiring a subsequent interest in the property may be bound by the action's outcome.

Another avenue of information is created when the foreclosure suit is actually filed. In almost every county seat there is a newspaper that routinely prints the details of newly filed suits. Become an avid reader of this publication and you will always be alerted to new opportunities. (If you can't find a paper that prints this information, ask an attorney—newpapers that cater to the legal profession *must* include these details.)

During the period between a foreclosure suit and the actual

decree, owners are likely to be more tractable than at any other time. A law suit is a sobering event—it forcefully brings home the reality of impending loss. Yet, the realization will not have existed long enough for the owner to have adjusted. Your proposal is likely to be viewed as a passport to safety, if not to virtual salvation.

The actual foreclosure decree will also be prominently heralded in newspapers that cater to the legal profession. Find out what paper is sold at the court house newsstand (other than general circulation papers), buy a copy, and read it thoroughly. Better still, ask for it at the public library's reference desk.

This paper will almost certainly contain a list of recent foreclosure decrees, with vital information such as the property address and the names and addresses of the defaulting borrowers. These notices also typically give such useful data as the reference numbers of the mortgage document and the decree, both of which are public documents that you will want to read before taking further action.

Between the decree and the foreclosure sale, a property still belongs to the defaulting borrower. But the loss is looming with ever growing clarity and certainty. The owner's options have been greatly circumscribed. The lender will have given up on the owner and will insist that the loan be paid off before the foreclosure action will be rescinded. The owner, however, will be unable to raise the necessary funds; who would advance money to an applicant that is already in foreclosure?

Should You Bid at Foreclosure Sales?

Your next opportunity comes at the foreclosure sale. The property will be sold to the highest bidder, with proceeds first applied to cover selling costs, then to satisfy the remaining loan balance. The owner gets whatever is left.

One competitor you can almost always count on at a foreclosure sale is the lender. To protect its interest in the property, the lender will usually bid the amount of the remaining balance on the mortgage. That way, it is assured of either getting its cash or of getting title to the property itself. In most cases the lender doesn't want the property; it would much prefer that someone bid even higher.

The lender is better off, however, taking title if the property is worth less than the loan balance. By bidding the amount of the loan, it can record the property on its accounting records at exactly the amount of the loan that it must write off. In this manner it will have simply swapped one asset for another and will not have to record any net loss.

Buying after Foreclosure

Some 27 states have enacted laws giving debtors one last chance to make good on their obligation and redeem foreclosed property before their rights are forever extinquished. This statutory right of redemption can be waived in some states—in other states a waiver is not enforceable.

Where the statutory right of redemption exists, it is a property right that can be sold or otherwise conveyed in the same manner as other property rights. This gives you an additional opportunity to step into the defaulting borrower's shoes and exercise the redemption right, thereby claiming the property for yourself. Owners who have no intention of redeeming will generally be willing to transfer their rights to you for a pittance— indeed, they may be willing to accept only a contingent consideration, such as a note that becomes due only if you actually exercise your newly acquired redemption privilege.

Strategies for Acquiring Redemption Rights

Whether you are negotiating for equitable or statutory redemption rights, the key idea is to pay little or nothing for them. This implies that you will be acquiring rights that owners have no intention of exercising, so that anything they receive will be "found money."

If your targets are small rental properties you will discover that many of the people with whom you deal will either not even know about redemption rights, or will completetly misunderstand them. The best approach seems to be a completely

forthright one. People who have been through a foreclosure pro-
ceeding are usually law-weary and financially shell-shocked.
They will have developed a protective veneer of scepticism that
will be difficult for even the most straightforward real estate
promoter to penetrate. Your toughest chore will be to establish
sufficient rapport so that they will seriously consider your proposal.

The most successful person I have known at this game
is a graduate of the real estate program at Chicago's DePaul
University. Paul acquired his first foreclosed property while
still a student at the university. He became so successful that
he later dropped out of law school at Northwestern University,
deciding that an early start on his real estate career was more
valuable than a law degree.

Paul's strategy was the epitome of forthrightness. He con-
centrated on single-family and small multiple-unit residential
properties. He approached defaulting owners from the perspective of a potential counselor. He asked if they were aware of how
their rights of redemption worked. If they were at all interested,
he explained in great detail how they could exploit the rules,
and the potential benefit of doing so.

He also told them that he regularly acquired rights of
redemption from property owners who did not intend to exercise
their rights on their own behalf, paying a modest amount for the
rights that, if not exercised in a timely fashion, quickly became
worthless. If owners indicated some interest in exploiting their
new knowledge for their personal gain, Paul's approach was to
leave his card and tell them to call if they decided against exercising the rights. Otherwise, he proposed an immediate transfer
of their rights.

Because he started as a virtually penniless student, Paul
was forced to innovate. He developed an approach that required
no front-end cash commitment. Compensation to property owners was always in the form of a promissory note, for which he
usually asked them to sign a quitclaim deed. In some cases the
promissory note had a due date as of the end of the redemption
period. In most cases, the note was payable in full only if Paul
actually exercised the redemption rights.

During the early months of his program, he routinely sold the properties and scheduled the closing before redemption rights were extinguished. This eliminated any need for funds to pay off the old mortgage lender, since the redemption rights were exercised simultaneously with closing of the subsequent sale. In this manner, proceeds from the sale were used to satisfy the old lien and clear the title.

With money he made that way, Paul began selectively redeeming rental properties from foreclosure and adding them to his own portfolio. Retained properties were usually improved by such simple, low-cost steps as refinishing hardwood floors and replacing broken wallboard. The finishing touch was usually a new coat of interior paint and touch-up exterior painting where appropriate. He then used his superb human relations skills to fill the units with reliable, creditworthy tenants. This of course created a reliable cash-flow stream from the property, which greatly increased its market value.

Based on these enhanced values, Paul usually found he could refinance his properties under favorable terms and walk away with more money than he had put in, yet with a healthy equity above the mortgage balance. In effect, he was liquidating a portion of this equity without incurring any income tax liability.

KEY POINTS

• Minor variations in purchase price make a big difference in average yields from real estate. In a very real sense, you make your profit when you buy. Expect to discard a score of proposed ventures for every one that you ultimately find acceptable.
• If you know the area intimately you can evaluate proposed acquisitions much more efficiently. Stake out a defined geographic area within which you become uniquely knowledgeable about prices, transactions, and rents. Exploit your superior knowledge by moving quickly when a really good deal comes on the market; reject with very little wasted analytical and data-gathering time those offers that hold little promise.

• Brokers can be your most valuable source of information about potential acquistions. Work with several brokers; give them your minimum acceptable criteria for new properties and let them do the initial screening for you. Break off relations with any broker who insists on wasting your time by bringing you deals that obviously do not fit your criteria.

• Landlords who are in financial straits can be your most valuable source of new acquistions. Follow local listings of new foreclosure actions, and offer to acquire defaulting owners' redemption rights.

CHAPTER 9

USING OTHER PEOPLE'S MONEY

Cash-flow estimates in our earlier examples are all predicated on using a substantial amount of borrowed money. That is an entirely reasonable assumption because most real estate investments do in fact involve mortgage financing. The jargon phrase is *financial leverage.*

A veritable cornucopia of real estate folklore tells of fortunes made by using financial leverage imaginatively. Stories of "go-for-broke" investors and developers building real estate empires on a financial shoestring are fascinating and inspirational, but can bewilder and discourage one who has just been denied credit at the local savings and loan association. It all sounds so easy in the wheeler-dealer biographies, and becomes so very complicated in practice.

Yet, few deals are consummated without at least some borrowed money. If no third-party lender is involved, it is usually because the seller agrees to take back a promissory note for a substantial part of the consideration. Financing arrangements are commonly a more sensitive issue than price, and financially sophisticated investors can often salvage a deal that would be lost by the less knowledgeable.

Harried investors trying to resuscitate deals smothered by lost mortgage commitments may be little interested in statistics. Nevertheless, as a matter of perspective we should note that real estate finance absorbs well over half the total credit in the United States. This makes mortgage lending truly big business. It also makes real estate particularly sensitive to credit cost and availability.

Real estate borrowing is an intricate—frequently arcane—

craft, the masters of which are eagerly sought by investors who appreciate the value of favorable financial leverage. Sophisticated real estate investors themselves understand the importance of an unusually keen grasp of financial markets, arrangements, and procedures.

COSTS AND CONSEQUENCES OF LEVERAGE

When borrowing increases the yield on equity funds, the leverage is said to be favorable; when it has the opposite effect, it is said to be unfavorable. Essentially, leverage is favorable so long as the effective after-tax cost of borrowing is less than the after-tax yield on the real estate. A simple example will illustrate.

Suppose a parcel of land can be purchased for $100,000 and leased perpetually for $10,000 per annum. To keep the focus on key issues, let's also suppose that our investor is a tax-exempt foundation and that the property's value is expected to remain fairly stable for the foreseeable future. This means the before-tax and after-tax consequences are identical and yield on *assets* will be 10 percent per annum:

$$\text{Yield} = \text{Annual cash receipts} / \text{Cost}$$
$$= \$10,000 / \$100,000$$

If our tax-exempt foundation buys the property on an all-equity basis (no borrowed money), the yield on *equity* will be the same as the yield on assets. But suppose the foundation can borrow $75,000 at, say, 8 percent per annum. This is an interest-only loan, with the principal never becoming due (an assumption designed, again, to keep the focus on the main issue). Borrowing at a rate below the 10 percent yield on assets will amplify the yield to the $25,000 of equity funds the foundation must put into the deal. Here's how the numbers look with the loan:

Equity cash flows:
Net receipts from operations	$10,000
Less debt service (.08 × $75,000)	6,000
Net cash to the equity position	$ 4,000

$$\text{Equity yield} = \text{Equity cash flow / Equity cost}$$
$$= \$4,000 / \$25,000$$
$$= .16, \text{ or } 16 \text{ percent per annum}$$

In this case, borrowing at 8 percent to acquire an asset that earns 10 percent has created a 16 percent annual yield on the equity. Since the leverage is favorable, the greater the ratio of borrowed to equity funds, the greater the yield to the equity position. Suppose, for example, our foundation could increase the loan to $90,000 under the same terms. The yield to the remaining $10,000 of equity funds leaps to 28 percent:

Equity cash flows:
Net receipts from operations	$10,000
Less debt service (.08 × $90,000)	7,200
Cash flow to equity	$ 2,800

$$\text{Equity yield} = \text{Equity cash flow / Equity cost}$$
$$= \$28,000 / \$10,000$$
$$= .28$$

Our illustration is oversimplified in several ways. In addition to assuming away income taxes, we have pretended the net operating income will continue forever, the property's market value will remain stable forever, and the principal amount of the loan will never have to be repaid. We also pretended the investor could increase the ratio of borrowed to equity funds without having to pay a higher interest rate.

Thanks to the Internal Revenue Code of 1986, which eliminated preferential tax treatment for capital gains, income taxes don't really complicate the illustration very much. Since our transaction involves raw land, there is no depreciation or cost recovery allowance to worry about. After-tax yields in this simple illustration are simply the before-tax yield multiplied by (1 minus the marginal income tax rate). If our investor pays taxes at the 28 percent rate, for example, after-tax yields will be:

With no leverage:

$$.10 \times (1 - .28) = .10 \times .72 = .072, \text{ or } 7.2 \text{ percent}$$

With a $75,000 loan:

.16 × (1 − .28) = .16 × .72 = .1152, or 11.52 percent

With a $90,000 loan:

.28 × (1 − .28) = .28 × .72 = .2016, or 20.16 percent

How Leverage Can Amplify Tax Shelter Benefits

Although recent tax law changes drastically curtailed benefits from tax sheltered investments, it did not completely eliminate them. Real estate is perhaps the best remaining opportunity to exploit special tax provisions. Using borrowed money can greatly amplify the shelter benefit that accrues to equity investments.

We saw in Chapter Six that depreciation or cost recovery allowances often permit deferring income taxes until you sell a property. An important point in this regard is that the depreciation deduction is based on the entire purchase price of the depreciable asset, regardless of the source of funds. Thus, an investor with $100,000 of equity funds could buy a $100,000 depreciable asset without using leverage. Or, with a 75 percent loan-to-value ratio loan, the investor could borrow $300,000 and buy a $400,000 depreciable asset. Using leverage in this case will have increased annual depreciation deductions by a multiple of four.

Let's look at some more numbers. Suppose we could earn 10 percent per annum before taxes and interest and are looking at an appartment building on leased land. Assume that we can borrow $300,000 at 8 percent per annum, to be repaid in equal annual payments over 30 years. Let's look at the after-tax yield on equity funds, if the market value of the property remains constant and we are in the 28 percent marginal income tax bracket (see table on page 133).

The first year's cash flow is 8.2 percent of the initial equity investment in the all-equity deal and 13.2 percent with leverage, a substantial benefit from borrowing. The interest expense and debt-service numbers were compiled from amortization tables, which are explained in Chapter Six. The depreciation deductions are based on writing off the purchase price over

	$100,000, All- Equity Deal	$400,000 Deal with $300,000 Loan
Net operating income @ 10%	$10,000	$40,000
Less: Interest expense @ 8%	–0–	23,909
Depreciation	3,636	14,545
Taxable income	$ 6,364	$ 1,546
Times tax rate	.28	.28
Income taxes, first year	$ 1,782	$ 433

27.5 years in equal annual increments. (These numbers are all approximate, of course. We have, for example, ignored the tax law that specifies only a half month's depreciation in the year of purchase, and we have assumed the purchase to have occurred in the first month of the taxable year.)

Only the first year's consequences are illustrated here. It should be noted that the leverage benefits decline gradually as an increasing percentage of the debt-service obligation becomes non-deductible principal payments rather than deductible interest expense. However, this is an extremely gradual shift, and when it progresses to the point of annoyance you can consider refinancing.

A more serious matter is the tax consequences of selling the property. All the depreciation deductions come back to haunt you if you sell for more than your adjusted income tax basis; a distinct possibility. In this case the benefit of depreciation deductions is measured by the value of deferring taxes until the year of the sale. You can, however, avoid the day of reckoning by never selling the property. Instead, adjust your portfolio with like-kind exchanges as explained in Chapter Thirteen.

When Is Leverage Favorable?

Giving up our other simplifying assumptions increases the complexity of the arithmetic, but does not alter the fundamental relationship; favorable financial leverage amplifies the yield to the equity position. Costs and yields, however, must be measured over the investment's life-cycle, rather than simply on a current basis.

Suppose borrowing imposes a repayment obligation of, say, 11 percent of the face amount of the loan, while the annual net cash flow from operating a property is only 10 percent of the price paid for it. Does this mean financial leverage is unfavorable? Not necessarily.

Whether the leverage is favorable or unfavorable depends on the relationship between the average annual cost of borrowing and the average annual yield on assets, measured on an after-tax basis over the entire investment cycle from acquisition through disposition.

Suppose, for example, that a property is generating a current yield on a before-tax basis of 7 percent (that is, the net operating income equals 7 percent of the purchase price). Suppose also that the property is increasing in value at about 4 percent per annum. If this continues throughout the investor's holding period, the average annual before-tax yield on assets will be about 11 percent; the current yield plus the appreciation rate.

If borrowed money costs less than 11 percent per annum, leverage will be favorable when measured on a before-tax basis. It will actually be even more favorable after tax because, as we have seen, leverage amplifies the tax benefits from depreciation deductions.

The Cost of Borrowing

As with most good things, financial leverage is not free. And, again as with most good things, overindulgence can be harmful. The cost of borrowing, as everybody knows, is interest. Interest is generally expressed as an annual rate, and appears self-explanatory. But this apparent simplicity is deceptive. Stated interest rates seldom tell the whole story. Understanding the real cost of borrowing requires a clear distinction between nominal and effective rates, and between contract rates and real rates.

The Real Interest Rate
In an inflationary environment lenders face a vexing problem. Loans are repaid in dollars with significantly diminished purchasing power. For example, suppose a lender advances $100,000 to be repaid several years hence, and during the

interim inflation erodes purchasing power by 20 percent. The lender only gets back 80 percent of the purchasing power advanced to the borrower—a bum deal unless there is sufficient other compensation.

To ensure an adequate reward for lending in inflationary times, interest rates always reflect expected inflation over the repayment period. Though the precise equation is more complex, the effective rate of interest (that is, the cost of borrowing expressed in purchasing power terms) can be approximated by subtracting the inflation rate from the contract interest rate. If a lender is charging 10 percent per annum and prices are going up at about 4 percent each year, the approximate real cost of borrowing is 10 minus 4, or 6 percent per annum.

Inflation, then, reduces the reward for being a lender under a long-term, fixed-rate promissory note. The possibility that inflation will ravage their profit is part of the risk for which lenders insist on being rewarded via interest income. The more likely it is that the rate of price increases (inflation) will accelerate during the loan period, the higher will be the interest rate you will be forced to pay.

Another way lenders approach this problem is more insidious. Many push adjustable-rate mortgages, or ARMs, where the contract rate of interest is altered periodically over the term to reflect changes in market interest rates. With an ARM, lenders need not be concerned that inflation will reduce the real rate of interest. ARMs, therefore, are an effective way for lenders to shift interest rate risk to borrowers. But, do you really want to accept this shift?

Lenders argue that ARMs enable them to lend at a lower initial rate. True. The question a borrower should ask is whether the difference in initial rates on ARMs and conventional fixed-rate loans justifies accepting the risk that has traditionally been borne by lenders. Most of the time the answer is no.

Nominal and Effective Interest Rates

Interest rate computations should be expressed in effective, rather than nominal terms. The *contract rate*, as the name implies, is the rate stated in lending documents. The catch is that these rates are computed on the face amount of a loan—

the amount referenced in the promissory note—and this is often substantially more than a borrower actually gets from the lender.

Lenders frequently charge a loan origination fee, expressed as a percentage of the amount borrowed. Additionally, they often deduct *points*, which are actually a discount from the face amount of the loan. The *loan proceeds*, which is the amount the borrower carries away from the closing table, is the face amount (on which interest will be computed) minus points and the loan origination fee.

Mortgage loans generally require monthly payments that include all the accrued interest for the month plus a small portion of the principal, so that the loan is retired gradually over the payment period. To determine the monthly payment on a fully amortizing loan, simply multiply the amount borrowed by a factor from a monthly mortgage amortization table such as that shown in Appendix B.

To use the table, scan the interest rate row at the top until you find a column corresponding with the contract interest rate. Then, read down the left side of the table to the row corresponding with the number of years over which the loan is to be repaid. The factor at the intersection of the row and the column is the monthly payment on a $1 loan. Simply multiply this by the size of the loan to determine the monthly payment.

Suppose you were considering a $100,000 loan with interest at 9 percent, to be repaid in equal monthly payments over 20 years. The factor from the table is .008997. Multiply this by the $100,000 face amount of the loan; the monthly payment will be $899.70.

Suppose, however, the lender is charging a 1 percent loan origination fee and three discount points. To determine the effective interest rate, first figure exactly how much money the lender will actually disburse:

Face amount of loan	$100,000
Less: Origination fee ($100,000 × .04)	4,000
Net loan proceeds	$ 96,000

In this case the borrower walks away from the closing table with only $96,000, but has to make monthly payments based on the entire $100,000 face amount of the loan. We saw earlier that the monthly payment will be $899.70. As a fraction of the amount actually received from the lender this is $899.70/$96,000, or .009372. Remembering that this is a fully amortizing, 20-year loan, you can estimate the effective interest rate by reversing the order in which you use the amortization table.

Glancing down the left-hand side of the table, start with the 20-year row. Read across the 20-year row until you find the amortization factor that most nearly approximates .009372. The number you should settle upon is .009321. Now, read up this column to determine the interest rate; you will discover it to be 9.5 percent. We conclude that, if the loan remains outstanding until maturity, the effective interest rate will be slightly above 9.5 percent per annum rather than the nominal rate of 9 percent.

Of course, most loans are paid off much sooner. Because property is sold or refinanced, typical loans have an average life of about seven or eight years. This increases the effective interest rate. In fact, the sooner the note is retired, the greater will be the lender's yield. Keep this in mind when you are deciding between contract interest rates and front-end fees.

WHERE TO FIND LOANS

Everyone knows that banks and savings and loan associations (S&Ls) are lenders, and they are usually the first recourse for would-be borrowers. These are not always enthusiastic lenders, however, and they will often flatly refuse loans to real estate investors. When this happens, where can you turn?

Who's Got the Money?

Other people's money (OPM) is the grease that makes real estate marketing machinery run smoothly. Prospective lenders, other than commercial banks and S&Ls, include insurance companies, savings banks, pension and trust funds, finance companies, private investors, and real estate sellers. The most likely lender for a particular deal depends on the property's size and location and the amount of money you need. Consistent success as a borrower depends on knowing which lenders to approach and what to include in the loan application package.

Predilections of Conventional Lenders

Savings banks, commercial banks, life insurance companies, and S&Ls have been the traditional sources of most real estate loans. Collectively, they account for well over 80 percent of all mortgage funds. Each type of lender has shown a preference for a distinct kind of loan arrangement and a particular class of real estate security, and most are loath to break with tradition. You need a high frustration threshold if you expect traditional lenders to consider innovative financing suggestions.

Other Lenders

Recalcitrant lenders are no cause for dismay. Other sources of mortgage funds abound. They include individual investors, personal finance companies, mortgage bankers, and—frequently the most promising source—the seller of the property you are trying to finance.

Dealing with Mortgage Bankers

When you are looking for a lender that will consider the unusual, that will evaluate your proposal on its merits rather than on its adherence to institutional policy, where do you go? Most of the time the answer is, to a mortgage banking firm. These companies are not lenders in the conventional sense. They usually have a small amount of capital at best, and they do not hold deposits the way banks and S&Ls do. Their importance to the mortgage-lending industry is disproportionate to the personal assets they commit to lending because they act primarily as go betweens, bringing together borrowers and lenders that might otherwise never make contact.

Mortgage bankers are a crucial link in the chain that connects pension funds and insurance companies to real estate borrowers. By its nature real estate lending is a local activity; someone has to solicit loan applications, check local public records, and inspect property. Since major lenders are usually too far away to do all this economically, they engage mortgage bankers to act for them.

As lenders' loan correspondents, mortgage companies solicit and process loan applications, check credit references, arrange for property appraisals, and handle the myriad local details attendant to closing loans. They often undertake the "servicing" of loans they originate, collecting monthly payments from borrowers and processing the related paperwork. For all this they are paid a modest annual fee; yet these fees in the aggregate constitute a major source of revenue.

Real Estate Brokers' Role in Mortgage Lending

Sophisticated real estate brokers often distinguish themselves by their ability to help you find money from unconventional sources. They understand sources of funds and the way lenders view loan proposals. They don't simply hand you a list of lenders and wish you luck. Instead, they "pre-shop" your loan application so that any lender to whom you are referred will have been sounded out on its attitude toward the loan proposal. Recognizing that financing is the key to success in difficult transactions, these brokers spend considerable time and energy considering financing alternatives. They understand that there are myriad ways to package a deal and that most alternatives are never explored or even recognized by less sophisticated competitors. If conventional lenders turn down a loan application, a knowledgeable broker considers how the transaction might be repackaged to make it more palatable to the next lender They also know about unconventional financing sources.

Asking about potential loan sources is a good way to separate sophisticated real estate brokers from the order-takers. If the broker isn't prepared to discuss the issue in terms other than referring you to a mortgage company, you might want to consider working with someone who has a greater appreciation for credit's role in commercial real estate transactions.

NEGOTIATING UNDER DIFFICULT CIRCUMSTANCES

People often panic when mortgage money is scarce and interest rates are high. Yet sophisticated investors recognize that many sellers don't have the luxury of waiting for a change in the financial climate before completing a transaction. For one reason or another, some property owners have to sell regardless of tight credit markets.

If overtures to traditional lenders prove fruitless, look for innovative ways to finance the deal.

Assume an Existing Loan

Long-outstanding mortgage loans may comprise an attactive source of borrowed funds for subsequent buyers of mortgaged property. Recently, lenders have routinely inserted a prohibition against selling mortgaged property subject to the existing loan without the lender's approval. There remain outstanding, however, a number of older loans that do not contain this restriction. Moreover, loans with such a restriction (a *covenant against alienation*) can still frequently be transferred with the lender's approval.

Restrictions against transferring mortgaged property subject to the existing loan are designed to protect lenders against extended holding periods on loans at interest rates substantially below the current market. When rates move above the contract rates on existing mortgages, lenders refuse to approve transfers, thus forcing buyers to acquire new financing and thereby liquidating existing loans. This of course permits the original lender to put funds back into the market at new, higher interest rates.

When money gets so scarce that loans are simply unavailable to new borrowers at affordable rates, the lender strategy of refusing to approve transfers can prove counterproductive. When this occurs, holders of existing loans might be prevailed upon to permit an assumption of the old loan by a buyer if the new owner pays an assumption fee sufficient to boost the lender's yield substantially above the old contract rate.

Your negotiating ability (or the persuasiveness of your representative) becomes critical at this point. The original lender has to be convinced that letting you assume the old loan with an attractive assumption fee is in the lender's best interest. This involves arguing that liquidating the loan is not an attainable goal; that the only alternative is for the existing owner to continue in possession of the property, with all that implies about the longevity of the old loan and yield rates to the lender. Recognizing that a reasonable assumption fee is the only alternative to an unappetizing status quo may make the lender more tractable.

Assumption with a New Second Mortgage

When new first mortgage loans are expensive or nonexistent, yet the difference between property value and the balance of an assumable loan exceeds available (or justifiable) equity funds, consider bridging a part of the gap with a second mortgage loan, perhaps held by the seller.

A problem occurs when the existing mortgage loan contains a clause precluding junior encumbrances such as second mortgages. A holder of such a first mortgage can sometimes, for sufficient compensation, be induced to waive the prohibition. The consideration might be an accelerated amortization schedule for the first mortgage, a revised interest rate, a pledge of additional security, a compensating balance placed on deposit, or any number of other inducements. Use your imagination.

Go Back to the Same Well

When new loans at viable rates are hard to come by, the holder of an existing loan on the property might be a responsive source. If rates have moved up considerably since the existing loan was placed, its yield (and its value on the secondary mortgage market) will have fallen far below the general market for new loans. The prospect of replacing such a loan with a new one at the current market rate may prove marvelously effective in focusing the lender's attention on your application.[1]

---

[1]We are presupposing that the holder of the loan is also in the business of loan origination. Many loans are sold to investors, who of course will not be in a position to originate a new loan. Just because a local lender is collecting the payments does not mean it owns the loan itself.

Suppose you are looking at a property that has a 30-year, 7 percent mortgage loan with 12 years remaining. If the old note was for, say, $100,000, the monthly payment will be $665.30 and the remaining balance will be about $64,694. You need $200,000 to acquire the property, but current interest rates of 13 percent per annum are too high to make the deal work. You point out that you must have a loan at no more than 12 percent to put the deal together, and that the alternative is for the present owner to continue in possession and the old loan to continue indefinitely.

You might find the lender amenable to your proposition, particularly if you discuss the incremental benefits of the arrangement. Note that the lender's net cash disbursement is the new $200,000 loan minus the $64,694 balance on the old, or $135,306. The new monthly payment, predicated on a $200,000 loan at 12 percent for 30 years, is $2,057.23. For the first 12 years this will be offset by the old monthly payment of $665.30, which of course will no longer be paid. The lender, therefore, will receive a net payment increase of $1,391.93 (the new payment minus the old) for the first 12 years and $2,057.23 for the ensuing 18 years (after the old loan would have expired). All this for a net disbursement of $135,306. Applying the mathematical procedure explained in Appendix A reveals that the effective interest on the incremental loan amount is just under 14 percent per annum; a competitive rate under current market conditions.

When Lenders Balk

If none of these strategies work, if lenders simply are not interested in any of the ideas reviewed, is it time to quit? Not yet. Additional strategies that might prod a reluctant lender include:

Open-end Mortgage
If a lender offers to lend less than the amount you need, but indicates that a larger loan would be available if you met specific objections to the original request, an open-end mortgage might solve the impasse. Such a loan provides for some immedi-

ate funds plus additional advances when you satisfy the lender's preconditions. This might be an appropriate strategy when the lender objects to deferred maintenance or to an unacceptably high vacancy rate.

Equity Kicker

If the problem is that the lender requires a repayment plan that is impractical given the property's early cash-flow projections, you might counter with a proposal for more lenient repayment terms combined with an equity kicker to give the lender a piece of the action if the deal works out as anticipated. A fairly typical arrangement gives the lender a percentage of the gain when you sell or refinance the property. Another is for the lender to share in operating income above some specified amount. An equity kicker converts a conventional mortgage loan into something analogous to preferred stock. It is a versatile way to tailor a deal to meet both buyer and lender needs.

Compensating Balances

If the lender is a depository institution such as a bank or S&L, try inducing the seller to place a portion of the sales proceeds on deposit with the lender for a specific time. The prospect of a large certificate of deposit (with "significant penalties for early withdrawal") can do wonders for a lender's disposition.

Pledge Depository Accounts

An extension of this strategy, and one to which many lenders will be more responsive, is for a seller to deposit funds with the lender (or purchase a large certificate of deposit with the sales proceeds) and pledge the account as collateral security for the buyer's mortgage loan. Typical provisions are for the pledged account to be released ratably as the principal amount of the loan is reduced or the market value of the mortgaged property is increased.

Pledge Additional Real Estate

If you have other real estate you can borrow funds in addition to those secured by a mortgage on the newly acquired property. The additional funds are secured by a pledge of your other real estate as collateral security. The pledged assets should be released when the supplementary funds are repaid, or when the market value of the new property reaches an agreed-upon level.

Pledge Securities
If you own stocks or bonds that are not margined, they will work nicely as collateral security for a real estate loan. Be sure the security agreement permits you flexibility to substitute new securities for old, so that your trading strategy will not be hampered by the security arrangement.

Negotiate a Blanket Mortgage
A reluctant lender might be reassured if you are willing to couple other property with the new parcel, encumbering both with the mortgage securing the new loan. There should be a provision to release the second property from the mortgage when the principal balance is reduced to an agreed level, or when you have increased the value of the new property so that the differential between the market value and the mortgage balance reaches an agreed level.

Credit from Sellers or Private Lenders

When conventional lending sources are exhausted, turn to sellers as possible sources of mortgage loans. Since a major portion of commercial and industrial property sales in fact involve some degree of seller financing, sellers are conditioned to such contract provisions. Also, there are in most cities a number of private parties who stand ready to lend funds to bridge the gap between conventional first mortgage loans and the available down payment. Sophisticated real estate brokers will usually know who these people are. Dealing with them opens new avenues for structuring loans.

Use a Repurchase Agreement
Under this arrangement you sell property to a private individual or firm that has available cash, and you take back an option to repurchase the property at a specified future date. The ini-

tial sale price will be substantially below current market value, so that the temporary buyer (a de facto lender) can be assured that either you will exercise your repurchase option or an open-market sale after the option expires will net the anticipated profit that serves as an inducement for the arrangement. The option-exercise price will be sufficiently above the initial sales price to compensate the buyer (lender) for parting with liquidity during the option period.

Wrap a New Mortgage around an Old
Because they remain contingently liable, sellers are sometimes reluctant to transfer title subject to an existing mortgage, even when lenders will agree. You may be able to overcome this reluctance by agreeing to remit payments on the old mortgage directly to the seller, who then makes payments to the mortgage lender. This permits constant surveillance on the loan's status and reduces concern that default will harm the seller's credit rating and perhaps instigate a foreclosure action. The mechanism is a *wraparound mortgage*, sometimes called an *all-inclusive mortgage*.

Borrow from the Selling Broker
Brokers work hard for their commissions, and any last-minute attempt to reduce their compensation will be received with justifiable hostility. A deferred commission, however, may be preferred to no commission at all. If the broker's commission (typically 5 to 10 percent of the sales price) will cover the gap between the required down payment and your available equity funds, don't be timid about proposing a loan secured by one of the arrangements described above.

Try a Lease with a Purchase Commitment
If you like the property and the price is right, but current interest rates are too high or loans are simply not available, propose a purchase option combined with a lease. You get immediate possession (subject, of course, to any preexisting leasehold interests) along with a chance of obtaining more favorable financing later in the purchase option period. The seller's inducement is the interim lease payments and the

escrowed option fee as assurance that a transaction will eventually occur.

Ask Sellers to Lease Back Vacant Space

If sellers contend that vacancy rates are abnormally high because of transient factors, and therefore should not affect the property's price, ask them to demonstrate their faith by leasing back the extra vacant units at just below what they contend is a fair rental value. If they really believe the market is better than the vacancy rate indicates, they should be confident that they can sublet the units and turn a modest profit. This relieves you of anxiety over the abnormally high vacancy factor and ensures an uninterrupted cash flow. If the sellers do not have stellar credit, insist that a portion of the sales proceeds be encumbered to ensure payment of their rent obligation.

THE DARK SIDE OF FINANCIAL LEVERAGE

Since favorable financial leverage amplifies equity yields, shouldn't you use all the borrowed money you can muster? This proposition's attraction is manifested by the commercial success of a host of books promising vast riches with *no money down.* Too often the no-money-down prescription proves a recipe for bankruptcy. As you borrow more and more money to finance a property, two undesirable side effects occur: You have to pay more for the additional dollars, and the likelihood of disaster multiplies.

Higher Leverage Costs More

If you are reasonably certain that you will earn, say, 14 percent per annum on a real estate asset and you can borrow 90 percent of the purchase price at 11 percent per annum, does it always make sense to take the loan? Not necessarily. Eleven percent is your *average* cost of borrowing, but you can't make a rational decision until you know the *incremental* cost. Incremental cost is the increase in total payments caused by borrowing additional sums, expressed as a percentage rate on the additional funds.

Suppose, for example, you could get a $200,000 loan at 10 percent per annum, to be fully amortized over 30 years. To keep the example simple, let's assume (unrealistically) that there is no loan origination fee. Now, suppose the lender offers an alternative arrangement that entails a $250,000 loan at 11 percent, amortized over the same 30-year period. What is the incremental cost of the additional $50,000?

Monthly payments on each loan can be computed by finding the appropriate factor on the amortization table in Appendix B and multiplying this number by the face amount of the loan. For the 10 percent, 30-year loan, the amortization factor is .008776; for the 11 percent loan it is .009523. Using these factors, it is easy to determine the monthly cost of borrowing the additional $50,000:

	Loan Proceeds	Monthly Payment
With $250,000, 11 percent loan	$250,000	$2,380.75
With $200,000, 10 percent loan	200,000	1,755.20
Increment	$ 50,000	$ 625.55

Noting that the additional $50,000 costs $625.55 per month for 30 years, you can find the appropriate amortization factor in the table in Appendix B and work backwards to estimate incremental cost. Since the payment is determined by multiplying the dollar amount by an amortization factor, it follows that dividing the payment by the loan will yield the factor. Here is the basic equation, with the incremental numbers:

$$\text{Payment} = \text{Loan} \times \text{Amortization Factor}$$
$$\$625.55 = \$50,000 \times \text{Amortization Factor}$$

Manipulating the equation algebraically, you can isolate the unknown amortization factor on one side of the equation and solve for it. Dividing both sides of the equation by the $50,000 incremental loan yields an amortization factor of .012511:

$$\text{Amortization Factor} = \text{Payment / Loan}$$
$$= \$625.55 / \$50,000$$
$$= .012511$$

Remembering that this is a 30-year loan, scan across the 30-year row of the amortization table in Appendix B until you find a factor as close as possible to .012511. Then read up the column to determine the approximate cost of the additional funds. The closest factor in the 30-year row is .012644, in the 15 percent column. We conclude, therefore, that the additional funds cost almost 15 percent per annum—a substantial premium over the 10 percent cost of the first $200,000, and more than the anticipated rate of return on assets.

In an actual lending situation you will almost certainly be asked to pay a fee that reduces the net proceeds below the loan's face amount, thus increasing the effective interest rate. Moreover, the size of the front-end fee usually increases disproportionately to the additional funds borrowed. This makes the incremental cost even greater, but the frequently exorbitant cost of additional money is not apparent unless you apply this type of analysis.

Between the Cup and the Lip, a Potential Slip

Financial leverage broadens the range of possible outcomes. Since variability is a measure of risk, it follows that greater leverage increases the risk attendant to equity investment.

To see how this works, suppose the possible net operating income (that is, gross rental revenue minus operating expenses, but before considering mortgage payments or income tax) of a certain property ranges from $250,000 to $350,000. If the property costs $2 million, possible before-tax current yields range from $250,000 divided by $2 million to $350,000 divided by $2 million, or from 12.5 percent to 17.5 percent. If you buy this property solely with equity funds (no borrowing), the current equity yield will be in this range.

But suppose you finance $1,400,000 of the $2 million purchase price with a mortgage loan that requires monthly payments over 25 years and carries a 13 percent per annum interest rate. Your monthly payments will be approximately $15,790, which means $189,480 of annual net operating income will be diverted to the mortgage lender. Your before-tax cash flow will be net operating income minus the debt service. Since the net operating income will range from $250,000 to $350,000, and since the debt service obligation is fixed at $189,480, your cash flow before taxes will range from $60,520 to $160,520. The current yield before taxes will be these amounts divided by the equity investment, which is the $2 million purchase price minus the $1,400,000 loan, or $600,000. Here is a summary of the math:

	Range of Possible Outcomes	
	Low Bound	Upper Bound
Net operating income	$250,000	$350,000
Less: Debt service	189,480	189,480
Before-tax cash flow	$60,520	$160,520
Current yield (before-tax cash flow/Equity investment)	10.1%	26.8%

If you assume that the expected outcome is the midpoint of the range of possible outcomes, then you can expect the net operating income to be $300,000. Without mortgage financing this is also the expected before-tax cash flow; with the mortgage, expected cash flow before taxes is $300,000 minus $189,480, or $110,520. The expected current yield without borrowed money is $300,000/$2,000,000, or 15 percent. Borrowing $1.4 million increases this to $110,520/$600,000, or 18.4 percent. Thus financial leverage that is expected to be favorable increases both the expected yield and the range of possible yields. Figure 9–1 illustrates financial leverage's impact on the expected outcome and the range of possible outcomes.

It's the possibilities that trip you up. Remember that when you are estimating whether leverage will be favorable or unfavorable, you incorporate a *certain* debt-service obligation and an *expected* operating result. If your operating forecast is off, so is your estimate of leverage's impact.

FIGURE 9–1
Possible Yields with and without Leverage

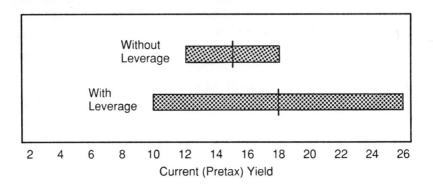

Current (Pretax) Yield

Borrowing also increases the likelihood that the property won't generate enough cash to pay the debt service. Expressed differently, the more you borrow the more likely it is that you will default on your mortgage and face foreclosure.

Consider another $2 million property; this one a 60-unit apartment house that rents for $9,300 per unit, per year. Assume also that variable operating expenses (those you incur only when the apartments are occupied) are $1,200 per occupied unit, and that fixed expenses (those, such as insurance, property taxes, and common-area maintenance and utilities, that you face even when the units are empty) total $276,000 per year. If all the units are rented and everybody pays up, your annual net cash flow will be $210,000 before accounting for mortgage payments.

But what happens if the market turns sour? With some units vacant, gross income and variable operating expenses will both drop, but fixed expenses just keep grinding. Variable expenses go down, but revenue slides even more. Specifically, each vacancy reduces net operating income an additional $8,100.

With enough vacant units, there obviously comes a point where the venture starts eating cash. The point where revenue and costs are equal—where there is no net inflow or outflow—is called the *cash break-even point*. The lower the occupancy level can fall before reaching the cash break-even point, the less the risk of financial catastrophe. But, borrowing money raises the cash break-even point. This is yet another way that mortgage debt increases risk.

Here's how to estimate the cash break-even occupancy level. First, estimate the per-unit gross rental revenue and variable operating expense. The difference is the *unit contribution margin*, the amount each unit is expected to contribute to fixed costs and profit. For our 60-unit apartment house the expected contribution margin is the $9,300 rental rate minus the $1,200 of variable expense per unit, or $8,100. Since we expect fixed costs to be $276,000 and each rented unit to contribute $8,100 to this total, we only have to rent 57 percent of the units to break even:

> Break-even occupancy level
> = Fixed Costs / Unit contribution margin
> = $276,000 / $8,100
> = 34.1 units
>
> Break-even occupancy percentage
> = Occupied units / Total units
> = 34.1 / 60
> = 57 percent

Figure 9–2 illustrates the relationship. Occupancy levels are measured on the horizontal axis; revenues and costs are on the vertical. Fixed costs are the same regardless of occupancy level, but variable costs and revenue are directly related to occupancy. The difference between revenue per unit and variable costs is, as we have seen, $8,100. Thus, moving out one unit on the horizontal axis moves us up $8,100 on the vertical axis, the relationship shown by the sloping (contribution margin) line. The point where the fixed-cost line and the contribution margin line cross is the cash break-even occupancy level.

Now, see what a mortgage loan does to the cash break-even point. We saw earlier that borrowing $1.4 million at 13 percent over 25 years generates an annual debt service obligation of $189,480. The debt service must be paid regardless of occupancy levels—it is an addition to fixed costs. Adding the debt service

FIGURE 9–2
Break-even Occupancy Level

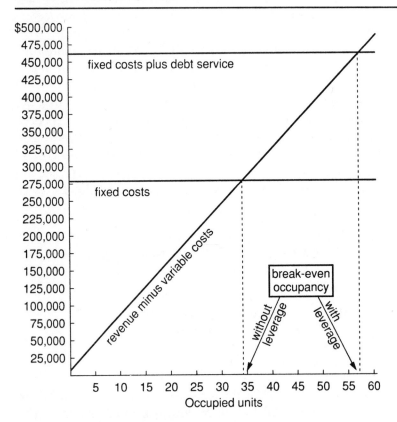

to other fixed costs, the revised fixed-cost element is $276,000 plus $189,480, or $465,480. With each occupied unit generating $8,100 above the per-unit variable cost, you now must rent at least $465,480/$8,100, or approximately 58 units, for the project to support itself on a cash-flow basis.

KEY POINTS

• If you can borrow money at a lower rate than you earn on real estate assets, then borrowing will amplify the yield on your equity funds. Remember, however, that borrowing also increases risk exposure.

• Borrowing enables you to control more property, and so to get larger annual tax deductions for depreciation expense. If you have sufficient income against which to offset the deductions, this tax shelter element is a valuable dimension of the benefits from borrowing.

• *Nominal* interest rates are those you are contractually obligated to pay; the *effective* rate includes the nominal rate plus a provision for amortizing the fees and discounts you pay when you close on the loan; *real* rates are effective rates adjusted for price-level changes. Effective rates are almost always higher than nominal, and real rates (except for adjustable rate notes) are invariably lower than effective rates.

• Instead of despairing when traditional loan sources dry up, explore unconventional sources. Also turn to other than depository lenders when you need special terms or conditions.

• Don't let the lure of favorable leverage blind you to costs and hazards. Remember that as the amount of borrowed funds mounts, you will probably face higher effective interest rates. Measure these as incremental rather than average rates and you will be less likely to negotiate an unfavorable loan.

CHAPTER 10

WORKING BOTH
SIDES OF THE STREET

Pick up any book or article on real estate investment and you will see emphasis on the magic of financial leverage: "Borrow your way to prosperity," or "Pyramid your wealth with credit." It makes no difference where the money comes from, it seems, so long as it doesn't come from your own pocket. The highly leveraged real estate deal is an idea discussed as enthusiastically in pool halls as in financial districts.

Investors accustomed to contrary thinking are always suspicious of ideas that become standard wisdom. Remembering that the way to buy at the right price is to buy when everyone else is selling and to sell when they are buying, perhaps when everyone is touting leverage the time has come to shift to the other side of the equation: to become a lender.

WORKING THE SPREAD

The *spread*, you will recall, is the difference between what you pay for funds and what you can earn. We saw in Chapter Nine that leveraging your equity makes sense when the spread between borrowing costs and expected yields on assets justifies the additional risk.

The concept of spread is broader than that, however. If leverage is unfavorable, or is not favorable enough to justify the added risk, you might want to consider shifting assets from real property into monetary assets. When the yield on lending exceeds the yield on real estate assets (after appropriate adjustments for risk differentials), it makes sense to become a lender—even if only temporarily.

We all do this, even though we may not realize it. When you put cash into a money market mutual fund you become a lender. You are also lending when you buy shares in Ginnie Mae pools or when you buy bonds or treasury bills. You might have thought of yourself as an investor rather than as a lender, but that is exactly the point; loans are investments too.

For a lender, the spread is the difference between borrowing and lending rates. Thus, if you can borrow at 9 percent and lend at 11, there is a favorable spread of 2 percentage points, or 200 *basis points* Financial leverage is favorable, and it might pay to be both a borrower and a lender. When you evaluate the implications of the favorable spread, however, don't forget that leveraging your creditor position increases risk in exactly the same way as does leveraging your equity position in real estate.

The idea that you can borrow at a lower rate than you earn from lending sounds heretical because we are accustomed to thinking that borrowing always costs more The usual difference between these rates is the favorable spread earned by lending institutions, which is their reason for existing. When you assume the lender's position you have to reverse this rela tionship

A ROLE FOR PRIVATE LENDERS

Private lenders are relegated to mortgage-lending backwaters because they can't compete with depository institutions such as banks and S&Ls or large financial firms such as life insurance companies and pension funds. Instead, they take what's left after the big guys finish feeding. The leavings, however, are hardly financial crumbs.

The industry's heavy hitters are uninterested in certain kinds of loans and some property types. This creates a niche devoid of major competition, a niche where lack of lender interest drives up borrowing costs—sure profit ingredients for private lenders. Similar yields in the mortgage-lending mainstream would create a lending frenzy and quickly drive profits back into the cellar. Opportunities lie in the interstices between major markets, either because big lenders are constrained by regulatory restrictions or because the interstices are simply too minuscule to interest them.

Redlined Areas

Large lenders need policies that reduce the problem of selecting properties on which to make loans. One common measure appears to be identifying areas in which loans will be made and, by implication, other areas where they will not. For a lender who does not know the local economic terrain, this is an altogether reasonable move.

Sensible as the strategy is for mainstream lending institutions, it creates opportunities for people like you. Redlined regions—the areas from which large lenders will not entertain loan applications—are not necessarily poor prospects for lenders; they just require you to weigh more carefully the merits of each individual parcel that a borrower wants to pledge.

If you intimately know the redlined neighborhood, you can exercise judgment without incurring the prohibitive research expense that makes a similar approach impractical for big lenders. Since you will expect to make loans repeatedly in the same geographic area, you can afford to spend some time and money mastering its economic eccentricities. The payoff goes on and on.

Bridge Loans

Commercial property loans are routinely layered. Second and third mortgage notes are not at all uncommon, but they are seldom provided by institutional lenders. That leaves sellers or people like you. Since sellers are often eager to put their money back into equities or, less frequently, are completely disillusioned with real estate and want out completely, individuals who will ante cash to bridge the gap between the balance of an existing first mortgage loan and the buyer's available funds are in demand. Because these loans typically are short-lived, coupling them with a front-end fee yields impressive returns, as we will see shortly.

Loans with Special Provisions

Borrowers often have special needs that could easily be accommodated by conventional lenders if they were not so hampered by regulators and by convention. Institutional lenders' inability or reluctance to meet these needs provides a sterling opportunity for anyone willing to be more innovative.

For reasons often deeply embedded in past tribulations, there is a maze of regulatory needles through which institutional loans must be threaded. Special borrower requirements often simply will not fit through the maze.

As lending institutions grow in size they tend to lose their ability to respond to their customers' needs even where there are no regulatory barriers. Policy manuals, designed to push decision-making down through the management hierarchy, virtually eliminate flexibility. The safe strategy for institutional lending officers is simply to reject any loan application for which the policy manual doesn't explicitly permit approval. Borrowers are forced to turn to untraditional loan sources—such as yourself.

What am I talking about? Possibilities are almost limitless. Every innovative investor has some ideas that will require lender cooperation. These needs often add nothing to lender risk, and may in fact make loans more profitable. Why not weigh each proposal on its merit, rather than comparing it with notes in a policy manual? Here are some examples:

Seasonal Payments
Cash flows in resort areas fluctuate widely with the seasons. You might permit high payments during the tourist season, with smaller—perhaps even zero—payments during the rest of the year. Why not, so long as the bottom line is the same?

Payment Moratoriums
A project might require some time before it starts generating cash flow. The borrower might ask that the interim interest be added to the principal amount of the loan and that amortization begin later. This makes consummate good sense as long as you judge the collateral to be adequate when based on the maximum amount to which the loan balance will grow.

Balloon Loans

Monthly payments on balloon loans are based on longer amortization periods than the loans actually run. For example, payments may be designed to retire the loan over ten years, but the remaining balance actually becomes due in six years. The final large payment is called a balloon payment for obvious reasons. Such a loan has appealing characteristics to an investor who is strapped for cash but has other property that can be liquidated before the due date of the balloon.

Substitutable Collateral

Your concern is that collateral security be adequate for the loan balance; what difference does it make to you precisely what property is pledged? Permit a borrower the flexibility of substituting different property when doing so will facilitate deal-making. You will of course reserve the right to approve or disapprove any specific substitute parcel.

Lifting Clause

This clause permits an existing senior mortgage note (one that has priority over yours in case of default) to be paid off and replaced with other senior debt. Without a lifting clause, paying off the existing senior note would elevate your note to the senior position, and any subsequent note would be junior to yours. This would make it impossible for the investor to borrow substantial amounts of money through refinancing without also paying off your note. Many financial institutions will balk at a lifting clause Yet it can be beneficial to both you and the borrower as long as the clause limits the total amount of mortgage debt that can be moved into the senior position

AMPLIFYING THE YIELD

There are basically three ways to increase the spread between your borrowing and lending rates.

1. You can shorten the term over which you borrow while extending the term of loans advanced to debtors. Longer-term loans usually carry a higher rate of interest.

2. You can make more speculative loans, while giving your creditors added assurance that they will not suffer losses on loans to you. Since the usual relationship is that the greater the risk of default the higher the interest rate or yield on a loan, this will enable you to borrow more cheaply while earning a higher rate of return on funds you place at risk.

3. You can position yourself to exploit market inefficiencies. Generally, the less efficient the market in which you operate, the greater will be your chances of earning above-market rates of return.

The Dangers of Playing the Yield Curve

Figure 10–1 shows the usual relationship between yield rates and the term until a loan matures. As the illustration indicates, the longer the term to maturity the higher the yield rate. There is a twofold reason for this: longer-term loans involve parting with liquidity, and—other things being equal—longer-term loans entail greater risk.

A legion of chastened lenders can attest to the risk associated with exploiting the yield curve to increase the spread between borrowing and lending rates. By borrowing in the short-term market and lending on the long-term notes, they reaped a bountiful harvest of profit—until the market double-crossed them. A rapid run-up in borrowing costs left them

FIGURE 10–1
The Usual Yield Curve

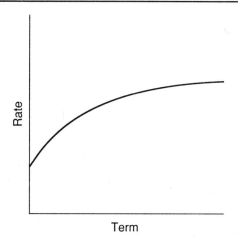

paying very high rates on short-term notes while they were locked into modest interest rates on longer-term credit they had advanced when money was easier to come by and thus less costly. Many lenders did not survive the debacle.

Hype the Yield with Risky Loans

The yield curve illustrated in Figure 10–1 has its characteristic shape because increasing the term to maturity exposes lenders to greater risk. Longer-term loans increase the probability that an increase in market interest rates will leave you holding assets with substandard yields. For assuming that risk, lenders insist on a higher expected rate of return.

There is another form of risk that is not necessarily associated with the term structure: the probability that borrowers will default on their repayment obligation. Figure 10–2 shows the characteristic tradeoff between expected yield and default risk. With virtually no default risk the expected yield is exceedingly modest. The prototypical loan free of default risk is one made to the federal government. Thus, short-term notes issued by the U.S. Treasury (Treasury Bills) offer very low yields and often serve as a proxy for the risk-free rate of return.

FIGURE 10–2
Risk–Return and Value with Altered Capitalization Rate

Moving out on the horizontal axis of Figure 10–2 will take you through the spectrum of loans guaranteed by very solvent governments and major corporations, through loans secured by liens on a borrower's assets, to unsecured loans. At the extreme end of the spectrum you will find pawnshop loans and promissory notes issued by governments that are considered unlikely to honor their obligations and have no assets exposed to seizure by creditors.

For lenders with virtually inexhaustible resources, moving along the risk–return axis makes consummate good sense. With a sufficiently diversified portfolio, the expected rate of default losses is a normal cost of doing business, and the statistically expected rate of return will almost certainly become a reality over time.

Private individuals who pursue such a strategy, however, court disaster. Limited resources make it virtually impossible to recover from the occasional string of losses that will inevitably occur. With your capital depleted there is no way to offset the losses with an equally inevitable string of successes. Where the market is functioning efficiently, participants who bear these risks must have a strong resource base. This is not a game in which you and I should participate.

A Niche Strategy Offsets Resource Limitations

Suppose you could find a situation where interest rates were predicated on a degree of risk that, for you, is not really there? If there is a general perception among market participants that risk can be avoided, the competition among lenders will drive interest rates down. If, on the other hand, most lenders overestimate the risk, they will insist on interest rates that you can easily undercut while still earning a handsome profit.

Such a market is said to be *inefficient* because there is crucial information (the information you have) that is not fully reflected in market prices—in this case, interest rates. Markets are rendered inefficient when information is expensive, or when some participants get the information sooner than others.

Your best chance of exploiting market inefficiencies is to pursue a niche strategy. You become familiar with all relevant data in a limited market area, or for a limited range of real estate project types, and use this information for repeated loan transactions that are limited to your niche and that you know more about than anyone else in the marketplace.

In his recent book, *Innovation and Entrepreneurship*, Peter Drucker calls this an "ecological niche" strategy. It aims, he says, at creating "a practical monopoly in a small area." The idea is to stake out turf that is very profitable for your size of operation but that is too small to attract competitors whose size and specialized marketing skills would enable them to wrest away your market with impunity.

For competitors more your size, who would be interested in your niche, it will be too late. You will have filled the niche so completely that they will have no hope of capturing a profitable market share.

LENDING STRATEGIES

It has been more than a decade now since Robert Allen wrote *Nothing Down*, a property investment primer that made the real estate world agog. Allen's book, which is subtitled *How To Buy Real Estate With Little Or No Money Down*, has probably been the best-selling real estate book ever published. It has spawned dozens of clones with similarly descriptive titles, each promising to reveal secrets that will let you build a real estate fortune almost overnight, with little or no equity investment.

If you decide to become a real estate lender, say a special thanks to Allen and authors of his ilk. They create a legion of prospective borrowers so dazzled with leverage's benefits that they don't bother to learn how to estimate the effective cost of borrowing. "Creative financing" can work wonders for a knowledgeable lender dealing with these investors.

Discount Paper Held by Sellers

Practically every financing strategy suggested by the "no-money-down" authors involves asking sellers to take back a promissory note as part or all of their consideration. The logic is that the greater the financial leverage the higher will be the yield to the equity investor. The ultimate outcome would be no equity investment at all, so that even a small positive spread would represent an infinitely large rate of return on equity. The presumption is that leverage will be favorable; the relationship between leverage and risk is virtually ignored.

The catch is that many sellers either don't want to hold paper or can't afford to do so. The motivation for selling is often a need for ready cash. The "no-money-down" boys assume you can always find sellers who will carry paper, but eliminating all those who are unable or unwilling to do so drastically limits the speculator's playing field. That is where you come in.

As a lender you can step into the breach by offering to buy acceptable paper from sellers—at a discount, of course. Since the creative financing gurus argue that terms are more important than price, sellers can simply increase the price of their property by the amount of the anticipated discount in order to net the target amount of cash.

Let's see how this might work. Suppose you are offered a $10,000 mortgage note that carries a 10 percent contract interest rate and is payable over five years with equal monthly payments. If you buy the note from the seller for $8,500 and hold it for the full five years, you will earn, not the 10 percent contract rate of interest, but 17.3 percent per annum.

If the borrower, for whatever reason, pays off the note before the full five years have elapsed (a distinct possibility) your effective rate of interest income will be even greater. If the note is retired after three years, for example, the effective yield will be 18.4 percent. Column two of Table 10–1 shows the

TABLE 10–1
Effective Yields on a 10 percent, Five-year Note Purchased at Discount

Discount Percentage	Effective Yield	
	Full Term	Paid after Three Years
10	14.7	15.4
15	17.3	18.4
20	20.1	21.7
25	23.2	25.3

effective annual interest rate on a 10 percent, five-year note
with various discounts when the note runs full term. The last
column of the table shows what the yield will be if the note is
paid off after three years.

Take Your Profit Up Front

If a note runs full term it really makes no difference whether
your interest comes as an annual receipt or is represented in
part by a payment made at the time the loan is created. The
effective interest will remain the same in either case. For example, you could earn about 12 percent per annum effective interest on a five year, monthly payment note either by charging
a 12 percent contract rate on the unpaid balance with no fee
up front, or by charging 9 percent per annum coupled with a 7
percent loan origination fee.

The situation changes drastically, however, if the loan is
paid off early. When this occurs, the more of your interest
income you have received in advance the higher will be the
effective interest rate. Yet most such loans are in fact paid
off early. Your challenge is to set a combination of front-end
charges and contract interest that will not discourage early payment yet will hype the average annual yield when early payment does occur.

Wraparound Loans

Perhaps the single greatest opportunity for private mortgage
lenders is in the area of second mortgage loans on commercial
properties that are sold subject to existing first mortgage loans.

As an investor's equity increases through the combination of gradual loan repayment and continual growth in the
mortgaged property's market value, the spread between market value and the balance of the first mortgage loan becomes
so great that few prospective buyers can or will pay the difference in cash. If the property is to be sold subject to the old first
mortgage, junior financing becomes imperative.

Buyers facing this dilemma have a limited range of options.
They can attempt to refinance with a new first mortgage loan,
but this is often prohibitively costly. They can ask the seller

to take back a second mortgage note for the difference, but as the size of the gap grows this becomes an increasingly difficult proposition for the seller, who must realize at least enough cash to pay the brokerage commission, legal fees, and income taxes, and whose need for additional liquidity is often the factor that motivated selling in the first place. A final alternative is to seek out an independent second mortgage lender such as yourself.

We saw earlier that second mortgage loans of this type, sometimes called bridge loans, can be lucrative. We also saw that the yield can be amplified by structuring the loan with a combination of front-end fees and contract interest rates that will make it advantageous to have the loan repaid early. Yet another way to hype the yield is to wrap the second mortgage around the existing first mortgage loan.

Here's how a wraparound loan (sometimes called an all-inclusive mortgage) works. Suppose the seller had borrowed, say, $80,000 on a first mortgage loan at 8 percent per annum, to be amortized over 20 years. The loan, which requires payments of $669.15 per month, is now 12 years old and the remaining balance has been reduced to $47,334. Meanwhile, the property has so increased in value that it could easily support a first mortgage loan of $120,000. Since interest rates, however, have climbed to about 12 percent per annum, the old 8 percent rate is very attractive and the ability to assume the existing note is a key selling point.

The buyer might arrange a $120,000 second mortgage loan with the understanding that the lender will disburse only the difference between this amount and the balance of the old note. The buyer will make payments on the $120,000 note and the new lender will take over payments on the old note. If the new note carries an interest rate of, say, 11 percent, the borrower and the new lender in effect share the benefit of the below-market interest on the old note.

The buyer saves money with this maneuver. The alternative of borrowing $120,000 at 12 percent on a new first mortgage note and paying off the old note from the proceeds would net the same amount of cash as the wraparound loan; $120,000 minus $47,334, or $72,666. But, whereas monthly payments on the $120,000, 11 percent wraparound note are only $1,504.27, payments on a new first mortgage loan would be $1,576.10.

(This assumes that the amortization period would be 12 years in either case.) With the wraparound alternative the borrower saves $71.83 each month for the next 12 years.

What's the attraction for the wraparound lender? By making a loan at a slightly below-market rate, the lender actually nets an effective rate of return slightly above the market. The actual amount of money disbursed at the loan closing, remember, is the difference between the new $120,000 note and the $47,334 balance on the old note: $72,666. For this the borrower will pay $1,504.27 per month for 12 years. Since the lender must make payments on the old loan for eight more years, during that period the net monthly revenue will be $1,504.27 minus $669.15, or $835.12. After eight years the old note will have been fully paid off; thereafter, the new lender keeps the entire monthly receipt.

Here is a summary of the deal from the wraparound lender's point of view:

| | Monthly Net Cash Flow to Lender | | |
Years	Inflow	Outflow	Net
At closing	$ 0	$72,666.00	($72,666.00)
1 through 8	1,504.27	669.15	835.12
9 through 12	1,504.27	0	1,504.27

The arithmetic to compute the effective rate of return on the lender's $72,666 is tedious but not complex. The easiest way, of course, is to crank the numbers through a computer or a financial calculator. If you do that you will discover the annual yield to the lender is about just slightly above 12 percent.

USURY LAWS

Some states have statutory limits on the annual rate of interest that real estate lenders can charge. Obviously, you have to avoid running afoul of these laws. The first step is to get good legal counsel in the state whose laws govern. Real estate lending is inherently complex, and you will need legal advice at every step. Initially, legal fees will seem oppressive. But your lending practice will become repetitive and the need for legal services will decline significantly through time.

Interest rate limitations usually apply to effective interest rates computed on a yield-to-maturity basis. You may be able to circumvent such laws by getting a substantial portion of your interest via discount points or loan origination fees and creating incentives for early prepayment of the principal. Of course, the earlier the loan is paid off the greater will be the effective interest rate based on amortizing the front-end fees.

Some examples of early prepayment incentives:

- Interest rebate.
- Limits on borrower use of property.
- Covenants against alienation.
- No lifting clause.
- Limits on additional financing.

MANAGING DEFAULT RISK

We saw earlier that one cannot expect to consistently earn yields greater than the T-bill rate without taking on some additional risk. Such is the nature of financial markets. Yet passive acceptance is an inappropriate response. Positive action can shift some risk to other parties, eliminate other risk, and ameliorate what remains.

Among the pantheon of risks borne by lenders—interest rate risk, purchasing power risk, and so on—default risk reigns supreme. This is the risk that borrowers simply will not repay.

My favorite real estate development commentator, the late James Graaskamp, often described a mortgage loan as a *put* to the lender. A put is an option that gives the holder the right to sell an asset at some specified price. In this case the price is the remaining balance of the mortgage note. The borrower exercises the put by the simple expedient of walking away.

In the absence of contrary provisions, lenders can sue defaulting borrowers for the remaining balance on a mortgage note. This, however, is scant recourse for a lender whose position is secured by a mortgage on rental property, because most such borrowers either find some way to protect their personal assets from attachment or personally own little or nothing of value.

The put option analogue is apt, but my preference is to view the lender-borrower relationship as a partnership. Both the equity investor (the borrower) and the debt investor (the lender) hope to earn a decent yield on the investment, and each party's success depends on much the same factors. They are in the same financial boat, but they inevitably have different perspectives on the voyage.

The Borrower's Perspective

Most of what you have read so far has been from the perspective of an equity investor, the borrower in a loan transaction. If you have been paying attention, you have a good idea of what it is that borrowers want in their relationship with a lender. We can summarize their aim as *spread, control,* and *bailout.*

Spread, the differential between the cost of funds and the yield on assets, is why equity investors use credit. Rational investors try to maximize the spread, consonant with their ability to bear risk. They do this by astutely marketing the property to prospective renters, by carefully controlling costs, and by minimizing the debt-service constant. This latter variable is the source of contention with lenders, who also want to control the constant.

The importance of the debt-service constant—the annual debt service as a percentage of the amount borrowed—is easy to overstate. As a lender, you should let the borrower have as much spread as is consistent with good lending practices, since the spread is the borrower's primary inducement to honor the loan agreement. Concentrate instead on other, more vital aspects of the relationship; control and bailout.

Control over operations is a vital issue to borrower and lender alike. So long as things are going well control resides comfortably with the borrower. When adversity strikes, you will need authority to wrest control away; that is your assurance that you will not be cast overboard as borrowers attempt to keep their financial ships afloat.

Borrowers' fall-back position is to simply walk away from their investments. This is the bailout provision so dear to every borrower's heart. It is also why Graaskamp characterized loans as puts to lenders. When a faltering market drains away the borrowers' equity in a property, there is little incentive to keep struggling if they have nothing except the extinguished equity at stake. Hence, borrowers will seek exculpatory language in loan documents—provisions that prohibit lenders from seeking judgments against borrowers.

The Lender's Perspective

Sophisticated lenders seek to impose pleasure, pain, and bailout provisions; pleasure to reward borrowers who honor their debt obligations, selective pain to pressure defaulting borrowers, and bailout to protect themselves if the deal turns completely sour.

The stage for borrower pleasure is set during negotiations over the loan constant. The smaller the annual constant, the greater the borrower's pleasure from continuing to honor all loan provisions. You give borrowers a low constant, while assuring yourself of a decent yield, by stretching out the term of the loan.

Lenders need ways to exert selective pain when borrowers fail to honor their commitments. A lender whose only weapon is the threat of foreclosure is like a nation that blows its entire defense budget on a doomsday weapon. If mutual assured destruction (MAD) is your only alternative to passive acquiescence, your adversary will have nothing to fear from constant petty aggression.

Your arsenal of remedies should enable you to impose both selective and progressive pain, short of foreclosure, on recalcitrant debtors. Your armory should include authority to impose late charges and penalties and to take control of projects and levy management fees.

Late charges should be automatic and should be featured prominently on the payment coupons you provide to borrowers. The coupon for a note with payments due on the first day of each month, for example, might cite the regular payment amount "if received prior to the first day of the month," and a higher amount that includes the regular payment plus the late charge "if received after the tenth day of the month."

Penalties other than a simple late charge should also be a standard part of your loan provisions. Otherwise, once the due date has passed and the automatic late charge is levied, there will be no incentive for a borrower to pay as soon as possible. The additional delinquency penalty should be progressive and should be an option for the lender. Your penalty clause might include a provision such as the following:

[*Selective pain*] Lender reserves the right to collect with each monthly payment an escrow payment for insurance and taxes if the mortgage becomes delinquent or if insurance or property taxes become delinquent, or if lender does not receive a paid copy of insurance and property tax bills within 30 days of the payment date.

[*Progressive pain*] If any payment is more than 10 days delinquent, a late charge of two cents for each dollar of such payment shall be due. In addition, if a loan payment is not received within 20 days of its due date, a default interest rate of the regular loan rate plus 6 percent will accrue on the entire outstanding principal balance, and this interest will commence to accrue retroactively as of the next day after the due date, and will continue to accrue until the late payment and all accrued interest are received.

The ultimate turn of the screw short of foreclosure is to take control of the borrower's rental operation. Control does not imply ownership, of course, and does not entitle you to keep operating profits. There should be no reason, however, why you cannot benefit (and thereby exert additional pain) from control. Your profit (and the borrower's pain) will stem from a reasonable management fee. A provision similar to the following should accomplish your objective:

If at any time this loan is 45 or more days in default, the lender reserves the right to approve and/or install professional management of this property at any time, and the borrower agrees that a normal management fee for this service shall be due and payable out of the operating revenue from the property or from the borrower's personal resources.

A note of caution: state laws vary drastically, and provisions that work well in one state may be unenforceable in another, or may be interpreted in an entirely different manner by the courts there. Moreover, penalty provisions might be construed as usurious interest in some jurisdictions. The moral should be plain: You need competent legal counsel in the appropriate jurisdictions.

Your fall-back position when all else fails is foreclosure, or a deed in lieu of foreclosure. The value and quality of collateral is your cushion against loss stemming from foreclosure. The essence of collateral stems from both the credibility of the appraiser who estimates its value, and a set of assumptions about the future.

With these considerations in mind, always evaluate a mortgaged property's operating efficiency and material quality as though you are going to own it. You might.

It isn't enough to be assured that the mortgaged property is worth considerably more than the amount of the mortgage. Remember that the mortgage will be outstanding for a number of years. You need reasonable assurance that the property's value will last at least as long. Toward this end, evaluate the trend of property values and anticipate where trends will be 10 years hence.

KEY POINTS

• When interest rates move above the yield on real assets, it makes sense to shift from borrowing to lending.

• Private lenders can carve out a lucrative position in the interstices between the markets over which major lenders fight. Look for niches that are too small or too unorthodox to attract institutional lenders. In a small market, seek to dominate as the major lender so that you will discourage other people from competing in your niche.

• To increase your yields, charge a loan origination fee or discount points (or both), then seek ways to induce borrowers to pay off the loan before it is due. The sooner the loan is retired, the higher will be your effective yield.

• To get higher yields, buy loans (at a discount) that have been originated by sellers of the property that secures the loan.

• Resist the temptation to borrow short term in order to lend long term. The strategy appears attractive because of the usual yield differential between long-term and short-term notes. But, if rates move up precipitously, you will be paying more for short-term money than you earn on your long-term notes.

• To secure your position as a lender, include provisions in promissory notes that levy a late penalty keyed to the length of the overdue period. Provide for transfer of operational control when the loan is in default for a specified number of days. This enables you to apply progressive pain short of foreclosure.

CHAPTER 11

ADDING VALUE
WITH MANAGEMENT
AND MARKETING

Real estate is often touted as unique among assets. Yet operating rental property is not that different from running other service businesses. Profitability depends on essentially the same factors. Whether your product is space in a high-rise building or advice on how to win friends and influence people, success requires you to scope out what customers want, plan carefully, acquire reasonably priced facilities, sell like mad, and pay attention to details.

The plain truth is that rental property is just the capital equipment in a business that sells occupancy rights—amenities and locational advantages. The only really unique feature is that the service has to be consumed on-site, a fact that makes minor locational differences loom large in your customers' eyes.

WHY GOOD MANAGEMENT PAYS, AND HOW

Most rental properties, however, are not well-run businesses. Owners often slight business fundamentals because they don't even recognize that they are running a business. They are passive investors who, unfortunately, have taken control of the operation and act as if it will run on automatic pilot.

Real estate is a microcosm that pretty much reflects the realities of the larger business world. As with other businesses, in a poorly run rental operation:

- Gross income (rental revenue) lags.
- Operating expenses climb.
- Net income drops precipitously from the double whammy of declining gross income and a narrowing gross margin.
- Market value of the firm (or the real estate) stagnates or declines.

The Management Payoff

Remember that purchasing real estate involves buying a set of assumptions about the property's ability to generate net cash flows, either from operations, from increases in value, or from both. Enhancing assumptions about a property's potential increases its market value, but only if subsequent buyers accept the revised assumptions. Management is the key.

Recall also that a common—and very useful—way of expressing the relationship between operating assumptions and market value is the capitalization rate, which is simply the ratio of income to value. If you follow the stock market you are used to thinking in terms of price/earnings ratios. The capitalization rate is the reciprocal of the price/earnings ratio. Here is the equation, which is explained in considerable detail in Chapter Three.

Value = Net Operating Income / Capitalization Rate

The greater the expected annual income (with a given, market-determined capitalization rate) the higher the market value. Thus, skilled management pays off not only by enhancing the stream of annual net cash receipts, but also by increasing the property's market value. In industry jargon, the enhanced income stream is *capitalized*.

But when astute management causes net operating income to increase, an amazing thing often happens: market-determined capitalization rates drop. Expressed another way, people are willing to pay more for each dollar of current cash flow when they become more optimistic about the future cash-flow stream. The consequence is that increasing your property's operating efficiency usually has a disproportionate impact on its market value.

Let's use some numbers to see how this works. Suppose

you own a property that commands a 10 percent capitalization rate in today's market. This means that every $1 of current income creates $1/.1, or $10 of market value. If the net operating income is $10,000 the market value will be $10,000/.10, or $100,000, and every dollar of additional earning potential will add $10 to market value—a multiplier relationship of 10. Hence, if you can increase income from the current $10,000 to $11,000, the market value will move from its current $100,000 to $110,000.

But if increasing income also alters the capitalization rate, the multiplier effect is amplified. Suppose that a consequence of making the property more profitable is a drop in the capitalization rate from 10 percent to 9.5 percent. Note that this lowered capitalization rate applies to the entire income stream, not just the increase. Increasing the income from $10,000 to $11,000 will now cause value to grow from $100,000 to $11,000/.095, or $115,789, a $15,789 increase. Measured incrementally, the multiplier relationship is 15.8. Figure 11–1 illustrates how this works.

Good management also reduces risk. Recall that we defined risk as the possibility of variance between actual outcomes and the assumptions on which an investment is based. It follows that risk can be reduced in two ways: by making better assumptions and by controlling outcomes. Better assumptions flow from more careful and appropriate research before you invest. Thereafter, carefully monitoring and constantly fine-tuning operations enables you to control outcomes within the limits imposed by the external environment.

Keys to Good Management

Whether your enterprise is an apartment building or a multinational manufacturing firm, the keys to management excellence are people, physical assets, and money. Each is a scarce resource, and the right combination handled in the most productive way ensures maximum long-range benefit. Start with good people and a thoroughly researched and carefully structured action plan. A reliable system that generates timely information will enable you to make certain the plan is implemented and to correct the plan itself when appropriate.

FIGURE 11–1
Income and Value with Altered Capitilization Rate

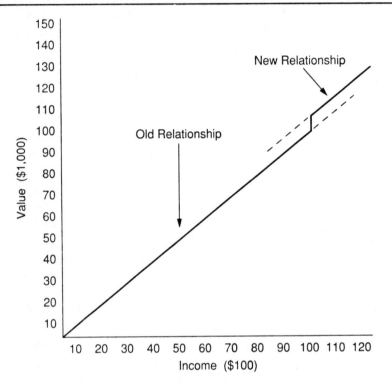

MANAGEMENT ACTION PLANS: BLUEPRINTS FOR PROFIT

A management action plan establishes the specific "who, what, when, where, and how much" of managing your property. Does everyone have a written management plan? No. But then, most properties are indifferently managed—some are handled downright poorly. Certainly it's possible to effectively manage a property without a detailed planning and control strategy, but the sure-fire way to consistently superior management performance is to have a specific, written plan for coordinating all activities necessary to solve your property's problems and exploit its advantages.

Why does the plan have to be written? At the outset, a written plan is almost certain to be more carefully thought-out, with no gaping omissions or inconsistencies. The mere act of committing it to paper forces you to be more precise. Moreover, it's easier to control progress and make midcourse corrections if you have a written record of what you intended at the time you laid your plans.

The amount of detail in your plan will vary depending on the property size and the degree of management involved. You will not have as extensive a document, for example, for a stand-alone commercial store as for a shopping center, or for a net-leased industrial property as for a self-storage warehouse complex. Large, multitenant developments will require more involved management plans because they have more complex problems.

Regardless of simplicity or complexity, however, the basic planning procedure is the same.

• Identify key management problems, their nature and causes. Rank them according to their relative seriousness, and specify what must be done to ameliorate or eradicate them.
• Estimate the time and cost to eliminate or solve each key management problem.
• Develop specific action plans in line with the cost and time allocations for each major problem.
• Develop a budget, and establish personnel responsibilities for each action step.
• Communicate your plan to everyone involved in its implementation. Make sure there is no misunderstanding, and seek agreement and collaboration on the details.
• Monitor activities. Note variations and exceptions from the plan, and take necessary corrective action. Revise the plan as appropriate when new information becomes available.

Developing Your Management Plan

You should sketch out a rough outline of a management plan as part of your property search process. By specifying particularly critical issues in a generalized plan, you can better determine whether a prospective acquisition is appropriate for your objectives. As soon as a purchase agreement has been signed, move purposefully ahead in developing the final, detailed plan. Your aim should be to have a completed plan ready to be implemented when you close the purchase.

Your planning will be greatly facilitated if the seller provides key information that frequently is not required in a property transaction. To ensure the seller's cooperation, have your attorney include an appropriate clause in the sales agreement. The following information will be particularly valuable and should be specifically mentioned in the agreement.

• Accounting data, including operating statements for the past three years and an interim statement for the current year through the date of the closing. These should be audited and certified statements if possible. The seller should be asked to retain all accounting records for at least two years after the closing, and to make them available for your inspection during that time.

• Leases and rent rolls that identify each rental unit, showing its occupancy status at the time of closing. This should include the tenant's name, rental rate, security deposit amount, and lease expiration date. It should also disclose any concessions made to the tenant, such as rent rebates, decorating allowances, or a free rent period. The seller should specifically warrant that all information is complete and accurate.

• Maintenance records for the past 12 months that show as much detail as the seller can provide. Copies of invoices from outside contractors and from parts and materials suppliers are potentially helpful and should be included.

• Tenant relations records, including a record of any tenant complaints, rent collection problems, or other issues of importance.

The seller should agree to announce the ownership change by sending a letter to each tenant and to all vendors. Follow the seller's letter with one of your own, introducing yourself as the new owner and giving sufficient background to reassure everyone of a degree of continuity in the relationship.

Your plan should have three main sections—physical, marketing, and financial—and should specify detailed steps to be taken in each area. In some of these areas little action will be required; others are likely to consume a major portion of your time and committed resources.

The Physical Plan

Data about the property come from a detailed physical inspection you will have made before you irrevocably committed yourself to buy the property. This inspection, completed with the help of outside specialists where appropriate, will have made you aware of all major and minor physical problems.

A second, more leisurely "walk-through" inspection during the interim between signing the purchase agreement and the actual closing on the deal will be required before you can put together the plan for physical maintenance and improvement. (This is separate from and in addition to the walk-through you will make immediately before the closing to identify any last-minute problems that might affect your willingness to close on the deal.) The purchase agreement should contain adequate provisions for access to the premises and the tenants so that you can go back as often as needed to assemble data for your plan.

With notepad and pen (or dictaphone) in hand, cover every inch of the building and grounds. Look critically at details; don't settle for a general impression. Inspect the property with an eye to what improvements are needed, and the best way to accomplish them. Concentrate on how to improve the property's appearance, housekeeping, and maintenance, and on what amenities should be added or enhanced. Note specific steps to be taken as well as your overall impression of the property's physical condition.

As you record property deficiencies, record also your impression of the most appropriate remedies and the results expected from the action. Be sure to note the degree of urgency of the work, because limitations of time and finances make it virtually certain that you will not be able to do everything right away. By establishing the estimated cost and the relative importance of each remedy, you can develop sensible priorities. Generally, low-cost, high-visibility steps should be taken first, because they offer the greatest payoff in terms of tenant impressions that the new landlord cares about their living conditions.

The Marketing Plan

Physical improvements to your property may be designed to reduce operating costs or to keep tenants satisfied. More frequently, improvements are aimed at making the space more marketable. You incur the cost of physical changes because you expect to be able to raise rents or to reduce vacancy levels.

Of all the steps in your plan, physical changes to buildings and grounds are the most immediately obvious to present and prospective tenants alike. Your program of physical improvements will yield maximum benefit, however, only if it is accomplished in tandem with an aggressive marketing program. There is little sense in spending money on improvements if you have no plans for marketing the improved space.

Pick a Market Segment. Don't be so eager to fill vacant units that you rent without questioning the tenants' compatibility. This is an important consideration in any multi-tenant property, whether residential, commercial, or industrial. A shopping center with too many shoe stores is in serious trouble; so is an apartment building with a mix of elderly retirees and exuberant undergraduate university students.

Deciding on the type of tenant that is most appropriate for your facility is perhaps the most basic marketing question you will face. Your answer will condition the physical improvements you will undertake and will largely determine the nature of your advertising program.

What you want in the way of tenants and what you can get are not always the same. Before preparing your property for a particular class of tenant, therefore, make sure there is adequate demand and your location will appeal to the tenant group you intend to target. Instead of deciding what type of tenant you want and then aiming your physical improvements and marketing strategy at them, why not study the market to determine what segment will find your facility most appealing?

Make Present Tenants Your First Marketing Target. Space marketing usually means advertising to selected segments of the space-using public. But this is only a part of the total package that comprises a well-crafted marketing plan. It may not even be the most important part.

Whether it is good or bad, your present tenants carry a far more powerful message about your facility than any paid advertisement ever can. They know other prospective tenants and will invite them to become neighbors or will warn them away, depending upon whether they themselves are satisfied or disgruntled. Let your tenants know what you are doing to make your property more safe and attractive, and why. Tell them when you expect a vacancy and invite them to nominate prospective new tenants. It may be appropriate to go an additional step and offer gifts for referrals that result in new leases.

Shop the Competition.   Value is always relative. With this in mind, inspect competing space. Ask questions. Take the perspective of potential tenants and make the same inquiries they would. Find out what the competition offers and how much they charge. Check their adds and note their sales presentations. You can learn a lot, not the least of which is the appropriateness of your rent schedules.

Monitor Advertising Results.   Have every prospective tenant indicate on a form how they discovered that you have space available. This will give you a measure of the effectiveness of your media and your message. Register every inquiry, whether it is a visit or a telephone call, by date and source. The most appropriate advertising media differ not only according to the type of buildings you own (what is right for offices will often not work for apartments, for example) and by geographic locale (what's best in Buffalo may be a bust in Boston), but also by prospective tenants' socioeconomic class (blue collar customers will be uncomfortable in white collar surroundings).

The Financial Plan
Since your goal is to earn a rate of return commensurate with your venture's riskiness, financial considerations are the backbone of investment success. Your physical and marketing plans

will spell out what actions are to be taken, but both are ultimately related to planned financial results.

Set Specific Financial Goals.   It isn't enough to intend
a venture to turn a profit; there are far more provisionally
profitable opportunities and alternatives than you can hope
ever to exploit. You need specific financial goals against which
to measure expected outcomes. Only then can you rationally
evaluate preliminary proposals for physical improvements and
marketing efforts. Every proposed action should yield financial
benefits in one of three measures:

- Increased rental revenue.
- Increased occupancy rates.
- Decreased operating expenses.

The measure of the advisability of any particular financial
expenditure should be the same as that employed in making the
initial commitment to the property: Does the expected return
match or exceed the return available from alternative uses of
funds that involve approximately the same level of risk? Using
procedures explained in Chapter Six, discount the expected
change in your cash-flow stream and compare the present value
with the amount of the proposed expenditure.

Appeal Your Property Taxes.   Property taxes are often
your single largest operating expense. Even a small reduction,
therefore, can make a big improvement in your bottom line.
Property taxes in most states are based on a percentage of the
property's market value as determined by an assessor. At best,
estimating property value is an inexact science; in many taxing
jurisdictions it is little more than a guess.

Overstated values will usually stimulate taxpayer complaints, but when values are understated taxpayers are silent.
Thus, there is a built-in stimulus for assessors to overestimate
values. Timid or careless owners bear the brunt of the system,
however, by paying more taxes than they need to.

If a seller gave you favorable credit terms, you probably
paid more for your property than its cash value. If so, it's up
to you to convert your deal into cash equivalent terms and con-

vince the assessor that the lower number is more representative of your property's value. The best way to do this is to engage a local real estate appraiser who has appropriate credentials.

If you discuss your position with the assessor before filing a formal appeal you may get an adjustment without going through the entire process. In any event, it is worth a try. Filing a formal appeal forces the assessor to defend a position that he or she might have been willing to compromise in an informal negotiating session.

If you believe your property is overtaxed and the assessor will not grant relief after an informal meeting, don't hesitate to go ahead with a formal appeal. Local tax appeal boards often compromise to avoid having the appeal shifted to the courts. As a last resort, investigate the credentials of local attorneys who specialize in property tax appeals.

Plan to Restructure Your Debt. Even if you buy your property under favorable financing terms, with a debt-service obligation you can easily handle with cash generated by operations, you may eventually find it profitable to refinance.

Keep in mind that borrowing costs fluctuate with economic conditions. When credit markets turn favorable, investigate the possibility of restructuring your debt to stretch out your payments, to borrow more money, or to reduce the interest rate.

Potential benefits from restructuring debt make it important to avoid provisions that render it prohibitively expensive to pay off your mortgage note before maturity. Negotiating prepayment penalty provisions is every bit as important as negotiating the tradeoff between interest rate and loan origination fees.

A standard part of your financial plan should be to check credit markets regularly to determine if you can benefit from restructuring your mortgage indebtedness.

MANAGEMENT INFORMATION SYSTEMS

Remember that your rental operation is a business, and good management in any business requires a reliable and timely information system. You will never know how well your plan is working unless you have information about your own operations as well as similar properties owned by other investors. There is simply no way you can establish control without a steady flow of accurate intelligence.

Information about your own property stems from well-crafted accounting records. If you are using a management firm, I suggest that you have your records designed by someone else. A key element should be an audit trail that enables you to monitor and check the management firm's performance.

Records

In addition to the usual operating statements that report cash receipts and disbursements, you will need a standardized format for information about who is renting space and who is looking at your buildings but rejecting them: What space are they currently occupying, what kind of business or profession are they in, what is their age group, how did they hear about your property?

You will need information about the rate and causes of tenant turnover. This means a steady flow of data on new rentals, lease cancellations, evictions, and rental applications. You will want to know about the rate and nature of tenant complaints, service calls, security problems, and rental delinquencies. In short, whether you are using a property management firm or having your property operated by your own employees, you need a steady diet of all the information required to tell you in advance of any impending problem.

Much of the information you need to monitor your property's fiscal and physical health is not routinely provided by property management companies. Get a firm understanding about what information they will provide, as well as the format and frequency of reports, before you sign a management contract. Until you sign you are in the driver's seat; after you sign, you're in control only if the contract says so.

Standards

Knowing *what* your property is doing does not, in itself, tell you *how* you are doing. For that you need comparison standards. Measuring your property's (and your property manager's) performance against industry standards lets you know where your strengths and weaknesses are and tells when corrective action is needed. Tracking industry performance not only tells you what is possible, it also lets you know when the market is shifting and suggests the direction in which you must move to remain competitive. Readily available sources of information about industry norms include the following.

BOMA Experience Exchange Report

(Building Owners and Managers Association International (BO-MA), 1221 Massachusetts Avenue, N.W., Washington, D.C. 20005). This annual report gives summary and comparative data on income, expense, and vacancy experience for office buildings owned or managed by BOMA members and nonmember respondents to the BOMA survey questionnaire. Most BOMA members' buildings are probably in better-than-average condition and have better-than-average management. Consequently, revenues may be upwardly biased and expenses downwardly biased. Coverage extends widely across the industry and includes buildings in both the United States and Canada. Canadian and U.S. statistics are shown separately, and data in each country are subdivided into private sector and government sector. Within each sector, data are categorized several ways:

- downtown/suburban
- size (square feet)
- average income and expenses per square foot
- component costs of the expenses

Dollars and Cents of Shopping Centers

(Urban Land Institute (ULI), 1090 Vermont Avenue, N.W., Washington, D.C. 20005). This publication, which is produced every three years, gives comparative income and expense data for shopping centers. Data are categorized by center size: neighborhood, regional, community, and super regional. Within each size category, data are broken into seven subcategories:

- gross leasable area
- total rental income

- sales
- common area charges
- percentage rental rate
- rent and common area charges as a percentage of sales
- total charges

Shopping center tenants are cross-listed by·

- type of business
- size of center
- center affiliation (national chain, local chain, independent)

Data are also cross-classified according to economic characteristics relating to income and expenses per square foot of retail space.

Data are derived from operating information reported by about 1,000 participating shopping centers throughout the United States, based on the cooperating centers' last completed fiscal year. All reporting centers have been operating for at least one full year. Data are voluntarily contributed by participating centers, and there is no audit or validity check by the publisher.

Expense Analysis: Condominiums, Cooperatives and PUDs
(Institute of Real Estate Management (IREM), 430 North Michigan Avenue, Chicago, IL 60611-4090). This annual publication reports operating expenses categorized by major type of expense and is cross-referenced for eight regions and 29 cities. Data are from reports submitted by IREM members and related practitioners and include information on about 1,300 different projects. Consistency of data between reporting firms is encouraged by having data reported on an IREM data collection form that includes detailed instructions.

Income/Expense Analysis: Apartments
(Institute of Real Estate Management, 430 North Michigan Avenue, Chicago, IL 60611-4090). This report gives a detailed annual breakdown of operating income and expense experience for four categories of apartment buildings. It includes separate tables for the United States, Canada, and 138 cities. It also

gives information on turnover rates, operating trends, and oper
ating ratios. Data are available in printed format or electroni-
cally via direct computer link-up. Information is cross-tabulated
by:

- building age
- furnished units
- unfurnished units
- building size

Data incorporated in the report come from IREM mem
bers and other cooperating practitioners and include results
from almost 9,000 buildings. However, the data are from professionally managed properties and therefore may not be representative of the entire universe of apartments from which the
sample is drawn.

Income/Expense Analysis: Office Buildings—
Downtown and Suburban

(Institute of Real Estate Management, 430 North Michigan
Avenue, Chicago, IL 60611-4090). This publication provides a
detailed annual breakdown of operating income and expense
data for office buildings. Separate tables are provided for the
United States, Canada, seven regions, and 51 cities. Data are
from IREM members and other cooperating practitioners and
cover almost 9,000 buildings. Data are cross-tabulated by

- building age
- building size
- rental type
- building height
- downtown or suburban

Additional data and analysis are given for:

- trends
- operating ratios
- leasing fees
- tenant alteration allowances
- energy consumption
- taxes
- heating fuel analysis

National C&I Report

(DAMAR Corporation, 3550 West Temple Street, Los Angeles, CA 90004, monthly). This report contains operating results and sales data on selected apartments; commercial, industrial, and agricultural property; and raw land that sold within the last two years. It includes data on special-use properties and those that sold for more than $1 million. Property information includes:

- principal's name and address
- principal's contact telephone number
- available financing
- property income and expense data
- ownership details
- property descriptive detail

It is developed in consort with the Society of Real Estate Appraisers Market Data Center, which provides all property sales information. Other, related data are collected from:

- institutional lenders
- Federal Housing Administration
- Veterans' Administration
- secondary mortgage market
- public records
- independent appraisers

PEOPLE–THE LINCHPIN

Probably the most difficult property management problem you will face involves people. You will have to rely on other people from the moment you start looking for your first property. After you close on your first building, your success will be increasingly at the mercy of people who act on your behalf.

When you first start building a real estate portfolio, your choices are to do your own management or turn the operation over to a professional real estate management firm. As the size of your portfolio grows, an additional option evolves; with a sufficiently large group of buildings you can afford to hire a skilled employee to handle management chores. In any case there is the continuing problem of ensuring that those directly involved in managing your property, whether they work for you or for a contractor, are reasonably qualified and honest.

Whom to Hire

The degree of competence you require in employees will depend in part on the amount of supervision you want to personally exercise. If you are qualified and willing to oversee day-to-day operations, you can employ any reasonably intelligent person as a general manager and subsequently train him or her to relieve you of responsibilities.

If, on the other hand, you want to be relieved of all except general oversight duties, you will need someone with knowledge and experience in real estate management. The best way to assure yourself that applicants have these capabilities is to insist on credentials from a legitimate professional or trade organization.

Numerous trade organizations are operated by or on behalf of real property managers, and most of the groups award designations that signify various levels of competence, experience, and education. The problem is how to efficiently sort through the alphabet soup of designations, whose validity ranges from sterling to dross. Some organizations grant a designation for little more than an initial membership fee. Others maintain impressive standards for education, experience, and demonstrated knowledge and maturity.

How does one separate the legitimate organizations from the mail-order mills? My recommendation is to stick with either the Building Owners and Managers Association or the Institute of Real Estate Management. Both award well-respected property management credentials, both have been long-established, and neither has compromised on the high standards required of their members.

Institute of Real Estate Management.
This is the oldest (founded in 1934) and largest association of real property managers in the United States. The Institute of Real Estate Management (IREM) sponsors a variety of courses,

seminars, and continuing professional education programs on a wide range of topics related to real estate management. It also publishes books, monographs, and journals on the topic.

Candidates who meet stiff experience and education requirements are awarded IREM's flagship designation: *Certified Property Manager* (CPM). Candidacy for the CPM designation is open only to members of the National Association of Realtors who are actively employed in real estate management (with appropriate licenses as required by state law), are at least 21 years old, have graduated from high school, and can gain the endorsement of the local IREM chapter. Endorsement depends on verification of high moral character and willingness to subscribe to IREM's code of professional ethics. To earn the designation, candidates must satisfy stiff educational and experience requirements and pass a battery of examinations.

IREM also certifies members as Accredited Resident Managers (ARMs). ARM educational requirements include course work in physical maintenance, handling tenant complaints, inventory management, personnel, administration, merchandising, physical security, community facilities management, communications, fiscal management, rent collection, handling delinquent accounts, payroll accounting and purchasing order processing, legal aspects of rental property management, residents' rights, owner-resident legislation, dealing with resident organizations, eviction procedures, and much more. Candidates must complete two years of experience as an on-site manager (or one year of experience under the direct supervision of a Certified Property Manager)

Building Owners and Managers
Association International.
The Building Owners and Managers Association International (BOMA) is concerned primarily with the management of office buildings, and membership is comprised mostly of office building owners and managers. There are approximately 70 BOMA chapters in cities around the United States and Canada. The Association publishes a journal, quarterly economic reports, and *The Office Building Exchange Report*, described earlier.

BOMA confers their Real Property Administrator designation on qualified candidates as a sign of professional accomplishment. Candidates must complete several approved educational courses, each accompanied by a final examination that must be completed with a prescribed minimum score.

National Apartment Association.
Apartment building owners and managers are eligible for membership in the National Apartment Association, which has more than 20,000 members. Candidates who pass a series of examinations, complete an acceptable analysis of operations of an apartment project, and meet experience requirements are awarded the Certified Apartment Manager designation. Other candidates, who meet the appropriate experience requirements and can demonstrate their technical expertise through a series of appropriate examinations (after completing required course work), are awarded the Certified Apartment Maintenance Technician designation. This indicates that they have attained a minimum level of knowledge and experience needed to maintain an apartment building in good physical condition.

National Association of Real Estate Brokers.
The National Association of Real Estate Brokers (NAREB) confers two management designations: Certified Resident Manager (CRM) and Certified Real Estate Manager (CREM). To qualify for the CRM designation, candidates must complete NAREB's course in Basic Property Management. Completing a second course, Advanced Property Management, qualifies candidates for the CREM designation.

Working with Property Management Firms

Can you avoid management decisions and management problems by contracting with a property management firm? Yes, you can, but this can be an expensive solution to the problem. I'm not talking about the fee the firm charges, though that does represent a big bite out of your gross income. The greater cost can come from missed opportunities and runaway expenses coincident to handing over operating authority to an indifferent or an incompetent contract manager.

Choosing a Property Management Firm

Selecting a firm to manage your property should be done the same way porcupines make love: very, very carefully. In a few states anyone can proclaim themselves to be a professional property manager. Most states require property managers to be licensed as real estate brokers, but this provides scant assurance of competence. Brokerage licensing standards are themselves abysmally low in many states, and in any case there is very little in licensing examinations or experience requirements that will screen out people with no knowledge or experience as property managers.

While all licensed real estate brokers (and in some states, any adult that breathes) can proclaim themselves to be property managers, they cannot bill themselves as an Accredited Management Organization (AMO). This is a special designation awarded to management companies that are headed by a manager who holds the CPM designation discussed earlier, has at least three years' experience in property management, and meets IREM's standards for integrity, financial stability, and employee education.

Problem: There aren't enough AMO management firms to go around. Most of us will have to settle for a company that does not hold the designation. Interview several firms; get to know their managers. Ask what they will do if you contract with them. Anyone who does not offer to work with a written management plan is not the manager for you. You don't need a caretaker; you want aggressive management.

One filtering mechanism will be your requirement for reports other than those the management firm routinely produces for clients. You should be able to get these at little or no additional cost because any competent firm will be generating the information as a by-product of their management activities. If they are not producing for their own use the same management information you need to monitor their operation, they can't be doing a professional management job.

A final observation. Large firms appear to have no advantages over small ones and may not be as eager for your business. In a small firm you will be dealing with the people who also actively handle your property; with a large company you may never know who actually represents you on the firing line.

KEY POINTS

• The greatest real estate profits are not a return on assets. Rather, they are a return on astute management and on innovation. Careful management can increase net operating income and the capitalization rate the market places on the income. This double payoff can greatly magnify your property's market value.

• Good management starts with a carefully crafted management action plan that identifies key management problems, estimates the time and cost to cure each, and establishes a priority list for action.

• Your management plan should have three dimensions: physical, marketing, and financial. The physical plan outlines your program for curing physical problems and upgrading the physical structure, the marketing plan lists the steps you will take to increase gross rental revenue, and the financial plan specifies your financial goals and the financial steps you intend to take to reach them.

• To be useful, your management plan must be based on good market information. You will need data about the operation of similar properties in markets like yours in order to set meaningful standards of comparison. You will need good information about your own operating results so that you will recognize incipient problems before they mushroom into crises. A well-developed management information system is every bit as crucial as a management action plan.

• Hiring good people and competent contractors is a problem that cannot be dismissed because the quality of those on whom you must rely will largely determine your success. Designations awarded by major trade organizations, signifying degrees of education and experience, are a useful way to assure yourself of minimum qualifications.

CHAPTER 12

DEVELOPMENT
AND
REDEVELOPMENT

A dress salesman, an accountant with a night-school degree, a high school football coach; these are the credentials of men who built three of America's biggest real estate empires. Each made his mark as a real estate developer; each amassed enormous personal wealth; and each appears to find his greatest joy in putting together new real estate deals.[1]

The high rollers aren't alone. Small-scale operators also find development and redevelopment their Jacob's Ladder to high yields and geometric portfolio growth. In many ways developers and redevelopers who operate on a more modest scale have advantages over the big guns. Competitors are likely to be less experienced and knowledgeable, for example. Moreover, opportunities to exploit special knowledge of local markets and low-cost access to information are more common.

Once you own your first rental property, you're virtually forced into the developer's role unless you are prepared to forfeit a major profit source. Development and redevelopment are more or less continuous processes in well-run projects.

This isn't to suggest that your premises should always be cluttered with trucks and scaffolding. But, remember, rental property is a form of cash-cycle enterprise, which involves converting management services and capital assets (land and buildings) into cash. The true profit centers in such an operation

---

[1]"Success Stories," *The Wall Street Journal* (March 24, 1986).

are the delivery of services and capital. Services (amenities and locational advantages) require appropriate capital equipment, namely, land and buildings. Since your property's most profitable use continuously evolves, development must be incessant.

Other than installing superior management systems, the principal way to add real estate value is to convert property to a more appropriate use. The landscape is literally cluttered with underutilized properties that cry out for conversion or modification to permit more effective use. They all represent redevelopment opportunities.

By converting existing buildings rather than building from scratch, you can often enter a market as the low-priced landlord, a circumstance that greatly facilitates establishing a market position. A Chicago developer, for example, was able to enter the Milwaukee market with a 135,000 square foot, combination office building and retail center with an attached marina at a rental rate about 25 percent below prevailing rents for comparable space. How did he do it? By converting a warehouse that occupied one of the few remaining large riverfront sites.[2]

THE GAME AND THE PLAYERS

Development and redevelopment involve dynamic interaction of investor-managers with two other decision groups: the general public and various public agencies. Each represents a distinct interest group that seeks to wield influence in pursuit of identifiable objectives, and each can be usefully viewed as a cash-cycle enterprise. A desirable solution to a real estate development problem occurs when all three groups achieve an acceptable level of satisfaction.

The General Public

Demand, and thus, ultimately, prices and the quantity of real estate services produced and sold, is driven by consumers of

---

[2]*Real Estate Times* (September 1987) p. 2.

space.   Consumers and developers interact on three distinct levels.

1. *Individual Consumers.* These are the tenants who rent or buy space that has been developed or redeveloped. They must be convinced that housing their activities (business or residential) in your facility will improve their status in terms of convenience, efficiency, security, or well-being at an affordable periodic cash cost.

2. *Collective Consumers.* Collectively, consumers operate in the political sector. They represent all members of society who will be (or think that they will be) affected by your project. You will have to convince this collective that regulators should grant you the necessary permits, zoning variances, and other approvals that enable you to proceed. Collective consumers are increasingly organized and vocal, and their effectiveness is growing. They should be your first marketing target.

Developers are discovering that they must deal with spreading no-growth and low-growth sentiment among those who must approve development plans. No longer can you count on the county or city to generously agree to widen roads or extend sewer or water lines to accommodate development. Wrathful citizens, driven by aversion to the inconvenience of increased traffic density and by fear of growing tax burdens, are blocking plans hither and yon.

Winning over these citizen groups is your first battle. To do this, identify the most likely opposition groups. Study their leadership structure and address the question of what the leaders want. Then ask yourself how you can satisfy their needs (or assuage their fears) at least cost to your development. Address these issues before opposition coalesces.

3. *Future Consumers.* These are tenants who will be attracted to your project at some future time. They will replace the first wave of tenants and will inevitably create some need for physical changes in your property. Keep these future tenants' needs in mind when designing your project. Meeting their requirements at an acceptable redevelopment cost requires that your site, structure, and services be flexible and adaptable. Only in this way can you expect to maintain the marketing edge that provides continuing profitability and resale liquidity.

The Infrastructure Group

Much of any project's value stems, not so much from the project itself, but from surrounding developments and from off-site improvements (public infrastructure). Infrastructure amenities are particularly crucial, and yet are only marginally under your influence. They include public and private utilities (streets, water, electricity, sewers, and so forth), government services such as fire and police protection, and the legal and social systems that control and support the transactional base of the private property system (deed registration, laws and governmental regulations, adjudication, and so on).

PROJECT FEASIBILITY

The degree of fit between any proposed course of action and the context in which it must operate is frequently called *feasibility*. A feasible proposal is one in which there is a reasonable probability that the proposed course of action will achieve your goals, given explicit constraints and limited resources.

Most feasibility questions can be addressed within one of three specific formats: a site in search of a use, a use in search of a site, or investment funds in search of an outlet.

Most Appropriate Development for a Specific Site

You or a colleague might have acquired a parcel of land that appears ripe for development or redevelopment. Or perhaps you have found a parcel you can acquire under reasonable terms and are wondering whether the opportunity is as attractive as it seems. In either case the following questions arise: What is the most appropriate way to exploit the locational and physical characteristics of the site, and will that use support the cost of site acquisition and development?

An Acceptable Site for a Specific Use

Perhaps your special skills and knowledge suggest a particular type of development, or analysis of current market conditions leads you to conclude that some specific project (apartment house, mini-storage, etc.) will meet with especially lucrative consumer acceptance. Having tentatively settled on the nature of your project, you must find the most appropriate site.

Most Appropriate Investment for Available Funds

More frequently, you will not yet have committed to a specific site and will maintain an open mind about the specifics of your development. (Although, as we have previously noted, most people are well advised to concentrate on some specific type of investment so that they can exploit superior product knowledge.) You have a limited amount of investable funds available and are searching for the best combination of anticipated yield and perceived risk.

The Common Denominator

The specific question to be answered differs in each of these formats. Yet procedurally they are virtually identical, as illustrated in Figure 12–1.

Market Analysis
The objective in market analysis is to measure the gap between potential demand and potential supply of the type of space in question over the forecast period. Market research is the firm bedrock on which all successful development or redevelopment projects must rest. This is where you determine the extent of the market for your prospective development; what rental rates will the market support, how long will it take to lease the space, and what average occupancy rates can you anticipate?

Your estimate of the project's feasibility will rest primarily on the consequences of market analysis. Therefore, the soundness of your investment decision depends on a sound market study. One of the more incredible features of the real estate investment and development culture is how frequently people put big money at risk without spending a modest amount for reliable information.

The information you will need divides logically into two

FIGURE 12–1
Project Feasibility Analysis

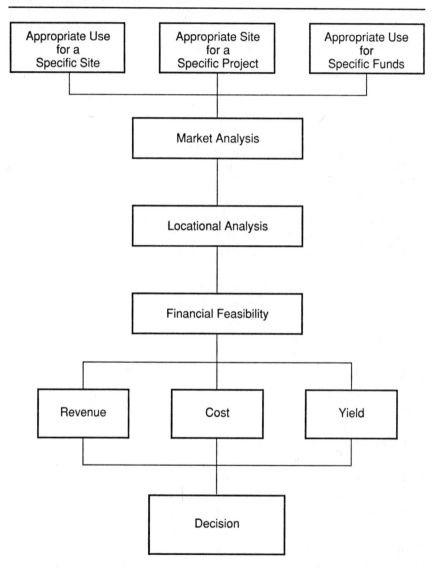

categories. *Merchandising intelligence* tells what you must do to establish a competitive edge over other projects. *Generalized market data* help establish the degree to which there is likely to be a gap between the amount of space needed by consumers and that supplied by developers and investors over the forecast period.

Merchandising Intelligence.   We cannot be very specific concerning market research because the information you will need is determined largely by the type of development or redevelopment project you have in mind.

Research for an office building project, for example, will focus on employment growth and the tastes and fashion prejudices of executives in charge of leasing decisions. Data will be segmented by class of space, location (downtown, office node, airport area, and so forth), and by type of building (medical, business services, research, for example).

In contrast, market research for a residential rental project is more likely to focus on household growth, segmented by categories such as owner or renter, household size, geographic preferences, income levels, and so forth. The consumers whose tastes will be of concern are heads of households.

Investors interested in retail stores will want data relating to localized retail expenditures; the number of households and disposable income per household. The consumer of concern may be either the household or the individual, depending on the type of retail establishments most likely to take space in the project. Data need to be segmented by types of stores (specialty or nonspecialty retailers, for example), size of shopping centers, and, in existing centers, the quality of anchor tenants.

Generalized Market Data.   This research will address broad market conditions affecting your prospective project. It includes such information as demographic and political trends.

The data you need will generally have been collected by someone else. Typical sources are federal and state census collectors, city and regional planning offices, local utility companies, and similar public and quasi-public sources. Examples of readily available information are population trends by age group, income category, business activity, and location of residence. Most of this information is free; occasionally the data-generating agency will levy a small charge to discourage browsers.

Free information? Yes; collected, categorized, collated, and presented in a neat package. There must be a catch! Of course there is. These data come in standardized formats that are almost never in exactly the form you need. Most of the time it is easier to adapt your research methods to locally available data than it is to adapt the data to your methods. So be flexible in your approach.

Chapter Seven includes an extensive catalogue of data sources, many of which are free, and others of which present information in a format of your choice—for a fee, of course.

Cost Estimating

Project cost is obviously a key feasibility factor. Many developers start with a rough cost estimate and work back into the monthly rental revenue a project would have to generate to make it feasible.

Cost information sources range from government documents to customized reports from commercial cost-estimating firms. The most commonly employed sources are cost guides published by American Appraisal Associates, F.W. Dodge, R.S. Means, and Marshall & Swift. These guides must be used with caution because of inevitable variances caused by terrain, climate, local building codes and construction practices, and local materials cost and availability. It should go without saying that any source you use must be adjusted to account for changes associated with time.

Here are several excellent sources of development cost information.

ULI Project Reference Files.

Quarterly project reference files from the Urban Land Institute give you in-depth facts on recent development projects. Files are generated in five different development categories: apartment and condominium, single-family homes, commercial, industrial, and special-use buildings. File contents include:

- Narrative description of architectural, planning, and engineering features.
- Narrative description of marketing experience.
- Extensive statistical data.

- Full-color site plan.
- Photographs of completed project and special features.
- Names, addresses, and telephone numbers of key development and design people.
- Analysis of the developer's experience with the project.

To order project reference files, contact:

ULI-The Urban Land Institute
1090 Vermont Avenue, N.W.
Washington, D.C. 20005
Telephone (202) 289-3381

Boeckh Building Cost Guides. Boeckh's guides give detailed cost information for various classes of construction and a wide range of building feature combinations. Localized cost estimates for all zip code regions, delineated by the first three digits, is categorized by four types of construction:

- Residential.
- Commercial, institutional, and light industrial.
- Mobile home.
- Agricultural

Order from:

American Appraisal Associates
525 East Michigan Street
P.O. Box 664
Milwaukee, WI 53201
Telephone (414) 271-5544

Building Construction Cost Data. Produced annually, this publication gives localized average construction costs, average unit prices for various building construction items, and labor and equipment costs for 162 cities Available from:

R.S. Means Company
100 Construction Plaza
P.O. Box 800
Kingston, MA 02364-0800
Telephone (617) 747-1270

Dodge Construction Cost Data Library. This five-volume reference library is updated annually. It provides extremely detailed cost breakdowns, with adjustments for local cost differentials, on all phases of development and redevelopment. The volume titles tell the story.

- *Dodge Assemblies Cost Data.*
- *Dodge Unit Cost Data.*
- *Dodge Square Foot Cost Data.*
- *Dodge Heavy Construction Cost Data.*
- *Dodge Remodeling and Retrofit Cost Data.*

These, and a variety of other cost-estimating aids, can be ordered directly from the publisher

Dodge Cost Systems
P.O. Box 28
Princeton, NJ 08540
Telephone (609) 426-7300 or (800) 257-5295

Residential Cost Handbook. This is a loose-leaf sub-scription service with quarterly updates that permits users to estimate construction costs for multifamily and single-family residential structures. The service includes local multipliers to adjust for differences in construction costs between geographi cal areas. It is available from·

Marshall & Swift
1617 Beverly Blvd.
P.O. Box 26307
Los Angeles, CA 90026-0307
Telephone (213) 250-2222

DEVELOPMENT STAGES

Development is best thought of as a process that proceeds through four distinct stages. The cycle starts with securing a position in land, proceeds through the approval process and the placement of improvements (buildings and other land alterations), and terminates with managing and marketing the space

Site Reconnaissance

Site analysis might begin with a specific site, sometimes with structures already in place. At other times, the starting point is a set of site specifications that will control a search for alternatives. In any case, a site suitability study will involve investigating a target site's *physical, legal, linkage,* and *dynamic* attributes. Most sites will have one or more of these attributes but will fall short in others, as illustrated in Figure 12–2. Eventually, you will identify a group of sites (the larger the group the better, but sometimes you will feel fortunate to find a single candidate) that meets minimum specifications with respect to all the attributes, represented by the shaded area in Figure 12–2.

Physical Attributes
Minimum acceptable physical characteristics (size, shape, topography, soil characteristics, and so on) will be determined

FIGURE 12–2
Overlapping Site Attributes

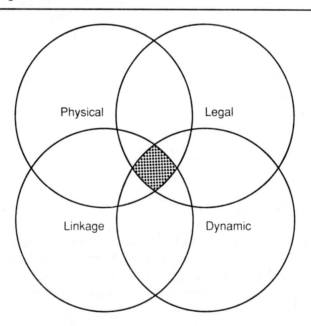

by the nature of your project. Because many physical characteristics are easily determined by casual inspection, these will be your initial specifications as you begin to narrow your search for an acceptable site (or to narrow the potential development alternatives if the problem is to determine the most appropriate use for an existing site).

Size, shape, and approximate lot area can usually be determined by casual inspection. These characteristics, and allowable land-to-building ratios, setback requirements, open space requirements, and other criteria set by regulatory authorities, determine the possible gross leasable area of your project. To a considerable degree, they also influence operating costs, particularly the costs of heating, ventilating, and air conditioning.

Sites that meet initial screening criteria for size and shape will warrant further investigation. The next stop will probably be at a public agency, which will provide information that might affect the site's development potential. Particularly vital information that is available to the public includes the following.

- Topography (Soil stability, compatibility, and load-bearing capacity, slope and drainage characteristics). Moving soil about, particularly having to haul landfill to the site, rapidly inflates development costs. These, therefore, are critical elements of initial land inspection.
- Water. The water table's level influences the nature and cost of construction; so does the location of wells, streams, and storm-water swales. Flood-plain designations determine whether you can build at all.
- Flora and Fauna. Existence of many species of plant, animal, and aquatic life can subject you to environmental impact litigation that will quickly escalate development costs.
- Utility Easements. Easements may limit a site's development potential.
- Utility Services and Capacity. The on-site availability of adequate utility services for the intended use should be ensured before you incur any significant expenses in pursuit of a nominally acceptable site. Bringing utilities to a

site from any distance will more often than not prove prohibitively expensive unless you are undertaking a very large-scale development project.
- Existing Site Improvements. Determine the extent to which existing improvements will have to be modified or removed.

Legal and Political Attributes

Remember that the law is what it is said to be by those charged with its interpretation and enforcement. The letter of the law is sometimes less important than the attitudes and powers of those to whom the political system has entrusted administrative and regulatory authority. Talk to key individuals in the political infrastructure; talk to developers who have experience with local authorities. Of particular concern are the following factors.

- Legal interests of others in the site. This includes interests of neighboring property owners who will be concerned with enforcing existing covenants that limit use, reuse, or modification of property improvements.
- Local ordinances that define alternative setback lines and height limitations. These determine permissible building envelopes.
- Applicable zoning codes that limit the uses to which the property may be put, and building codes that place constraints on such critical factors as floor-area ratio, parking requirements, allowable number of dwelling units, and so forth. Some jurisdictions have valuable zoning options such as rezoning, planned-unit-development zoning, and so forth.
- Special constraints imposed by state and federal authorities. These are frequently imposed by airport landing authorities, harbor and river commissions, environmental protection agencies, the Department of Health, Education and Welfare, the Department of Housing and Urban Development, and many more than you will care to encounter.

Remember that your project will unfold over time and will be subject to subsequent as well as current legislation and rules. This makes impending legislation fully as important as laws currently on the books. Recent regulations require interpretation and feedback from public hearings so that public officials can administer them in accordance with public attitudes and expectations.

Don't overlook the indirect governmental regulation that stems from the rules and protocols that control lending institutions. Examples include rules governing designated flood plains, quotas for government funds that are to be distributed along political subdivisions, and geographic dispersion guidelines for local, state, and federal housing finance agencies.

In many jurisdictions, planners' views of appropriate control over urban sprawl are a major influence on governmental regulators' attitudes. Solicit those views early in your site reconnaissance program.

Linkage Attributes

Functional relationships that require people (or things) to move between sites are often called linkages. These relationships may involve interactions with other activity centers that will generate users for your site (movement between home and entertainment centers and between work and shopping, to cite two examples). The relationships also include interaction with facilities that provide the infrastructure to support your site (streets and sidewalks, transit systems, utility services, and so forth). Comparing the linkage characteristics of the proposed site with those of competitive alternatives will provide a measure of the site's competitive advantages.

Dynamic Attributes

Mental or emotional responses that a site induces will affect users' decision-making behavior. The users may be potential tenants, shoppers who will buy at tenants' stores, or your tenants' professional clients. All affect the competitive position of your project, a fact that makes the site's dynamic attributes a key site-selection issue. Examples of dynamic attributes include:

- Neighborhood history and public image; the reputation and values attached to the site by prospective users.
- Prevailing air currents and airborne pollutants (fumes from mills and factories, for example).
- Noise and congestion adjacent to the site, which affect the reality or the perception of inconvenience and discomfort associated with site access.
- Anxiety factors associated with security for tenants and their customers.
- Visual factors associated with the prominence of the site and views from the site.

Site Acquisition

You have found a site that has a satisfactory confluence of attributes and that enables your project to meet your feasibility parameters. You now face the challenge of controlling the site so that you can pursue the necessary approvals and financing, yet at the same time avoiding an irrevocable purchase commitment in case the approvals and financing are not forthcoming.

The idea is to gain control but defer payment. You don't want to be locked into ownership of a site for which you have paid a price based on development potential, only to discover the potential isn't really there.

What can go wrong? The possibilities are legendary. Here are two common hazards that must be avoided.

- Invalid title. Make sure you are buying from the real owner, and obtain title insurance to protect yourself from losses stemming from title defects. Do this early enough in the acquisition process that any title defects can be cleared before the scheduled closing date for title transfer. Since attorneys for lenders are notoriously slow in clearing titles, it will be up to you and your development team to push the process to the front.

- Hazardous Wastes. Who is responsible for cleaning up any hazardous wastes detected on the site? Generally, whoever owns the property when the issue surfaces. Protect yourself by having a good chemical engineer thoroughly check the site before you obligate yourself to go through with the transaction. In most jurisdictions, title insurance will not protect you from losses stemming from the discovery of hazardous wastes. Test for wastes early; then test again just before the deal closes.

The most common alternatives for controlling a site until you have determined whether it is an acceptable alternative are an outright purchase, a ground lease, and a joint venture with the land owner.

Purchase
Price is too often the focus of early negotiation. Yet price is usually less important than terms and conditions surrounding a contract of sale. Land owners (obviously) want to maximize the value of their land. To benefit from the maximized value, they must somehow share the risks associated with obtaining necessary development permits, or they must give the developer the necessary time and freedom to eliminate these risks. Intelligent land owners understand this, and will be interested in your proposal of how you both might benefit from a cooperative approach.

Perhaps the most common strategy is to obtain an option to purchase at a price based on obtaining the permits and approvals. The option itself will be relatively inexpensive and will run for a period sufficient to enable you to exhaust all prospects for getting the sought-after affirmations. The option price is often based on a percentage of the value of the property. For example, a one-year option might cost 12 percent of the property's value. This compensates the land owner for taking the property off the market while you negotiate with the appropriate regulatory authorities.

The most common developer error at this stage is negotiating an option that runs for too short a period. Remember that the regulatory maze gets thicker every year, and approvals always take more time than experience suggests they should. To insulate yourself from this hazard, include a provision for option renewal. The renewal rate will probably have to be considerably higher than the initial option price, but remember that you don't anticipate having to lap over into the renewal period; it's there for insurance.

An alternative to a purchase option, and a response to land owners who object to the uncertainty of option arrangements, is an immediate purchase with a two-tiered price. The purchase itself is engineered at a base amount that represents what the property will be worth if necessary development permits and approvals are impossible to acquire. Layered over this basic price is a conditional bonus payment that becomes effective only if you are able to get the approvals you need to go ahead with your development plans.

Leasing

Development ground leases are often used for major developments. The leases run for 45 or more years and typically provide for one or more renewals. The leasehold interest will usually be subordinated to the interests of the mortgagee who provides financing for the development. Leases of this type are exceedingly complex, as is the lease process itself. Few small-scale developers use the ground-lease alternative.

Joint Venturing

Another increasingly popular alternative to direct land purchases, and one that is employed as frequently by small firms as by development behemoths, is a joint venture with the land owner. Joint-venturing land owners usually get a preferred return plus participation in additional profits. They might, for example, receive all the cash flow from a project until their annual return reaches, say 8 percent of the value of the land. The developer might get any cash flow above that level, until the developer's compensation reaches some predetermined amount. Thereafter, developer and land-owner might share additional cash flow at an agreed-upon ratio.

Many developers feel the biggest problem with joint-venture arrangements is that of the land owner's role in development and management decisions. They caution that a land-owner should be made an active (as opposed to a silent) part-ner only if the owner is also an experienced developer. In any event, it's vital that the agreement include a buy-out arrange-ment that permits you to either buy out a dissident land-owner or personally abandon the project without prohibitive financial penalties.

Approvals

Winding your way through the regulatory maze is becoming an increasingly crucial and difficult aspect of development and redevelopment. As with any lengthy, complex, yet vital opera-tion, this one is growing ever more costly, and specialists adept in the process are courted by developers. Securing the necessary approvals adds significantly to a land parcel's market value, and some entrepreneurs are engaged in acquiring land, secur-ing the necessary approvals, and selling the completed package to a developer.

The process will be immensely facilitated if you keep in mind that regulatory authorities are political creatures. They react most assiduously to pressure from collective consumers because that is the source of the regulators' rewards and penalties. The key to successfully navigating the regulatory sea, therefore, is to determine what collective consumers want.

Astute developers try to identify the most influential mem-bers of collective consumer groups and determine what they want. You should do this *before* opposition to your project coalesces. Then, the collective consumers' leadership can abort nascent opposition without losing face.

Construction

Key construction strategies include *fixed-fee*, where the devel-oper commissions a complete set of plans and specifications from an architectural design firm and then chooses a contrac-tor based on competitive proposals; and *cost-plus*, where the contractor agrees to complete the project according to specifica-tions in exchange for cost reimbursement plus a fee based on predetermined criteria. Construction provisions and detail can become extremely complex and require an experienced hand to stave off catastrophe. The Urban Land Institute sponsors a number of training events (seminars and short courses) that will be extremely useful if you contemplate becoming involved in development.

REDEVELOPMENT PROBLEMS

One of America's most colorful pioneers in rejuvenating old buildings is George Bockl, a real estate broker, developer, writer, and teacher from Milwaukee, Wisconsin. In *Recycling Real Estate* (Prentice Hall, 1983), Bockl recounts lessons he learned in more than 30 conversions of old buildings to new uses. Perhaps the most useful part of his book for a neophyte redeveloper is the final chapter. In it, he lists key problems and recommends solutions. What follows is a summary of some of his more cogent observations.

• *The neighborhood is more important than the building.* A good building in a bad location is a dangerous temptation. You might make it work if you are able to buy cheaply enough, can market the space with sufficient imagination, and are extraordinariiy lucky. But why take a chance? You control the building that you are rehabilitating, and you can make whatever changes the market suggests; you do not control the neighborhood and are powerless to make needed changes. Don't subject yourself and the value of your portfolio to the whims of chance.

• *What about a bad building in a good neighborhood?* This combination greatly increases your odds of success, but danger lurks in buildings that require more than cosmetic alterations. Compute rehabilitation cost estimates very carefully, with generous provisions for cost overruns. With this information, and with conservative estimates of revenue during the rent-up and subsequent operating periods, work backward to estimate the most you would be justified in paying for the building. Don't be swayed by romanticism or preservationist fervor—yours or anyone else's.

• *What combination of building and neighborhood is ideal?* What you should be looking for is a basically sound and serviceable but neglected or underutilized building in a good neighborhood. The most valuable, yet least costly, ingredient you can supply is imagination and innovation to determine the building's most appropriate use.

• *Is it better to modernize buildings, or to preserve old features?* Preserving old features often adds value. It is also frequently the least costly approach because it economizes on materials and labor. Yet preservation also contributes to aesthetic considerations that are much valued in today's culture.

• *How can I protect myself from ruinous cost overruns?* Your first line of defense is to get the building at a bargain price. Then, establish working relationships with subcontractors—electrical, plumbing, heating, and so forth—rather than always going with the absolute low bidder. Too often, the low bidder expects to make a profit by using substandard materials and slipshod workmanship and by charging exorbitantly for the inevitable changes from original contract specifications. Reliable subcontractors who expect to get work from you on a continuing basis can help keep costs down by working with you to refine your redevelopment strategy and by showing your architect less costly alternatives.

This is not to suggest that you blindly use a contractor with whom you have established satisfactory relationships. Projects should still be let out for bid, but the primary purpose will be to assure yourself that your established subcontractor's charges are reasonable. Don't change contractors simply because a new bidder is able to undercut others by a few dollars.

• *Doesn't the possibility of hidden defects make redevelopment prohibitively risky?* Hidden problems are the Damoclean sword hanging over every rehabilitation project. It is a risk that new developments avoid, and it partially explains the difference in potential rewards. No matter how carefully you study a building, you are almost certain to overlook some problems that will cause cost overruns.

Incur some costs to minimize the risk of overruns from hidden defects. Sign purchase agreements that permit you to rescind the contract within a specified time if you uncover hidden problems. Then spend time and money with a knowledgeable and cooperative engineer to test such key building components as foundations, footings, floor load capacity, roof, elevators and other mechanical components, plumbing and heating, electrical, and sprinkling systems. Have the city building inspector look at the building and note what you will have to do to bring it up to current standards.

KEY POINTS

• After good management, the most effective way to add value to real estate is to convert it to its most appropriate use. For raw land this entails initial development; for developed parcels the process is redevelopment.

• Converting underutilized buildings to their most appropriate use is often less costly than constructing comparable buildings. This allows you to underprice the competition and establish a commanding market presence.

• Project design should consider the needs of three categories of consumers. Collective consumers work through the political process and can stymie efforts to get necessary public approvals unless their concerns are addressed. Individual consumers are the tenants who make the project financially feasible. Future consumers are tenants you will need to attract some years hence, and your building design should incorporate sufficient flexibility to be adaptable to their needs.

• Project feasibility refers to the likelihood that a proposed project will achieve your goals. It involves (1) market analysis to measure the need for the type of space your project will include, (2) locational analysis to ascertain that the site is appropriate for the intended use, and (3) financial analysis to determine whether the cost and revenue projections will support the project at a level of profitability consonant with your minimum acceptable yield.

• An appropriate site must meet multiple criteria. It must be physically feasible to build on the site at an acceptable level of site-preparation costs. Size, topography, vegetation, utility cost and availability, and existing site improvements are key cost determinants. Legal and political issues must be manageable. Conflicting ownership claims, local ordinances, and state and federal building and use regulations must be reconcilable within time and cost constraints. The site must be appropriately located with respect to others between which people and things will regularly move, and the site must be appealing to prospective tenants and their clients.

• The optimum site-acquisition strategy is to acquire an option to buy the property without incurring substantial expenses until you determine the site's development potential. Make sure your option runs for enough time for all details to be nailed down. Alternatives to an option (and eventually, a purchase) include a long-term land lease or a joint venture with the landowner.

CHAPTER 13

TRADE–DON'T SELL

Our analysis so far has been based on selling your property after several years. Most of the time, though, you will be better off not selling. When it is time to adjust your portfolio, to dispose of one property and acquire another, the Internal Revenue Code permits you to make the adjustment without incurring any income tax liability. The secret ingredient is a like-kind exchange. In a word, trading.

Let's illustrate. Suppose you bought vacant land a long time ago for say, $10,000. Suppose also that you can sell it today for $55,000 (we may as well think positively) and that your selling costs will be $5,000. If you are in the 33 percent income tax bracket, selling this land means you will have only $36,800 of equity to put into a new parcel. Here is the math:

Sales price		$55,000
Less: Tax basis	$10,000	
Transaction costs	5,000	15,000
Taxable gain		$40,000
Times income tax rate		.33
Income tax consequences of selling		$13,200

Sales price		$55,000
Less: Income taxes	$13,200	
Transaction costs	5,000	18,200
After-tax cash proceeds		$36,800

If you trade, instead, your equity will be $50,000:

Trade-in value, net of transaction costs	$50,000
Less income taxes	0
After-tax equity in new property	$50,000

PLUMBING THE BENEFITS BARREL

Conserving equity by not paying taxes on your gain when you adjust your holdings is an impressive benefit of trading, but you can get more—much more—out of the like-kind exchange strategy.

Increase Tax Shelter by Releveraging

After several years of ownership, you run out of tax basis for depreciation deductions. Suppose you bought a rental property when depreciation write-offs were taken over 15 years. Now, 15 years later, your depreciation deductions end, but taxable income continues. If you used the accelerated depreciation methods permitted under prior tax law, you will have encountered this dilemma even sooner. Because much of your taxable income will be going to service the mortgage debt, and because an increasing portion of the debt service will be going to (nondeductible) repayment of the principal amount of the loan, taxable income will soon exceed before-tax cash flow.

Meanwhile, with a little bit of luck the property will have increased in value over the years. Let's assume you paid $100,000 for the property; $20,000 for the land and $80,000 for the building. Assume further that the purchase was financed with a $75,000 loan. If the property has doubled in value over the years, and the mortgage loan has been paid down to, say, $50,000, your equity in the property will have grown over 15 years from an initial $25,000 to a current $150,000:

	15 Years Ago	Today
Market value	$100,000	$200,000
Less mortgage balance	75,000	50,000
Equity	$ 25,000	$150,000

Over the same 15-year period your tax basis in the property will have declined drastically. If you initially opted for a 15-year recovery period, your basis in the building (cost minus accumulated depreciation) will in fact have been reduced to zero. Your only remaining basis, therefore, will be in the land. (Remember our basic assumption that $20,000 of the $100,000 purchase price was attributable to the land.) The tax code requires that the initial tax basis reflect these relative values. Here's what the tax basis will have looked like when you purchased the property 15 years earlier, and how it will stand today:

	15 Years Ago	Today
Tax basis: land	$ 20,000	$ 20,000
building	80,000	0
total	$100,000	$ 20,000

Because your tax basis in the building has been reduced to zero, no further tax deductions are allowed for depreciation. Therefore, taxable income will be the before-tax cash flow plus the principal portion of mortgage payments; you are paying taxes on income that does not represent cash flow. Moreover, your mortgage loan now represents only 25 percent of the property's market value. This combination of circumstances, plus the fact that, over 15 years, the desirability of the area in which the property is located will have changed, suggests that this may be a good time to dispose of the property and acquire a substitute. We have seen that the least taxing way to do that is with a like-kind exchange.

Putting aside for the moment the mechanics of how it is done, let's suppose that you trade your equity for equity in a substitute property that has a 75 percent loan-to-value ratio mortgage loan. Here is what your position will look like before and after the transaction if you incur transaction costs totaling $12,000 (6 percent of the value of your old property):

	Before	After
Market value	$200,000	$552,000
Less mortgage balance	50,000	414,000
Equity	$150,000	$138,000

Your tax basis in the substitute property will be its market value minus the deferred gain on the old property. Since the gain on the old property ($168,000, comprised of its $200,000 market value minus the $20,000 adjusted tax basis and the $12,000 transaction cost) is totally deferred, the substitute tax basis will be $552,000 minus $168,000, or $384,000.

Tax law requires you to allocate the substitute tax basis between the substitute land and building in accordance with their relative market values. If the substitute land accounts for, say, 20 percent of the total value, then 20 percent of the substitute basis, or $76,800, will be allocated to it. The other $307,200 is allocated to the substitute building and becomes the basis for computing depreciation deductions. Here is a summary of your tax basis before and after the transaction:

	Before	After
Tax basis: land	$20,000	$ 76,800
building	0	307,200
total	$20,000	$384,000

Shifting from Land to Income Property

Suppose you have been holding land for a number of years, and now you would like to use your growing equity to generate a partially tax-sheltered income stream. Part or all of the land can be exchanged for rental property, which will generate annual rental revenue and annual depreciation deductions; all without incurring any current income tax liability for the gain on disposal of the land.

You might, for example, agree to transfer ownership of a portion of the land to a developer in exchange for an apartment building to be built by the developer on the remaining portion.

Reducing Property Management Problems

Busy professional or business people don't have time to devote to property management. Investors who have acquired a port-folio of real estate that requires disproportionate allocation of their time can use like-kind exchange techniques to move into property capable of supporting professional management.

Perhaps you have, over the years, built considerable equity in a melange of small rental units more or less randomly dis-tributed over your chosen market area. For a variety of reasons, such properties are uneconomical to operate, and it is difficult to engage a really competent professional management team at an acceptable price. Exchanging a portfolio of such buildings for one or more larger rental parcels will yield management economies without the attendant burden of the large income tax liability that would stem from selling the old properties and buying the substitutes.

Shifting from Management Intensive to "Self-Managing" Property

As you approach retirement you will ask yourself whether you want to continue holding a portfolio of rental properties that require attention. If you want to move to another locale and would be uncomfortable as an absentee landlord depending on a commercial management agent, or if you simply want to be free of management responsibility, a like-kind exchange of your management-intensive property for property under a net lease to creditworthy tenants will accomplish your purpose without generating any income tax liability.

Shifting Geographic Locales

A frequent objection to real estate as an investment is its lack of mobility. A portfolio of stocks and bonds presents no complication when you move from New York to San Francisco, but what about land and buildings? Transcontinental trips to check on your real estate can be discomfiting as well as expensive. Yet selling the New York property and investing after-tax proceeds in San Francisco property may represent a major reduction in the total value of a portfolio, depending upon the size of the tax bite.

The answer, of course, is a like-kind exchange. By trading your New York equity for equity in a desirable West Coast property, you can preserve your entire real estate portfolio undiminished by income tax liability and will be able to conveniently keep tabs on your investment. It sounds complicated at this point, but it really isn't.

Estate Building

Like-kind exchanges enable you to defer taxes until you dispose of the substitute property in a taxable transaction. At that point, all the deferred tax liability becomes due and payable. The solution to this potential problem is to *never* engage in a taxable transaction that involves the substitute property.

Does this mean you must hold the property forever? No, it can be disposed of in another like-kind exchange, then the new substitute can be traded for yet another, and so on in as long a chain of like-kind exchanges as you wish.

In this manner you can adjust your portfolio as frequently as seems prudent with no concern about taxes. Thus, as your investment objectives change (from estate building to cash flow, for example) the type of real estate in your portfolio can be altered apace, without having the portfolio decimated by income taxes.

Figure 13–1 illustrates how portfolio management objectives typically change over time. Each phase suggests a different asset mix. Moving from one stage to the next implies altering the type of real estate you own as well as adjusting your

FIGURE 13–1
Time and Portfolio Objectives

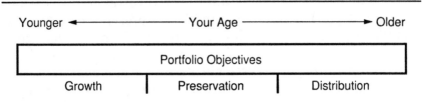

degree of diversification. Portfolio shifts to accommodate new objectives can often be done with least damage to your net worth by using like-kind exchanges.

During your early adult years, rapid portfolio growth is typically an overriding goal. This implies assets that are positioned for extraordinary appreciation—a category not generally associated with safety of principal. During this phase you are likely to favor real estate that has been underutilized or mismanaged: "workout situations," in the industry vernacular.

A typical pattern of change in asset value is diagramed in Figure 13–2. Maximum gain involves spotting property in the predevelopment or redevelopment stage and holding it until the growth curve begins to flatten. At this point, an aggressive acquisitor will exchange the asset for other property judged to be on the development or redevelopment cusp. Avoiding the sizeable income tax liability that would result from selling greatly appreciated parcels has obvious implications for the rate of increase in aggregate portfolio value; it is done with like-kind exchanges.

When shooting for growth, speculators will often sacrifice the benefits of diversification to reap the rewards of specialization. They will deliberately shoulder risk that could be eliminated by diversification so as to concentrate limited resources on opportunities that offer the greatest potential.

A dash of prudence and a dollop of luck will eventually take you to the stage on Figure 13–1 that some social commentators have described as the most pathetic of all human conditions: the point where you have something to lose. Growing affluence tends to transform attitudes about assets as well as about

FIGURE 13–2
Real Estate Growth Stages

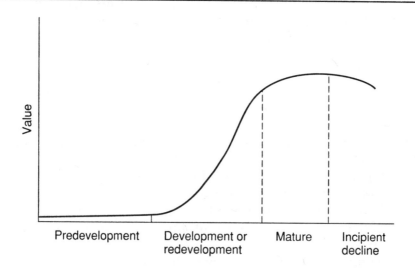

Predevelopment   Development or   Mature   Incipient
                  redevelopment   decline

political and social issues. Having joined the establishment in at least one dimension, we become concerned with preserving what diligence and good fortune have wrought.

At the portfolio conservation stage, illustrated on Figure 13–1, earlier strategies of concentrating assets in high-growth areas may be counterproductive. For conservators, diversification is a prime objective.

Once again, the mechanism is a series of like-kind exchanges. Large properties can be exchanged for a portfolio of smaller, spatially diverse parcels for geographic diversification, or for different types of properties (a mix of residential, commercial, and industrial, for example) for economic diversification.

But, for successful investors, a further shift in portfolio emphasis is inevitable. There comes a time when you begin recognizing more and more of the names in the obituary columns, and with growing persistence your thoughts turn to what will happen when friends recognize your name there. How much of your diligently accumulated and carefully preserved estate will be diverted to the tax collector's coffers, and how much will remain for your heirs?   Concern with this issue will spark additional portfolio adjustments.

At this stage, most investors will begin disengaging from many of the activities that consumed their earlier years. Many will want to be free of concern with investment management. The very successful will want to cap the size of their estates so as to minimize estate and inheritance taxes. Most will want an assured lifetime income stream sufficient to sustain them in reasonable style for their remaining years.

Toward these ends, net-leased properties (those where tenants pay all operating expenses, including property taxes) rented to creditworthy, national tenants will likely prove attractive. Long-term leases of this sort will free you from management and marketing concerns. Modern leases contain escalator provisions to protect you from inflation that can decimate the purchasing power of your rental income stream or the value of your portfolio.

Using real estate to accomplish these goals carries additional dividends. Like-kind exchanges permit you to shift your portfolio's composition to accommodate altered objectives without incurring income tax liability. By continuing to hold substitute real estate assets, you can in fact defer the income tax liability for the rest of your life. Moreover, your death completely eliminates the potential tax liability. Heirs will take title to your real estate with a stepped-up tax basis equal to the value of the property as determined for estate tax purposes. They begin anew with depreciation allowance schedules based on this value.

THE LOGIC OF EXCHANGE RULES

Whether special tax provisions are praised as incentives or condemned as loopholes often depends on who holds the microphone or television camera. It also often depends on the size and direction of congressional contributions from special interest groups; it may even depend on whether an election is looming.

Like-kind exchanges, whose provisions are found in Section 1031 of the Internal Revenue Code, have survived countless encounters with special interest legislators and a great many elections. Its survival in an era in which loophole-closing has political cachet is a testimony to the economic soundness of the underlying rationale. It reflects the wisdom of not encouraging misallocation of capital by taxing away resources when the nature of employed assets is unchanged. (They are not, for example, being converted into more liquid form.)

Business enterprises regularly use like-kind exchanges to defer taxes when they trade old capital equipment for new, more efficient production facilities, and when they shift the locus of business activities from one geographic locale to another.

In the final analysis, the like-kind exchange provisions of Section 1031 do not represent special interest legislation, or a tax loophole. This is a transaction method open to everyone. Its benefits are available without distinction to all businesses and to every investor.

From a national economic perspective, these rules make consummate good sense. They encourage productive reallocation of resources without distorting the decision process with tax avoidance issues.

BASIC REQUIREMENTS

The enabling language in Code Section 1031(a)(1) says: "No gain or loss shall be recognized on the exchange of property held for productive use in a trade or business or for investment if such property is exchanged solely for property of a like kind to be held either for productive use in a trade or business or for investment." As you might expect from documents created by the modern legislative process, the section then elaborates in painful detail on this basic sentence.

Specific Exclusions

The range of possible options is narrowed drastically by a list of special exceptions enumerated immediately below the code's enabling sentence. Excluded are exchanges of:

- Assets held primarily for resale.

- All securities or evidence of indebtedness or interest.
- Partnership interests.
- Trust certificates, or beneficial interests in a trust.

Intended Use

Both the old and the substitute property must have been held specifically for productive use in a trade or business, or as an investment. Neither property can be held, for example, for your personal use as a residence or for other uses not related to business or professional activities. Investment purposes and productive use in a trade or business, however, are considered interchangeable purposes.

Productive use in a trade or business refers to employing the asset in furtherance of business activities, not to selling the asset itself as a part of your business or trade activity. Thus, assets held for resale in the normal course of business would not qualify for tax-deferred exchange treatment under Section 1031.

The requirement that both the old and the substitute property be held either for productive use in a trade or business or as an investment relates strictly to the intended use during your ownership; what the subsequent owner of your old property intends to do with it is irrelevant, as is the use to which the substitute property was put by its previous owner.

Don't be distracted by the tax status of other parties to a trade; their position doesn't matter. Whether you qualify for like-kind exchange treatment is determined independently of whether others qualify. The property acquired in an exchange may have been held by the previous owner primarily for resale, or perhaps as a personal residence. Either motive means the other party will not qualify under Section 1031. But that has no bearing on whether you qualify. In fact, the other party to a typical like-kind exchange probably will not be at all interested in tax deferral.

The proscription against tax deferral where either the old or the substitute property is held primarily for resale poses a potential trap for the unwary. Remember that if the IRS challenges your motives, the burden of proof is on you. You must, therefore, establish a trail of documents establishing your intent.

A property advertised for sale and subsequently exchanged for a substitute parcel probably will not qualify for like-kind exchange treatment. The fact that you advertised the old parcel for sale, or listed it with a broker for that purpose, will almost certainly be adequate evidence that, at the time of the transaction, you held it primarily for resale.

Likewise, a property acquired in a trade and sold soon after presents a special disqualification risk. You will need evidence (such as internal memos or letters to your broker, attorney, banker, or other third party) that your intention at the time of the original transaction was to hold the property for business or investment use, and that you subsequently changed your plans.

Property Must Be of Like Kind

Only like-kind property qualifies for tax deferral under Section 1031, regardless of ownership motives. This excludes exchanges of realty for assets that would be considered personalty under state law, but the general rule is that any real estate will be considered like kind with any other real estate. In an important clarification of the law, a federal court judge ruled that the law ". . . was not intended to draw any distinction between parcels of real property however dissimilar they may be in location, in attributes and in capacities for profitable use."[1]

In its implementing regulations the Treasury Department gives a number of examples. They include [in Treasury Regulation 1.1031(a)(1)(b)]:

- Property held for use in a trade or business, together with cash, for other property for the same purpose.
- Urban real estate for a farm or ranch.
- Improved for unimproved real estate (held for investment purposes).
- A leasehold (with not less than 30 years to run) for a freehold.

---

[1]Commissioner of Internal Revenue Service v. Chrichton, 122 F. 181 (1941).

- Mineral interest in land (not merely an assignment of payments) for a fee title in real estate.

Consequences of Receiving Unlike Property

Any consideration that is not considered like-kind property is called *boot*. If you receive boot in a transaction that otherwise qualifies for like-kind exchange treatment, any gain (but not a loss) must be recognized for tax purposes to the extent of the net boot received; the balance of the gain (and the entire amount of any loss) will be deferred.

Boot includes anything of economic value other than the like-kind assets involved in the transaction. Examples include cash, services rendered or an obligation to render services, debt forgiveness, or a promise to convey something of value in the future.

A special rule applies when properties are traded subject to existing mortgage loans. If only one of the properties is encumbered, the party relieved of debt is treated as having received boot in the amount of the mortgage balance. If both parties transfer realty subject to mortgage loans, however, only the one who receives *net* debt relief (that is, the person whose remaining mortgage balance was the larger) is treated as receiving boot in the amount of the difference between the remaining balances. Moreover, if an investor receives net debt relief but pays cash as part of the deal, the boot received via net debt relief is offset by the amount of cash paid; only the difference is treated as boot.

Only *net* boot triggers recognition of the gain. To determine net boot received, subtract your transaction costs from any unlike property you have received in the deal. Transaction costs, recall, include items such as brokerage commissions, recording fees, transfer taxes, and attorney's fees required to complete the transaction and ensure that you have a good and marketable title. They do not include any costs associated with getting a mortgage loan.

Balancing the Equities
It helps to keep in mind two fundamental ideas: Only equities are exchanged, and transactions always involve equal

values. Your equity is the only thing of value you have to offer with respect to any asset (but of course your equity can equal 100 percent of the property's market value). If equal values are not involved, one party will be making a gift to the other.

Prior to a trade, the market value of equities will almost never be exactly the same. An early step in putting together the deal, therefore, is deciding how to compensate for differences in the value of equities—a step often called *balancing the equities*.

Several alternatives other than boot are available. If the party with the smaller equity is transferring a property subject to an existing mortgage, for example, the mortgage balance can be paid down sufficiently to make the equities equal. Alternatively, the party with the smaller equity could offer equity in an additional property.

YOUR SUBSTITUTE TAX BASIS

You have a tax basis in everything you own, though the basis is sometimes zero. The basis of property received in an exchange is called a *substitute* basis to reflect the fact that it incorporates the basis of your old property adjusted for the circumstances of the exchange.

Tax accountants have a complicated procedure to determine the substitute tax basis. After completing their computations they prove the math by noting that the substitute basis is always the market value of the substitute property minus the amount of the deferred gain (or plus the amount of any deferred loss). For our purpose the proof alone is adequate, so we can leave the complexities to the CPAs.

For example, suppose you trade a property that has an adjusted basis, prior to the exchange, of $24,000. Assume your property is worth $145,000, and your transactions costs are $12,200. The other party's property is worth $250,000, and since both properties are being transferred free and clear of any mortgage indebtedness, you agree to pay $105,000 cash boot. How you raise the money is irrelevant to the example. You may choose to mortgage the substitute property for this purpose, and in fact may borrow enough so that you can cover all costs and walk away from the closing with cash in your pocket. None of this affects the tax consequences of the transaction.

The simple way to compute your substitute tax basis is to determine the amount of your deferred gain and subtract this from the $250,000 value of the substitute property. Your realized gain is the value of the substitute property minus your tax basis in the old, after adjusting for transaction costs. Here are the numbers:

Market value of property received:		
Real estate		$250,000
Other consideration		0
Total		$250,000
Less basis of consideration tendered:		
Real estate (adjusted basis)	$ 24,000	
Add: Transaction costs	12,200	
Cash	105,000	
Other	0	
Total		141,200
Realized gain		$108,800

Since you received no boot, none of your realized gain will be recognized and you will incur no income tax liability. Your substitute tax basis will be the $250,000 market value of the substitute property minus the $108,800 deferred gain, or $141,200.

As always, the tax basis (in this case, the substitute basis) must be allocated between land and buildings in accordance with their relative market values. For example, if $50,000 of the $250,000 market value is properly attributable to the land, then $50,000/$250,000, or 20 percent, of your $141,200 substitute will be attributed to the land.

KEY POINTS

• Like-kind exchanges are almost always less expensive than sales and purchases when you want to adjust your portfolio. The difference is that you defer taxes on your gain until you sell the newly acquired (substitute) property in a taxable transaction. If you never do so, the tax will never be due. If you die holding the last property in a chain of like-kind exchanges, the accumulated deferred tax liability is forgiven and your heirs take title with a clean slate.

• Like-kind exchanges can help you achieve a multitude of investment objectives without incurring income taxes. You can, for example, shift from one type of real estate to another, or from one geographic locale to another. You can move from a collection of small properties to a few large ones, or vice versa. You can get out of management-intensive properties and into those that are essentially the same as holding a highly secured bond.

• To avoid taxes on exchanges you must not receive anything except like-kind property. This means only real estate that is to be used in a trade or business or held as an investment. The property you tender must also be real estate held for one of these purposes.

CHAPTER 14

LIMITED PARTNERSHIPS

Until 1986 real estate limited partnerships (often called *syndicates*) were the glamour segment of the securities industry. Because of a substantial "cottage industry" element, no one really knows the total amount of partnership shares offered to the investing public during this period. The visible part of the phenomenon, publicly registered partnerships, experienced a compound annual growth rate of about 34 percent for 10 years, reaching a zenith of about $8.5 billion in 1986.

Major revisions to the Internal Revenue Code ravaged the industry, as did overbuilding in most of the real estate sectors of interest to the largest syndicators. Real estate promoters adjusted to the new tax environment by shifting emphasis from tax shelter to cash flow. Their response to overbuilding has been to look for less-exploited areas of investment and development and to move from their traditional geographic locales (major cities in high-growth areas) to middle-sized cities that offer promising if unspectacular growth prospects.

For individual investors, real estate syndicates offer a mixed bag of overblown hyperbole, analytical imponderables, and genuine opportunities. Your problem as an investor will be to determine which is which

SYNDICATION SYMBIOSIS

Limited partnerships bring together promoters with energy, ideas, and dreams and investors with money and optimism. The idea people become general partners and the moneyed participants become the limited partners. (In every limited partnership there must be one or more general partners and one or more limited partners.) The object is to package or repackage real estate deals to satisfy everyone's aspirations.

The General Partners

The general partners are the venture's sponsors and managers. They raise money by selling shares to individual investors, who become limited partners. The general partners are charged with conducting partnership business affairs and have unlimited personal liability for partnership obligations.

Perhaps the most numerous promoters during the early days of real estate limited partnerships were real estate brokers. Their place in the center of the industry uniquely positions them for the role. They know what properties are available, the sources of loanable funds, the condition of the market, and the telephone numbers of people interested in investing. And, depending on the laws of the state in which they do business, they are usually in a position to collect a commission or fee at every step in the process of forming the partnership and carrying out its intended function.

The formation of a limited partnership often occurs to a broker who finds he or she has an exclusive listing on a property that requires more cash than most individual investors can raise. To sell the property and collect a commission, the broker might form a limited partnership to pool funds from enough investors to swing the deal.

In addition to collecting a commission when selling property to the syndicate and another when selling on the syndicate's behalf, the broker will usually collect a management fee for operating the property during the partnership period. With appropriate licensing the broker might also be able to collect a commission from the partnership for selling the shares to individual investors.

Real estate developers are probably the next most frequent group to engage in real estate syndication. Developers can use equity funds raised from limited partners, leverage this with mortgage loans, and put together larger developments than they could ever hope to swing if they had to rely on their own financial resources. In addition to the same compensation available to brokers, developers will get a fee for putting the project together.

The smell of real money inevitably attracts the big boys. By the mid-1970's most major real estate development firms and several major investment banking firms were in the real estate syndication business. They offered syndication shares as major public security offerings and attracted a nationwide investor following.

The Limited Partners

Limited partners are passive investors, in the sense of having absolutely no role in determining a venture's success or failure. They put up their money and hope for the best. Limited partners are attracted to real estate syndicates for the same reason they might be lured into any other venture: the prospect of an investment bonanza.

What makes limited partnership shares different from stock market investments, other than the fact that real estate has a reputation as a high-yield investment opportunity, is the special income tax advantages this entity offers. Real estate has always been afforded special treatment by the Internal Revenue Code, and limited partnerships permit investors to get those tax advantages without direct real estate ownership.

Because of their special tax status, partnerships are called *tax conduits*. Unlike corporations, partnerships are not taxable entities. Instead, the tax consequences of real estate ownership pass through the partnership (thus the conduit designation) directly to individual investors.

This benefit proved so attractive and profitable to investors that the Internal Revenue Code was revised to 1986 to prevent the limited partners' net losses from offsetting income from any source except another passive investment. This represented a massive reduction in the income tax incentive to invest as a limited partner, but promoters merely shifted emphasis from tax shelter to cash flow and continued to furiously market their shares.

Partnership Assets

There is no such thing as a favored partnership asset. The most appropriate property depends in part on the partnership's nature and, of course, on the partners' objectives. Assets range from undeveloped land through shopping centers and high-rise apartments to industrial parks, office complexes, and rehabilitation projects.

The variety of syndication projects reflects the disparity in the partnerships themselves, which range from a few friends who pool their resources to control a small local rental project to multimillion dollar deals pooling the investments of thousands of individuals.

THE LURE OF LIMITED PARTNERSHIPS

Limited partnership interests give you the same limitation of personal liability that you would have as a corporate shareholder, yet you avoid the double taxation that makes the corporate form less than desirable for many purposes. This propitious melding of corporate and propriertorship characteristics alone would probably ensure the partnership form's popularity. But several traditional problems of real estate as an investment medium can also be mitigated by limited partnership arrangements

Partnerships Are Tax Conduits

Partnerships are not taxable entities. They function instead as conduits for passing gains and losses directly to the tax returns of individual partners. Furthermore, individual income and loss items maintain their character on partners' personal tax returns; what would have been a tax preference or a tax credit item for the partnership, for example, is a tax preference or tax credit for the individual. From an income tax perspective, this is the essential feature distinguishing partnerships from corporations or other associations.

Partnerships must file tax returns, but the purpose is

purely informational. They report the amount and nature of partnership income, expenses, and deductions and indicate how each of the items is allocated among partners. The partners must in turn report their distributive shares of these items on their personal returns. Income tax consequences of partnership business transactions thus accrue directly to partners, rather than to the business entity.

Since 1986 the Internal Revenue Code has imposed a severe restriction on the tax benefits accruing to limited partners. They must pay income taxes on their share of partnership profits, yet often find they cannot deduct net losses. Income and losses from activities the Code characterizes as *passive*, a designation that always applies to limited partnership activity, must be segregated from income generated by portfolio-type investments such as stocks and bonds and from general income sources such as wages, salary, and profit from a trade or business. With only very limited special exceptions, net losses from these passive activities cannot be offset against income from other sources.

Instead, net losses must be carried over and offset against passive income in future years. Any passive loss carried over and not yet offset against passive income becomes deductible when the related asset is sold or otherwise disposed of in a taxable transaction.

Other Limited Partnership Benefits

Instead of committing your whole bankroll to one deal, as you might have to in order to make an individual real estate investment, you can make smaller investments in each of several limited partnerships. This lets you diversify, both geographically and across types of real estate, and diversification is an important way to reduce risk. In effect, you avoid putting all your eggs in one basket. One sour deal doesn't devastate your portfolio the way it might if you had to put in enough money to control a real estate project by yourself.

We saw earlier that properly managing real estate assets is a time-consuming proposition, even if you have hired on-site managers. Professional management is often too expensive to be practical for a small-scale apartment or office complex

Pooling several investors' funds lets your syndicate control a large enough project so that professional management is both practical and economical.

YIELD EXPECTATIONS

Someone once described limited partnerships as arrangements where limited partners contribute money and the general partner contributes experience. The most frequent outcome, they continued, is that the general partner gets the money and limited partners get experience. Research findings indicate that there is more than a germ of truth in this generalization.

We saw in Chapter One that, over the long term, real estate assets tend to generate a rate of return (on average) slightly above that on common stocks. If the ownership entity is a limited partnership, a big piece of these earnings goes to the general partner, with the leavings to the limited partners. It seems reasonable to expect, therefore, that limited partnership interests will, on average, do somewhat more poorly than common stocks. Research teams have concluded that this expectation is borne out by market experience.

Public Syndications

An unambiguous distinction needs to be made concerning yield evidence for public syndications and for private placements. All the evidence relates to the public offerings, where securities law and SEC regulations force disclosure. Private placements are by their nature impossible to trace. Nevertheless, after examining available information about the public offerings' performance, we will speculate about how private placements fare.

Stephen Roulac and Robert Hatheway[1] looked at several public real estate syndications that had sold all their property

---

[1]Stephen E. Roulac and Robert Hatheway, "Investment Returns to Limited Partners of Public Real Estate Programs," *Real Estate Securities Journal* 3 (Summer 1982), pp. 7–17.

by 1981, and found average rates of return to be little short of breathtaking. This old information is useless for predicting what you might reasonably expect today, and we mention it here only so that you will not be misled if you find the study cited elsewhere.

Syndicates included in the Roulac study all bought their assets before the big inflationary runup of the 1970s. They were all highly leveraged deals and benefited immensely from a situation that will almost certainly not exist again during our lifetime; savers were forced by law to subsidize borrowers. Interest rates were kept artificially low by laws that limited the rates banks and S&Ls could pay to depositors. Long-term fixed-rate mortgage notes were routinely available at after-tax rates below the inflation rate of the 1970s. Consequently, the real (that is, inflation-adjusted) cost of borrowing was negative—debtors were in effect being paid to borrow.

Financial institutions' deregulation has eliminated this ridiculous and unfair arrangement. Depository institutions now must compete for savers' assets, and this competition is reflected in lending rates. Moreover, while inflation remains a problem, the double-digit rates of the late 1970s don't appear imminent. These are the reasons not to dwell on the leveraged yields real estate earned in the 1970s.

What do we know about syndicate yields in the 1980s? Considerable. We know, for example, that, on average, about 25 percent of investors' contributions are siphoned off before any real estate investments are made.[2] Where does all that money go? Syndicators have developed ingenious ways to strip off dollars.

In a typical publicly registered syndication deal about 8 percent of the shareholders' investment goes to pay securities sales commissions. The sponsor (general partner) usually gets an acquisition fee (ranging from about 10 percent to as much as 18 percent) for finding a property, in addition to reimbursement

---

[2]Ronald C. Rogers and James E. Owers, "The Investment Performance of Real Estate Limited Partnerships," *AREUEA Journal*, Vol. 13, No. 2 (1985) pp. 153–66.

for out-of-pocket costs for legal, accounting, and organizational expenses associated with putting the partnership together. A major syndicator, in the disclosure required by SEC regulations, listed the following additional ways it intended to claim limited partners' funds for itself: property management fees, a share of operating cash receipts, a share of proceeds on sale or refinancing, sales commissions, management services fees, and a share of partnership profits and losses.

Roughly three-quarters of your funds, then, actually work for you in a typical public syndication. If these are invested with a level of competence equal to that of the professionals who handle real estate investments for pension funds, we can infer the approximate average before-tax yield to equity investors.

We saw in Chapter One that Commingled Real Estate Funds (CREFs) are large real estate investment war chests handled by professional managers on behalf of pension funds. One could make a good argument that the incentive structure induces CREF managers to do a better job for their investors than does that of the syndication industry. Certainly, there is no reason to expect them to do worse. Conservatively, therefore, we estimate that equity yields to CREFs give a good measure of the upper limit of average yields to limited partners *on equity funds actually invested in real estate.*

Brueggeman, Chen, and Thibodeau have estimated average annual yields to CREF real estate investments during the period 1972 through 1983 to be about 11.5 percent.[3] These findings are close to what Ibbotson and Siegel found when they investigated a separate data base.[4] If public syndicates were able to do as well, their average before-tax yield on limited partners' equity would be about 8.6 percent. Here is how the estimate is derived:

---

[3]W.B. Brueggeman, A.H. Chen, and T.B. Thibodeau, "Real Estate Investment Funds: Performance and Portfolio Considerations," *AREUEA Journal*, Vol. 12, No. 3 (Fall 1984), pp. 333–54.

[4]Roger G. Ibbotson and Laurence B. Siegel, "Real Estate Returns: A comparison with Other Investments," Ibid, pp. 215–18.

Source of Yield	Yield Rate	Percent of Total Equity	Weighted Rate
Equity in assets	11.5%	75	8.6%
Equity siphoned off	0	25	0
Total invested equity		100	8.6%

Researchers have used the embryonic secondary market for limited partnership shares to infer likely yields to limited partners over the life-cycle of syndicated ventures. Separate researchers have used this approach to derive yields remarkably close to those we estimated above.

Steven Kapplin and Arthur Schwartz[5] looked at 53 publicly offered real estate limited partnerships whose shares are traded on the National Partnership Exchange (NAPEX). Incorporating actual annual cash flows with the value of anticipated future cash flows as indicated by prices on the NAPEX, they estimated average annual yields on the partnership shares.

Yields, after income taxes (with investors in the 50 percent marginal tax bracket), ranged from a high of 16.8 percent down to *minus* 24.4 percent per annum. The average after-tax yield for all 53 syndicates was 3.1 percent, which is less than you could have earned by simply holding 90-day T-bills over the same period. Kapplin and Schwartz concluded, with typical academic understatement, "Real estate limited partnership returns do not appear to be very competitive with other investment vehicles."

We are, of course, looking at averages. Buried in the average statistics are specific investment opportunities that the averages simply don't reveal. The range of possible outcomes exhibits a pattern similar to that shown in Figure 14–1. Maybe, instead of an average yield, your investments will be in the upper end of the distribution—yielding you the kind of returns

---

[5]Steven Kapplin and Arthur Schwartz, "Investing In Real Estate Limited Partnerships," *AAII Journal* (September 1986), pp. 8–12.

FIGURE 14–1
Probability Distribution of Partnership Yields

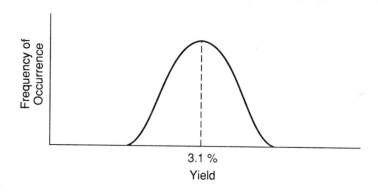

that make good cocktail party conversation. Sure, and you also might win the Irish Sweepstakes. If you want to gamble, Las Vegas is lots more fun and offers more favorable odds.

How about some careful investment analysis to identify the deals most likely to be in the upper end of the distribution? Won't eliminating the obvious dogs improve your odds of hitting a real winner? Sure. All you have to do is get information and process it in much the way we outlined in earlier chapters.

There's the catch. Study almost any syndication prospectus, and you will find virtually no information useful in developing rational cash-flow forecasts. Many of the deals simply invite you to write a check and hope for the best. They say very little about where your money will actually go. In these deals, called *blind pools*, you are merely told in general terms the kind of property and the geographical area in which assets will be located.

Luck and the Illusion of Omniscience

Why not rely on the general partner's track record? Most syndicators have been in the business for a while and must have closed out one or more earlier ventures. Aren't you justified in assuming that a promoter who did well in the past will also outperform the market in the future?

If you really believe that having picked winners in the past increases the probability that a promoter will pick more of them in the future, the *Forbes* Dart Board Fund is for you.

In 1967, the publisher and two editors of *Forbes* magazine pinned a copy of *The New York Times* stock market page to their wall and threw darts at it to select a stock portfolio. They invested a hypothetical $1,000 in each of 28 stocks picked on the basis of their randomly tossed darts, and adopted a passive management style: if one of the firms merged, they took shares in the acquiring firm; if a firm sold out for cash they reinvested their hypothetical shares of the sales proceeds in the remaining stocks in their dart board portfolio. In effect, they just sat on the portfolio.

As luck would have it, they compiled an amazing performance record. By the summer of 1984 their hypothetical investment of $28,000 had grown to almost $132,000, not including dividends. Compare their 370 percent gain with the 76 percent run-up of the New York Stock Exchange composite index for the same period, or the 37 percent gain for the Dow Jones industrial averages, before you belittle their stock-picking strategy. Many professional money managers and most mutual funds were thoroughly trounced by the *Forbes* Dart Board Fund.

If you like relying on an investment manager's track record, you should love the *Forbes* Dart Board Fund. You sneer? Would you be more impressed with their record if the *Forbes* editors had quoted impressive statistical studies or a convoluted theoretical basis for their selections? There's really no more reason to put your faith in a syndicator's track record than in that of the *Forbes* editors—the editors have simply been more forthright.

Suppose 200 people participate in a coin-tossing contest— heads win and tails lose. Odds favor half the contestants getting heads on the first toss. Of these 100 winners, chance favors half winning again on the next toss. Winners twice in a row—pretty good. Twenty-five of these will probably flip heads in the third round; ten will succeed again on the fourth try. These ten stellar performers can boast of four outstanding ventures in a row—a truly impressive record.

On the next try about five will draw tails; two of the remainder will get heads on the sixth toss. Odds favor one of these getting heads on the seventh toss as well. What a performer; what skill, what adroitness, what an unbelievable ability to manipulate nature! If you were betting on the eighth round, surely you would give odds that this seven-time winner will do it again. She has a track record, she deserves your confidence. What more can she do to show you that you're riding a sure thing?

Absurd? Of course. In the next round your champion has no better chance than someone who lost in all seven prior rounds. Far from being a natural winner, she is a random product of blind chance.

But consider real estate syndication. In any given year chance decrees that half the ventures will outperform the averages and half will fall short. After seven years one syndicator out of a hundred will have beaten the averages every single year, purely by chance. This accomplishment (but not the cause) will of course be trumpeted in press releases and will be the source of countless news stories. It will also attract a huge investor following. The promoter's blind pools will routinely be oversubscribed, and investors who are able to put their money at risk will deem themselves blessed—until a project goes into receivership.

Even if superior performance stems from skill rather than luck, it is likely to be temporary at best. If the syndicator's employees are especially skillful, they will eventually be hired away by someone else, or will decide to break away and run their own shows. In either instance the skill element of the syndicator's performance is dissipated and only the dim prospect of luck remains.

Specific Asset Syndications and the Cost of Information

For most investors in publicly registered syndications the situation is only slightly improved when the syndicator identifies specific assets to be acquired and their cost. Fundamental analysis then becomes theoretically possible, but is likely to be economically unfeasible.

Information is costly to come by and can be accumulated and verified economically only if the prospective investment is large relative to information search costs, or if the information can be reused in connection with other projects. For most investors in publicly registered ventures neither of these conditions holds true. Hence, it is frequently impractical to generate the information you need for fundamental analysis even when specific assets are identified.

Syndicators often include a cash-flow forecast in their promotional material. At first blush this seems to solve your data collection problem. The difficulty, of course, is that you have no way to evaluate the accuracy of the forecasts without replicating the research—which once again brings you hard against the reality of economies of scale.

A Horse of a Different Hue

So far we have looked at peculiarities of publicly registered limited partnerships. This is the industry's highly visible segment, but it may account for less than half the dollar amount of real estate syndication activity. It certainly amounts to considerably less than half the number of syndicated ventures.

The majority of real estate syndicators seek to avoid having to run the full gamut of Securities and Exchange Commission (SEC) registration requirements. They do this by claiming exemption either as private placements or as intrastate offerings. Most claim both exemptions.

Many investors find it a novel concept that limited partnership shares are securities, just as are stocks and bonds, and therefore subject to regulatory oversight by the SEC. The Securities Act of 1933 says *securities* include:

> ...any note, stock, treasury stock, bond, debenture, evidence of indebtedness, certificate of interest or participation in any profit-sharing agreement, collateral-trust certificate, preorganization certificate or subscription, transferable share, investment contract, voting-trust certificate, certificate of deposit for a security, fractional undivided interest in oil, gas, or other mineral rights, or in general, any interest or instrument commonly known as a 'security', or any certificate of interest or participation in, temporary or interim certificate for, receipt for, guarantee of, or warrant or right to subscribe to or purchase any of the foregoing.

That's almost comprehensive enough to include joint ownership of your home with your spouse. The Supreme Court removed any lingering doubt about the sweep of SEC authority by ruling in 1946 that an investment contract (and, therefore, a security) exists if individuals invest in a common enterprise and are led to expect profits, and profits come about as the result of the activity of a third party or the promoter. Clearly, limited partnership shares fit this description.

To avoid the considerable expense of compliance with SEC registration, most syndication sponsors seek exemption both as intrastate businesses and as private placements. By claiming both, they have a fallback position if one of the exemptions is denied.

To qualify for a private placement exemption, syndicators have to refrain from general solicitation or advertising and are permitted to sell the securities to only a few investors. Hence, you hear very little about these ventures. All purchasers must acquire securities solely as personal investments, with no resale intentions. The SEC places severe restrictions on the nature of investors to whom the securities may be offered.

The rules are complex, but, essentially, investors must be either wealthy or wise. A "wise" investor is one who understands the risks and potential rewards, or is represented by a designated *purchaser's representative*. To be considered wealthy (an *accredited investor*), you must:

• Be wealthy enough so that your purchase (which must total at least $150,000) does not exceed 20 percent of your net worth, *or*
• have a net worth (in concert with your spouse) in excess of $1 million, *or*
• have had income in excess of $200,000 for each of the last two years, and expect your income to exceed $200,000 in the current year.

To get the intrastate offering exemption, syndicators must be residents of the state in which the offering is made and must sell partnership shares only to residents of that state. The responsibility for determining investors' residency status rests solely with the sponsor. Moreover, there can be no out-of-state resales within nine months of the offering. Also, at least 80 percent of partnership assets must be in the state, and at least 80 percent of partnership income must originate there.

An important consequence of these rules is that most private placement real estate partnerships are local deals. You can visit the property, kick the bricks, drive the neighborhood, and get a feel for the venture. Moreover, you will usually be required to put up a big hunk of cash, and this warrants some investment in research and analysis. With private placements you will usually find it prudent to proceed in much the same manner as if you were to be the property's sole owner.

A nice aspect of most private placements is that much more of your money actually finds its way into the property. There should be no commissions to securities firms, and organizational fees should be modest relative to the venture's size. Look for deals where the general partners will take their compensation on the back end, or where compensation is firmly tied to performance. Don't allow a sponsor to take a property acquisition fee up front.

ENSURING CONDUIT TREATMENT

A number of serious income tax problems can befall the unwary or unfortunate partnership investor. Being treated by the IRS as an "association to be taxed as a corporation" may be the most serious of these. The size of publicly registered syndicates, the degree of regulatory oversight, and the amount of legal and accounting experience of professional advisors generally preclude this disaster. Private placements, particularly small ventures where there might be a temptation to economize on the degree and quality of professional guidance, are more vulnerable.

An organization is treated as a partnership for tax purposes if it does not have more corporate than partnership characteristics. IRS regulations spell out six characteristics, two of which—the existence of associates and the objective to carry on a business and divide the profits—are common to both partnerships and corporations. The remaining four, therefore, determine whether the entity is treated as an association or a partnership. The four critical corporate characteristics are:

- Continuity of life.
- Centralized management.
- Limited liability for all partners.
- Free transferability of interests.

Treasury Regulation 301.7701-2 contains rules for determining whether these corporate characteristics exist. It states that continuity of life does not exist if an organization is not continued in the event of death, insanity, bankruptcy, retirement, resignation, or expulsion of any member, without the express agreement of all remaining members. Since such a provision is included in the Uniform Limited Partnership Act, continuity of life does not exist for limited partnerships in states having statutes corresponding to that act. In other states, an article in the partnership agreement to the effect that unanimous agreement is required to continue the partnership under these circumstances should ensure that the partnership lacks continuity of life.

Centralized management is deemed to exist under Regulation 301.7701-2 when a general partner resembles "in powers and functions the directors of a statutory corporation." This implies that management is empowered to make independent business decisions on behalf of the organization without need for ratification. The regulation goes on to state that limited partnerships generally do not have centralized management unless ". . . substantially all the interests in the partnership are owned by the limited partners."

The corporate characteristic of limited liability exists if partnership creditors may look only to the assets of the organization for satisfaction. In a limited partnership, of course, debtors may look to the general partner or partners for satisfaction when debts exceed the assets of the partnership. If general partners are not possessed of substantial assets from which to satisfy such claims, however, their personal liability may be ruled a sham by the IRS. The partnership would then be considered to provide limited liability for all partners. Just what constitutes substantial assets is not specified by the IRS. The IRS has, however, specified net worth requirements for general partners before it provides an advance ruling on the question.

Free transferability of interests is the final corporate characteristic not always present in partnerships. If a member's interest can be transferred to an outsider without the consent of other members, conferring on the outsider all rights and privileges of the transferer, then free transferability exists. A mere assignment of rights to share in profits does not constitute free transferability as defined by the regulation. It is generally relatively simple to avoid the free transferability of interests characteristic by making the transfer to outsiders subject to a consent requirement, though the consent requirement may be ruled a sham if it is routinely given.

Remember that to be treated as a taxable association the partnership must have more corporate than partnership characteristics. This means that three of the four characteristics must be present. A carefully drawn agreement should circumvent this without sacrificing the flexibility general partners need to ensure successful pursuit of investment goals. Treasury Regulation 301.7701-3(b)(2) contains two examples of real estate organizations that qualify for treatment as partnerships. These examples are reproduced here as Examples 14–1 and 14–2.

Example 14–1. Three individuals form an organization that qualifies as a limited partnership under the laws of the state in which the organization was formed. The purpose of the organization is to acquire and operate various pieces of commercial and other investment property for profit. Each of the three individuals who are general partners invests $100,000 in the enterprise. Five million dollars of additional capital is raised through contributions of $100,000 or more by each of 30 limited partners. The three general partners are personally capable of assuming a substantial part of the obligations to be incurred by the organization. While a limited partner may assign his or her right to receive a share of the profits and a return of his or her contribution, his or her assignee does not become a substituted limited partner except with the unanimous consent of the general partners. The life of the organization as stated in the certificate is 20 years, but the death, insanity, or retirement of a general partner prior to the expiration of the 20-year period will dissolve the organization. The general partners have exclusive authority to manage the affairs of the organization but can act only unanimously. The organization has associates and an objective to carry on business and divide the gains therefrom, which characterize both partnerships and corporations. While the organization has the corporate characteristic of centralized management since substantially all of the interests in the organization are owned by the limited partners, it does not have the characteristics of continuity of life, free transferability of interests, or limited liability. The organization will be classified as partnership for all purposes of the Internal Revenue Code.

Example 14–2. Three individuals form an organization that qualifies as a limited partnership under the laws of the state in which the organization was formed. The purpose of the organization is to acquire and operate various pieces of commercial and other investment property for profit. The certificate provides that the life of the organization is to be 40 years unless a general partner dies, becomes insane, or retires during such period. On the occurrence of such death, insanity, or retirement, the remaining general partners may continue the business of the partnership for the balance of the 40-year period under a right stated in the certificate. Each of the three general partners invests $50,000 in the enterprise and has means to satisfy the business obligations of the organization to a substantial extent. Five million dollars of additional capital is raised through the sale of freely transferable interests in amounts of $10,000 or less to limited partners. Nine hundred such interests are sold. The interests of the 900 limited partners are fully transferable; that is, a transferee acquires all the attributes of the transferer's interest in the organization. The general partners have exclusive control over management of the business, their interests are not transferable, and their liability for debts of the organization is not limited to their capital contributions. The organization has associates and an objective to carry on business and divide the gains therefrom. It does not have the corporate characteristics of limited liability and continuity of life. It has centralized management, however, since the three general partners exercise exclusive control over the management of the business and since substantially all of the interests in the organization are owned by the limited partners. While the interests of the general partners are not transferable, substantially all of the interests in the organization are represented by transferable interests. However, since it does not have three of the four corporate characteristics, the organization will be classified as a partnership for all purposes of the Internal Revenue Code.

KEY POINTS

• Limited partnerships are tax conduits, which means the income tax consequences pass directly through to the partners rather than being attributed to the partnership itself. Income and losses from limited partnership shares, however, are treated as passive items under the current Internal Revenue Code. This means you will be able to deduct net losses from partnership shares only if you have enough income from other passive sources to offset the losses. Any remaining passive losses must be carried forward until you either generate passive income or sell the passive asset.

• Publicly registered limited partnerships usually work out well for the general partner no matter what happens to the limited partners. As a limited partner you have no control over the investment outcome and no assurance that the project will be operated in your best interest.

• Your limited partnership shares must be considered essentially illiquid. Under most circumstances you can sell your shares only at a substantial discount.

• Research findings suggest that average annual after-tax yields on publicly registered limited partnerships are not significantly greater than you could get from holding T-bills. Yet the partnership shares are much less liquid and entail substantially greater risk.

• Private placement syndicates often represent a better deal than do publicly registered ventures. Make sure that the sponsor's compensation in your private placement deal is rigidly tied to partnership performance, so that your success is mutually dependent. Also, plan to put enough money into the deal that you can afford to economically commission a professional analysis of the proposal before you commit your funds

CHAPTER 15

REAL ESTATE INVESTMENT TRUSTS

Like Henry Higgins in *My Fair Lady*, investors often ask, "Why can't real estate be more like a mutual fund?" They would like the positive characteristics of real estate assets—such as inflation protection and a relatively predictable income stream—but are not anxious to give up the convenience, liquidity, and freedom from management chores characteristic of mutual funds.

Well, now you can have the best of both worlds. Real estate investment trusts (REITs, pronounced "reets") sell shares in themselves and invest in real estate assets. The concept is very much the same as closed-end mutual funds, except for the nature of the assets held in the portfolio. One key difference from mutual funds is that REITs borrow against their equity—they use financial leverage much as an individual investor would.

THE REIT ADVANTAGE

Buying a direct ownership interest in real estate or taking a position in a private placement syndication takes a lot of cash. You can get in with less money when you buy shares in publicly registered syndications, but, as we saw in the previous chapter, vou may pay dearly in terms of fees and expenses.

With REIT shares you can get in cheaply without the penalty that accompanies public syndications. Since REIT shares come in easily affordable denominations—typically $10 to $30 per share—you can add to your portfolio whenever you have more money to invest.

REITs' big advantage over more conventional approaches to real estate investment, though, can be summed up in a single word: *marketability*. Shares of the larger REITs are actively traded on secondary securities markets. Direct ownership of real estate equities or mortgage instruments creates serious (though not necessarily insurmountable) barriers to partial liquidation, and limited partnership shares are usually even less liquid than are direct ownership interests. In contrast, REIT shareholders can sell as few or as many of their shares as they wish by the simple expedient of a telephone call to their securities broker.

Another big REIT advantage is professional management at an affordable price. Centralized management is by knowledgeable professionals who operate under the direction of a board of directors or trustees, a majority of whom do not have any affiliation with the managers. Publicly registered limited partnerships may have equally skilled and knowledgeable managers, but the limited partners pay a much higher price for the service. Moreover, syndicate management is often a captive of the sponsor, and one cannot escape the impression that management decisions are often designed more to benefit the sponsoring general partner than the limited partners who provide the funds.

With REITs you can get diversification on a budget. Since many REITs hold a geographically diversified portfolio of real estate assets, even a small investment buys you an interest in a large diversified portfolio. Because REIT shares are so inexpensive, you can further diversify with a limited budget by buying shares in several REITs whose portfolio composition differs. This reduces the risk of economic downturns in any single geographic area or type of business.

Variety in REIT operational objectives enables you to structure a REIT portfolio to fit virtually any financial goal. For example, you can buy into REITs that generate high levels of current income or that hold real estate with substantial appreciation potential. You can find REITs whose assets comprise an excellent inflation hedge or whose assets are a comfortable cushion against recession.

VARIETY IN REIT OPERATIONS

REITs are required by law to hold at least 75 percent of their assets in real estate-related assets, cash items, or government securities, and to derive at least 75 percent of their gross income from rents, mortgage interest, or selling real estate assets. Within the limits imposed by these provisions, REIT investment powers are broad. Most have shown a distinct preference for certain types of assets, however, and specific investment policies are embedded in articles of incorporation so that a policy change requires shareholder approval.

Consequently, REITs can be conveniently categorized according to broad investment policy. Those with a revealed preference for mortgage-secured lending are frequently called *mortgage REITs*; those that show a preference for ownership of real estate are usually called *equity REITs*. Others, termed *hybrids*, defy such simple categorization because they favor a mixed portfolio of mortgage notes and equities, altering the mix as opportunities and market conditions dictate.

The National Association of Real Estate Investment Trusts recently reported that about 29 percent of REITs invest primarily in equities, approximately 60 percent prefer mortgages, and the other 11 percent hold hybrid portfolios.

How Mortgage REITs Operate

Mortgage REITs lend funds for property construction and development and for permanent mortgage financing. Development loans are used to finance site improvements such as clearing and grading land and for building roads and sewers. Construction loans finance the construction phase of housing developments, apartments, and commercial structures and are secured by first mortgage liens on the property.

Construction and development lending has an almost irresistible attraction: high yields. Even so, this represents a relatively small portion of mortgage REIT assets. Recent data from the National Association of Real Estate Investment Trusts showed construction and development loans accounted for less than 8 percent of all REIT mortgage loans. In contrast, data compiled by independent researchers some 20 years ago showed these loans represented about half of all mortgage-secured REIT loans.

Why the shift away from high-yielding construction and development loans since the decade of the 1970s? REITs found the high yields carried substantial risks, revealed in widespread distress and a number of REIT failures during that decade.

Today, the overwhelming preference of mortgage REITs is for long-term mortgage notes—so-called *permanent* loans. Permanent mortgage lending yields are somewhat lower but are considerably less risky. Yields on long-term loans are still higher than those earned by most equity REITs. But there is substantial risk associated with a portfolio of fixed-income securities such as mortgages. Many mortgage REITs hedge the risk by holding loans with equity kickers, provisions that give the lender a share of any increase in the mortgaged property's appreciation.

Eclectic Equity REITs

Equity REITs hold a portfolio of income-producing properties; residential, commercial, or industrial. Most REITs specialize in a particular type of property such as shopping centers or office buildings, and many concentrate their portfolio in a particular region of the country. Others hold a diversified portfolio that includes a variety of property types (warehouses, shopping centers, industrial buildings, and so on). Very large REITs often own properties scattered from coast to coast.

Equity REITs outshine their mortgage REIT cousins in their reputation for steady growth and capital appreciation coupled with regular dividends. They generally avoid highly leveraged deals, a strategy that has served them well during cyclical economic downturns.

The Hybrids

Hybrids hold a combination of equity interests and mortgage-secured notes. They expect this to deliver a higher dividend record than the equity REITs yet provide some inflation protection coupled with appreciation potential. Property ownership gives them a conservative anchor while their mortgage portfolio gives their earnings a boost.

Hybrids seek to capture the best of both worlds. But as an investor you have no control over the balance between equities and mortgages. In contrast, you can construct your own hybrid portfolio by owning both mortgage and equity REITs. If you adopt this alternative approach, you control the mix and can alter it as changing economic conditions dictate.

REIT SELECTION SUGGESTIONS

As with any investment, REIT shares are far from a sure thing. You can improve your chances of a decent yield by following some common-sense suggestions designed to avoid major REIT mishaps.

Stick with Actively Traded REITs

One big advantage REITs have over limited partnerships is liquidity. REIT shares are like those of closed-end mutual funds—they are bought and sold on secondary securities markets. But not all REITs are equally liquid. If your shares are not actively traded there is likely to be a substantial spread between bid and asked prices. The wider the spread the greater the penalty you pay for liquidating your position.

To avoid liquidity problems associated with inactively traded shares, you might want to concentrate your investments on those REITs with a substantial volume of shares widely distributed over a large number of investors.

Avoid Initial Public Offerings

Internal Revenue Code provisions in 1986 radically altered the comparative advantages of REITs over limited partnerships. One consequence has been a proliferation of new REIT issues. As a general rule, new issues carry higher risk relative to yield possibilities.

In most cases no properties will have yet been acquired when new shares are being sold. You will be buying into a blind pool, and there is no guarantee that the REIT will be able to acquire quality properties at a price that makes the investment reasonable. There is no established dividend stream, no management performance record, and no established appreciation trend. In short, the venture is untested.

New stock issues are costly to peddle. Someone has to pay the investment bankers who push the shares on investors. That someone is the first group of shareholders. This capitalization of underwriting costs is one of the reasons most stocks decline in price shortly after an initial public offering. The best way to avoid bearing the underwriting costs is to wait and buy your shares on the secondary market. Doing so does not guarantee you an advantageous price, but it does give some assurance that the price reflects careful evaluation after reasonable market exposure.

Beware of Finite-Life REITs

Recently a new form of REIT has become popular. It has a fixed life rather than an indefinite one. These finite-life REITs (called FREITs) have a stated life at their inception, after which managers must sell the assets, distribute the proceeds, and dissolve the fund. This gives the investor a time frame for expecting to receive the underlying value of the shares.

The average FREIT has a life of 10 to 15 years; some have a fixed number of years, while others have a range of three to four years during which they must be dissolved. Some charters permit shareholders to vote on extending the fund's life.

Some people prefer FREITs over traditional REITs because the forced sale of FREIT assets assures investors that they will eventually receive the full value of underlying assets. They claim that REITs often own real estate that is worth considerably more than book value, and observe that REITs usually sell at a discount below asset value.

We find the counterargument more compelling. Because FREITs are locked into a dissolution date set seven to ten years in advance, there is no way to determine what the real estate market will be like during the liquidation phase. Real estate is a cyclical industry, and the liquidation may well occur at the bottom of the cycle.

It seems more prudent to avoid FREITs. The typical discount at which REITs sell is no disadvantage when buying on the secondary market. Having bought at a discount, you should not be distressed if you have to sell at an equally sharp discount. Historically, well-managed equity REITs have appreciated impressively. You can expect a steady dividend and comfortable inflation protection without subscribing to funds with flashy frills that offer more *show* than *go*.

REIT BACKGROUND NOTES

REITs are a relatively new phenomenon; they did not exist before 1960. Enabling legislation passed that year (the Real Estate Investment Trust Act, comprising sections 856 through 858 of the Internal Revenue Code) permits trusts that meet the act's criteria to be treated as intermediaries rather than corporate entities for tax purposes. This makes it possible for them to avoid the double taxation that plagues corporate shareholders.

To qualify as a tax-exempt intermediary, REITs must meet a detailed and exacting set of requirements. The principal criteria are the following.

• At least 95 percent of net annual earnings must be distributed to shareholders within one year.
• Shares must be held by at least 100 persons, with more than half of the outstanding shares not held by five or fewer individuals at any time during the last half of each taxable year.
• At least 75 percent of assets must be in real estate, loans secured by real property, shares in other REITs, cash, cash items, or government securities.
• At least 75 percent of gross income must come from rents, mortgage interest, and gains from selling real estate.
• The REIT must be a passive investor rather than an active participant in property operations and must engage *independent* real estate professionals to carry out certain management activities.

• The trust cannot engage in speculative, short-term holding of real estate for the purpose of selling for quick profits.

Investors, of course, may owe taxes on their share of distributed REIT earnings. Distributions fall into three categories: income, capital gains, and capital recovery. Distributions above the net income and capital gains level are considered a return of capital and are not taxed, although they are deducted from the investors' cost basis when they sell the REIT shares.

Initial REIT legislation permitted ownership solely of real estate equities. The law was revised in 1967 to permit ownership also of mortgage notes, and this ushered in a decade of almost frenetic REIT activity. As traditional sources of real estate financing—banks, S&Ls, and insurance companies—found in the late 1960s and early 1970s that depositors and policy holders who traditionally served as primary sources of funds were moving their money in search of higher yields, the lenders turned increasingly to newly formed mortgage REITs as an alternative source.

With no legal limit on the interest rates they could pay, REITs were able to compete successfully with the bond and money markets for available funds, which they then loaned in the mortgage markets. The spread between the interest earned and the interest paid made mortgage REITs very profitable, especially those active in high-rate construction and development lending.

The IRS requirement that they disburse at least 90 percent (now 95 percent) of net income to shareholders each year essentially deprived REITs of retained earnings as a way to finance growth. Their principal alternative was to borrow, mostly short term. Much of the money the REITs loaned for construction and development was raised by issuing short-term notes and commercial paper. (In 1973, 10 percent of all outstanding commercial paper in the United States had been issued by REITs.) This worked profitably and well so long as developers were able to secure end loans upon completion of construction and use the proceeds to retire their construction and development loans.

Disaster struck in the early 1970s. Many developers were unable to find long-term lenders to provide money with which to retire construction loans. The real estate market sank into recession and many completed projects sold for less than the amount of the outstanding construction loan. At the same time, interest rates began to rise and the REITs' spread became negative. Many builders could not afford the higher rates and defaulted on their loans. Most mortgage REITs with sizeable construction and development loan portfolios had severe cash-flow problems. Eventually, many faced bankruptcy.

In 1975 the American Institute of Certified Public Accountants established procedures for loan-loss provisions and valuing defaulted loans at their future recovery values. These very conservative accounting procedures drove total REIT assets down from $20.5 billion (in 1974) to $9.7 billion by the end of 1976. Many REIT shareholders saw their entire equity erased in the space of two years. One result has been a long-lasting investor aversion to REIT shares.

By the 1980s the whole approach to investing in real estate had changed, and REITs posted a comeback performance. The debacle of the 1970s gave management a valuable appreciation for the relationship between profit potential and risk. REITs are no longer as vulnerable to interest rate changes as they once were, and mangers are more adept at analyzing the safety and value of assets.

The Tax Reform Act of 1986 contains several provisions that will probably affect investor attitudes toward REITs. The main effect on real estate is the replacement of accelerated cost recovery by straight-line depreciation methods. Losses from passive investments will no longer shelter earned income. Since REITs have always used straight-line depreciation, there will be no need to reevaluate their assets, and since they have never been used to shelter income, they should benefit from the new tax laws. While there is no guarantee that real estate will be a good investment in the 1990s, REITs should be very appealing to those who are interested in real estate.

REIT CAPITAL STRUCTURE

REITs' capital structure can have a tremendous effect on their return and risk. All REITs use some equity ownership; those capitalized as trusts will issue shares of beneficial interest and those that are corporations will issue common stock and possibly preferred stock. Since REITs are required to pay out at least 95 percent of their earnings in dividends to retain their tax-exempt status, retained earnings can never be a major funding source. Those who include growth as an objective, therefore, must either borrow extensively or issue new equity.

When a REIT chooses to borrow funds to finance its assets, it is leveraging its investment portfolio. Favorable financial leverage occurs when the return on a debt-financed asset exceeds the cost of the funds borrowed to finance that asset. This increases the return on equity and the earnings per share available to stockholders.

Leveraging can increase an investor's per-share earnings, but it also increases risk exposure; it can multiply losses as well as profits. REITs that use short-term credit to finance long-term assets face having to renew the credit periodically. If rates rise in the interim, rolling the debt over may cost more than the REIT earns on its assets. Leverage that turns unfavorable in this fashion will reduce per-share earnings and probably cause share prices to fall. REITs facing higher debt costs may decide to sell assets rather than to renew the debt.

Interest rate risk can be reduced somewhat by carefully matching the maturities of the debt and the assets, a maneuver that will also reduce liquidity problems. Even the matching of maturities, however, will not solve all problems associated with leveraged investments. When debt costs remain stable but asset yields decline, leverage can still turn negative. Generally, the more leveraged a REIT, the more likely it is to fail under adverse conditions. Conversely, the more highly leveraged REITs will generate the most impressive returns under favorable conditions.

REIT EVALUATION PROBLEMS

Choosing a REIT involves estimating which fund has the highest return in relation to risk. This is not an easy task because the nature of the underlying assets generally causes REIT shares to trade at less than book value.

Since real property is not traded on a regular basis, appraisers estimate the value of income-producing property with one of several methods. *Market data* valuation uses the prices of recently sold buildings with similar attributes to evaluate the property. *Replacement cost* valuation estimates what it would cost to replace the building today, taking into consideration its age and condition. And the *income method* estimates future cash flows and uses the net present value of these cash flows to estimate value. Since all of these methods require subjective judgments, the appraised value may not reflect an accurate market value. These discrepancies can compound over a period of years.

Another valuation problem stems from the common appraisal practice of using price index trends to estimate price appreciation. If a property is in an area that suffers adverse economic conditions or less than the expected growth patterns, this practice greatly overstates the property's real value. This lack of standardization makes it difficult to arrive at a basis for comparison for REITs that own different types of property in different areas.

WHERE TO GET INFORMATION

Investing in REITs poses a special problem because there is a dearth of useful information. The industry is in its infancy, and new information sources will undoubtedly emerge as share ownership becomes more widespread.

The National Association of Real Estate Investment Trusts has developed a REIT share price index using 1972 as a base year. They also publish a monthly newsletter, *REIT Line*, which contains the share price index.

Even though it is difficult to compare measures of value and return between REITs and other stocks, some useful operating measures are published. Value Line Investment Surveys, Moody's Investors Service, and Standard and Poor's Corporation all provide potentially valuable data pertaining to prices, earnings, and the composition of assets and liabilities.

No single information source provides data on all REITs, but the largest ones are covered by one or more of these publications. *Value Line* summarizes key information relevant to each fund the service tracks, and gives a brief summary of recent developments that may point to where the fund is heading. *Moody's Financials* reports the operating statements of each REIT that it tracks. *Standard and Poor's* furnishes annual reports of several REITs.

Clues to REIT managers' experience and ability can be found in the various *Who's Who* books and in *Dun's Reference Book of Corporate Managements*. Reviewing managers' records may give you an idea of how experienced and successful they have been in the past, and this is often the best indicator of what they will do in the future.

KEY POINTS

• REITs are superior to limited partnerships in at least one dimension: They are infinitely more marketable. If you limit your holdings to REITs that are actively traded, they will be just as liquid as common stock.

• REITs are similar to closed-end mutual funds in that they hold a portfolio of assets yet pay no income tax. Taxable income, if distributed to shareholders, is taxable directly to the shareholders rather than to the REIT.

• The pass-through of taxable income to shareholders is similar to the tax treatment of limited partners. But, unlike limited partnerships, REITs cannot pass losses through to shareholders. Moreover, REIT income is treated as portfolio income by the IRS. In contrast, partnership income is treated as passive income.

• Some REITs specialize in rental property, others in mortgage-secured promissory notes, and others hold a combination of realty and debt. You can indirectly manage the relative percentage of realty and debt by altering the composition of REIT shares in your portfolio.

APPENDIX A

THE SIMPLE MATHEMATICS
OF REAL ESTATE FINANCE

All of modern investment and financial theory rests firmly on the concept of compound interest and discount. Thus, a thorough grounding in the subject is an essential prerequisite to understanding investment decision-making processes. Failure to master this analytical tool will render any modern investment text utterly incomprehensible.

Conceptual Basis for Discounting

Two fundamental propositions form the theoretical basis for discounting: more is better than less, and sooner is better than later. The first proposition is so obvious that it needs little elaboration. The second becomes equally evident with a minimum of consideration.

Better More than Less. That more of a good thing is better than less is disputed only by philosophers and mystics. Economists have considered this a self-evident proposition since the dawn of their discipline. If one bottle of champagne is gratifying, two will be even more so; three are even more desirable than two, and so forth. Fundamental to the concept (and certainly to our example) is that one need not consume the greater quantity if one wishes not to do so. Increased gratification, therefore, stems from certain knowledge that more is readily available if desired. Two bottles thus provide the same option as one, plus the additional option of continued imbibition.

Better Sooner than Later.   A preference for present over future consumption is only one step further into abstraction. Who would not (other things being equal) prefer $5 today to the certain promise of $5 next week? Choosing the promise reduces one's options without offering something in return. Current receipt, in contrast, permits consumption either now, next week, or any time in the distant future. Clearly, a good's want-satisfying power is enhanced by current receipt.

Compound Interest

If a $1,000 loan for one year requires a payment of $1,070 at the end of the year, the amount of interest is $1,070 less $1,000, or $70. The rate of interest is $70/$1000, or 7 percent per annum. This simple example incorporates all the mechanics of compound interest. The general relationship may be expressed as

Amount repaid = amount borrowed + interest

Since annual interest is usually expressed as a rate or percentage of the amount borrowed (the principal), the same relationship may be expressed as

Amount repaid
= amount borrowed + (amount borrowed × interest rate)

Rearranging the right-hand terms yields

Amount repaid = amount borrowed × $(1 + i)$

where i is the interest rate. In the earlier illustration of a $1,000 loan for one year at an interest rate of 7 percent, this becomes

$$\$1,070 = \$1,000 \times 1.07$$

Suppose the $1,000 loan was for three years, with interest at 7 percent per annum and with the entire payment (principal and compound interest) due at the end of the third year. Table A–1 illustrates how compound interest accumulates so that the amount to be repaid after three years equals $1,225.04. If we express the calculations in Table A–1 in terms of the equation

$$\text{Amount repaid} = \text{amount borrowed} \times (1 + i)$$

the amount to be repaid after three years is:

After 1 year:

$$\$1,000 \times 1.07$$

After 2 years:

$$(\$1,000 \times 1.07)(1.07) = (\$1,000)(1.07)^2$$

After 3 years:

$$
\begin{aligned}
(\$1,000 \times 1.07)\,(1.07)\,(1.07) &= (\$1,000)\,(1.07)^3 \\
&= \$1,000 \times 1.22504 \\
&= \$1,225.04
\end{aligned}
$$

This relationship between principal, compound interest, and time is summarized in more general fashion as

$$V_n = P(1 + i)^n$$

where V_n is the amount to be received in the future (value in period n), P is the initial amount deposited (or present value), i is the interest rate, and n is the number of time periods involved.

In Table A–1, P is the initial \$1,000 loan and V_n is the \$1,225.04 due at maturity. But the formula applies equally when P is the amount of a deposit or an investment of any kind, and V_n is the expected amount to be received at a future date. The only laborious arithmetic in the formula is raising $(1 + i)^n$ to the nth power. For the problem illustrated in Table A–1, there are only three periods over which to calculate the

TABLE A–1
Accumulation of Compound Interest

Year	Amount Owed at Start of Current Year	Plus Interest at 7 percent	Amount Owed at Year-End
1	$1,000.00	0.07 × $1,000.00	$1,070.00
2	$1,070.00	0.07 × $1,070.00	$1,144.90
3	$1,144.90	0.07 × $1,144.90	$1,225.04

TABLE A–2
How $1 Left on Deposit at Compound Interest Will Grow

Period	6%	7%	8%	9%	10%	12%	14%
				Compound Interest Rate			
1	1.0600	1.0700	1.0800	1.0900	1.1000	1.1200	1.1400
2	1.1236	1.1449	1.1664	1.1881	1.2100	1.2544	1.2996
3	1.1910	1.2250	1.2597	1.2950	1.3310	1.4049	1.4815
4	1.2625	1.3108	1.3605	1.4116	1.4641	1.5735	1.6890
5	1.3382	1.4026	1.4693	1.5386	1.6105	1.7623	1.9254
6	1.4185	1.5007	1.5869	1.6771	1.7716	1.9738	2.1950
7	1.5036	1.6058	1.7138	1.8280	1.9487	2.2107	2.5023
8	1.5938	1.7182	1.8509	1.9926	2.1436	2.4760	2.8526
9	1.6895	1.8385	1.9990	2.1719	2.3579	2.7731	3.2519
10	1.7908	1.9672	2.1589	2.3674	2.5937	3.1058	3.7072

compound amount. But suppose there had been 75 periods. In the absence of a good calculator or a set of tables, calculating $(1 + i)^{75}$ would be tedious in the extreme.

Fortunately, tables are readily available that give solutions to $(1 + i)^n$ for various values of both i and n. An excerpt from such a table, for some representative values of i and n, is reproduced above as Table A–2. The time periods in the table are expressed as years, but they could just as well be days, months, quarters, or any other period appropriate to the problem being considered. A more complete table can be found in almost any standard finance textbook.

The earlier problem of the amount to be repaid on a $1,000, three-year loan with compound interest at 7 percent per annum can be solved quickly by reference to Table A–2. Simply extract the value for $(1 + 0.07)^3$ by reading down the 7 percent column and across the third (three-year) row. That factor (1.2250) is the compound amount of $1 left on deposit for three years at 7 percent. Multiplying this factor by the initial payment P of $1,000 yields the value for V_n: $1,225.00. (Note the four-cent cumulative rounding error in the table.)

Let's work another example. Suppose a vacant lot in a local subdivision is available for $5,000. The lot is expected to increase in value at a compound rate of 10 percent per annum for the next several years. What is the expected value of the lot after seven years? A solution is given by the equation

$$V_n = (\$5,000) \times (1.10)^7$$

where V_n is the expected value at the end of the seventh year. The factor $(1.10)^7$ can be read from Table A–2 at the intersection of the 10 percent column and the seven-year row. This factor, 1.9487, multiplied by the initial $5,000 market value of the property gives its expected value of $9,744 after seven years.

Present Value of a Future Amount

The equation for the future value of an initial amount can easily be altered to solve for a known future value and an unknown initial amount. The restructured equation is

$$P = V_n[1/(1 + i)^n]$$

where the symbols have the same meaning as before, but the initial amount P is the unknown. In this form, the equation is used to solve problems involving the present value of known or estimated future amounts or the interest (discount) rate required to equate known present values with known or estimated future amounts.

Suppose a parcel of land is expected to sell for $1,500 per acre when sewer lines are extended five years hence. What is the most an investor can pay for the land today if he expects to earn 12 percent per annum on his investment?

When we place the known interest rate (12 percent per annum) and future value ($1,500) into the equation for determining the present value of a known or estimated future amount, we get

$$P = \$1,500(1/1.12^5)$$
$$= \$851$$

Solving for the value of $1/(1 + i)^n$ would be laborious when n is a high number were it not for precalculated tables of values for this factor. The solution to $1/1.12^5$, used to solve the last equation, can be read directly from Table A–3 by reading down

TABLE A–3
Present Value of $1 Due at a Future Date

				Discount Rate			
Period	6%	7%	8%	9%	10%	12%	14%
1	0.9434	0.9346	0.9259	0.9174	0.9091	0.8929	0.8772
2	0.8900	0.8734	0.8573	0.8417	0.8264	0.7972	0.7695
3	0.8396	0.8163	0.7938	0.7722	0.7513	0.7118	0.6750
4	0.7921	0.7629	0.7350	0.7084	0.6830	0.6355	0.5921
5	0.7473	0.7130	0.6806	0.6499	0.6209	0.5674	0.5194
6	0.7050	0.6663	0.6302	0.5963	0.5645	0.5066	0.4556
7	0.6651	0.6227	0.5835	0.5470	0.5132	0.4523	0.3996
8	0.6274	0.5820	0.5403	0.5019	0.4665	0.4039	0.3506
9	0.5919	0.5439	0.5002	0.4604	0.4241	0.3606	0.3075
10	0.5584	0.5083	0.4632	0.4224	0.3855	0.3220	0.2697

the 12 percent column and across the five-year row. The factor at the intersection of the column and row is 0.5674. Multiplying this by the expected future value of the land ($1,500) gives the present value of $851.

Note the distinction between Tables A–2 and A–3. The first gives values for $(1 + i)^n$, while the latter gives values for $1/(1 + i)^n$. Because these are reciprocals, separate tables are not really needed. All the values for either table can be derived by dividing the corresponding values from the other table into 1. Both tables are generally provided, however, because it is easier for most people to multiply than to divide.

A by-product of the added convenience of two tables is the attendant problem of determining which to use. One way to keep this straight is to remember that the solution to factors on the future-value table $[(1 + i)^n]$ is always greater than that for the present-value table $[1/(1 + i)^n]$ for the same interest rate so long as the rate is greater than zero. This reflects the basic idea that an amount received in the present is always more valuable than the certain promise of receiving the same amount at a future date. A more extensive set of values for $1/(1 + i)^n$ is given in Appendix B.

Present Value of An Annuity

Any series of periodic payments received or paid at regular intervals may be termed an *annuity*. Examples include pension checks from a retirement fund or payments on a fully amortized installment note. While all such regular periodic streams of cash technically qualify as annuities, not all are popularly known as such.

The present value of an annuity is best thought of as the amount that, if invested today at a given interest rate, would provide the known periodic payments for the prescribed period. Suppose, for example, funds are placed on deposit with interest at 6 percent per annum (compounded annually) and are to be withdrawn in $1,000 increments at the end of each year for three years. To determine how much has to be deposited if the balance of the account is to be exactly zero after the third annual withdrawal, you can use the factors in Table A–3 or you can refer to an annuity table.

To answer the question using Table A–3, first divide the problem into three subsections.

• *Question 1*: How much must be deposited today to provide $1,000 in one year?

To solve this problem, restructure the basic equation to solve for the present value, P_1:

$$P_1 = V_1 \times [1/(1 + i)^n]$$

where V_1 is the first periodic withdrawal, i is the interest rate, and there is just one compounding period. Substituting the appropriate numerical values into the equation, we have

$$P_1 = \$1,000 \times [1/(1.06)]$$

• *Question 2*: How much must be deposited today to provide $1,000 in two years?

Again, substitute the appropriate numbers into the basic equation. We determine that

$$P_2 = \$1,000 \times [1/(1.06)^2]$$

• **Question 3**: How much must be deposited today to provide $1,000 in three years?

Numerical substitution results in the following equation:

$$P_3 = \$1,000 \times [1/(1.06)^3]$$

The total amount to be deposited to provide for the three annual withdrawals is the sum of the three values just calculated. Therefore the total present value, P, is

$$P = \$1000 \times 1/1.06 + \$1000 \times 1/1.06^2 + \$1000 \times 1/1.06^3$$
$$= \$1000 \times [1/1.06 + 1/1.06^2 + 1/1.06^3]$$

Values for $1/1.06^t$, where t varies from 1 through 3, are found in the 6 percent column of Table A–3. Summing these three factors, we get

$$P = \$1,000 \times (0.9434 + 0.8900 + 0.8396)$$
$$= \$1,000 \times 2.6730$$
$$= \$2,673$$

The general form of the preceding computation can be expressed as

$$P = R[1/(1 + i) + 1/(1 + i)^2 + \ldots + 1/(1 + i)^n]$$

where R is the amount of a level periodic receipt, P is the present value, and i is the discount (interest) rate.

Alternatively, the same concept can be expressed as

$$P = R \sum_{t=1}^{n} 1/(1 + i)^t$$

where t indicates the time periods from 1 through n.

The practical problem in solving this type of calculation is the time required to do the computations when the number of compounding periods, and thus the exponent for $(1 + i)^t$, is very large. Precomputed tables for the troublesome factor again simplifies the problem. The preceding example can be solved quickly and simply by reference to the annuity factors in Appendix B, an excerpt of which is presented in Table A–4.

TABLE A–4
Present Value of an Annuity of $1

Period	Discount Rate						
	6%	7%	8%	9%	10%	12%	14%
1	0.9434	0.9346	0.9259	0.9174	0.9091	0.8929	0.8772
2	1.8334	1.8080	1.7833	1.7591	1.7355	1.6901	1.6467
3	2.6730	2.6243	2.5771	2.5313	2.4869	2.4018	2.3216
4	3.4651	3.3872	3.3121	3.2397	3.1699	3.0373	2.9137
5	4.2124	4.1002	3.9927	3.8897	3.7908	3.6048	3.4331
6	4.9173	4.7665	4.6229	4.4859	4.3553	4.1114	3.8887
7	5.5824	5.3893	5.2064	5.0330	4.8684	4.5638	4.2883
8	6.2098	5.9713	5.7466	5.5348	5.3349	4.9676	4.6389
9	6.8017	6.5152	6.2469	5.9952	5.7590	5.3282	4.9464
10	7.3601	7.0236	6.7101	6.4177	6.1446	5.6502	5.2161

To find the value for an annuity of $1 per annum, simply read down the column headed by the appropriate discount rate and across the row for the appropriate number of periods. The intersection of the column and row is the value of the summation of $1/(1 + i)^t$, where t ranges from 1 through n.

Using Table A–4 to solve the previous problem involves finding the factor for a discount rate of 6 percent for three years. That factor, 2.6730, multiplied by $1,000 gives the amount that must be initially deposited: $2,673.

Payments to Amortize a Loan

To determine the monthly payment needed to retire a level amortizing loan over a specified number of years, multiply the loan amount by the payment that would retire a $1 loan. A table of payment factors for a $1 loan is given in Appendix B, and an excerpt is presented here as Table A–5.

The factors in Table A–5 are often called *loan-repayment factors*, or *debt constants*. The table itself is referred to as an *amortization table*. Here's how you would use the table to determine the monthly payment necessary to retire a $100,000 loan if equal monthly payments are made over five years, with inter-

TABLE A–5
Installment to Amortize $1 (Monthly Payments)

Period	Interest Rate						
	6%	7%	8%	9%	10%	12%	14%
1	0.08607	0.08653	0.08699	0.08745	0.08792	0.08885	0.08979
2	0.04432	0.04477	0.04523	0.04568	0.04614	0.04707	0.04801
3	0.03042	0.03088	0.03134	0.03180	0.03227	0.03221	0.03418
4	0.02349	0.02395	0.02441	0.02489	0.02536	0.02633	0.02733
5	0.01933	0.01980	0.02028	0.02076	0.02125	0.02224	0.02327
6	0.01657	0.01705	0.01753	0.01803	0.01853	0.01955	0.02061
7	0.01461	0.01509	0.01559	0.01609	0.01660	0.01765	0.01874
8	0.01314	0.01363	0.01414	0.01465	0.01517	0.01625	0.01737
9	0.01201	0.01251	0.01302	0.01354	0.01408	0.01518	0.01633
10	0.01110	0.01161	0.01213	0.01267	0.01322	0.01435	0.01553

est at 8 percent per annum on the unpaid balance. At the intersection of the 8 percent column and the five-year row, find the amortization factor: 0.02028. Multiplying the factor by the $100,000 loan gives the required monthly payment: $2,028.

Remaining Balance on a Note

To determine the remaining balance on a fully amortizing loan, use the contract interest rate and discount the remaining payments as a level annuity. Payment periods for the discounting, however, must be the same as those required by the note.

Suppose you wanted to find the remaining balance after four years of a $10,000, 7 percent, ten-year note that requires monthly payments. First determine the amount of the monthly payment. This amount, $116.10, is found by multiplying the $10,000 face amount by the amortization factor at the intersection of the 7 percent column and the ten-year row from Table A–5. After four years, six years remain on the note. Therefore, discount the monthly payment as a six-year, monthly annuity.

A monthly annuity factor can be derived from the amortization table by taking the reciprocal of the amortization factor: 1/0.01705, or 58.6510. The present value of the remaining payments is therefore $116.10 × 58.6510, or $6,809.38.

APPENDIX B

FINANCIAL TABLES

TABLE B–1
Present Value of $1

Period	1%	2%	3%	4%	5%	6%	7%	8%	9%	10%
1	.9901	.9804	.9709	.9615	.9524	.9434	.9346	.9259	.9174	.9091
2	.9803	.9612	.9426	.9246	.9070	.8900	.8734	.8573	.8417	.8264
3	.9706	.9423	.9151	.8890	.8638	.8396	.8163	.7938	.7722	.7513
4	.9610	.9238	.8885	.8548	.8227	.7921	.7629	.7350	.7084	.6830
5	.9515	.9057	.8626	.8219	.7835	.7473	.7130	.6806	.6499	.6209
6	.9420	.8880	.8375	.7903	.7462	.7050	.6663	.6302	.5963	.5645
7	.9327	.8706	.8131	.7599	.7107	.6651	.6227	.5835	.5470	.5132
8	.9235	.8535	.7894	.7307	.6768	.6274	.5820	.5403	.5019	.4665
9	.9143	.8368	.7664	.7026	.6446	.5919	.5439	.5002	.4604	.4241
10	.9053	.8203	.7441	.6756	.6139	.5584	.5083	.4632	.4224	.3855
11	.8963	.8043	.7224	.6496	.5847	.5268	.4751	.4289	.3875	.3505
12	.8874	.7885	.7014	.6246	.5568	.4970	.4440	.3971	.3555	.3186
13	.8787	.7730	.6810	.6006	.5303	.4688	.4150	.3677	.3262	.2897
14	.8700	.7579	.6611	.5775	.5051	.4423	.3878	.3405	.2992	.2633
15	.8613	.7430	.6419	.5553	.4810	.4173	.3624	.3152	.2745	.2394
16	.8528	.7284	.6232	.5339	.4581	.3936	.3387	.2919	.2519	.2176
17	.8444	.7142	.6050	.5134	.4363	.3714	.3166	.2703	.2311	.1978
18	.8360	.7002	.5874	.4936	.4155	.3503	.2959	.2502	.2120	.1799
19	.8277	.6864	.5703	.4746	.3957	.3305	.2765	.2317	.1945	.1635
20	.8195	.6730	.5537	.4564	.3769	.3118	.2584	.2145	.1784	.1486
25	.7798	.6095	.4776	.3751	.2953	.2330	.1842	.1460	.1160	.0923
30	.7419	.5521	.4120	.3083	.2314	.1741	.1314	.0994	.0754	.0573
40	.6717	.4529	.3066	.2083	.1420	.0972	.0668	.0460	.0318	.0221
50	.6080	.3715	.2281	.1407	.0872	.0543	.0339	.0213	.0134	.0085
60	.5504	.3048	.1697	.0951	.0535	.0303	.0173	.0099	.0057	.0033

* The factor is zero to four decimal places.

TABLE B-1—Continued

12%	14%	15%	16%	18%	20%	24%	28%	32%	36%
.8929	.8772	.8696	.8621	.8475	.8333	.8065	.7813	.7576	.7353
.7972	.7695	.7561	.7432	.7182	.6944	.6504	.6104	.5739	.5407
.7118	.6750	.6575	.6407	.6086	.5787	.5245	.4768	.4348	.3975
.6355	.5921	.5718	.5523	.5158	.4823	.4230	.3725	.3294	.2923
.5674	.5194	.4972	.4761	.4371	.4019	.3411	.2910	.2495	.2149
.5066	.4556	.4323	.4104	.3704	.3349	.2751	.2274	.1890	.1580
.4523	.3996	.3759	.3538	.3139	.2791	.2218	.1776	.1432	.1162
.4039	.3506	.3269	.3050	.2660	.2326	.1789	.1388	.1085	.0854
.3606	.3075	.2843	.2630	.2255	.1938	.1443	.1084	.0822	.0628
.3220	.2697	.2472	.2267	.1911	.1615	.1164	.0847	.0623	.0462
.2875	.2366	.2149	.1954	.1619	.1346	.0938	.0662	.0472	.0340
.2567	.2076	.1869	.1685	.1372	.1122	.0757	.0517	.0357	.0250
.2292	.1821	.1625	.1452	.1163	.0935	.0610	.0404	.0271	.0184
.2046	.1597	.1413	.1252	.0985	.0779	.0492	.0316	.0205	.0135
.1827	.1401	.1229	.1079	.0835	.0649	.0397	.0247	.0155	.0099
.1631	.1229	.1069	.0930	.0708	.0541	.0320	.0193	.0118	.0073
.1456	.1078	.0929	.0802	.0600	.0451	.0258	.0150	.0089	.0054
.1300	.0946	.0808	.0691	.0508	.0376	.0208	.0118	.0068	.0039
.1161	.0829	.0703	.0596	.0431	.0313	.0168	.0092	.0051	.0029
.1037	.0728	.0611	.0514	.0365	.0261	.0135	.0072	.0039	.0021
.0588	.0378	.0304	.0245	.0160	.0105	.0046	.0021	.0010	.0005
.0334	.0196	.0151	.0116	.0070	.0042	.0016	.0006	.0002	.0001
.0107	.0053	.0037	.0026	.0013	.0007	.0002	.0001	*	*
0035	.0014	.0009	.0006	.0003	.0001	*	*	*	*
.0011	.0004	.0002	.0001	*	*	*	*	*	*

TABLE B–2

Present Value of an Annuity of $1 per Period for n Periods

Number of payments	1%	2%	3%	4%	5%	6%	7%	8%	9%
1	0.9901	0.9804	0.9709	0.9615	0.9524	0.9434	0.9346	0.9259	0.9174
2	1.9704	1.9416	1.9135	1.8861	1.8594	1.8334	1.8080	1.7833	1.7591
3	2.9410	2.8839	2.8286	2.7751	2.7232	2.6730	2.6243	2.5771	2.5313
4	3.9020	3.8077	3.7171	3.6299	3.5460	3.4651	3.3872	3.3121	3.2397
5	4.8534	4.7135	4.5797	4.4518	4.3295	4.2124	4.1002	3.9927	3.8897
6	5.7955	5.6014	5.4172	5.2421	5.0757	4.9173	4.7665	4.6229	4.4859
7	6.7282	6.4720	6.2303	6.0021	5.7864	5.5824	5.3893	5.2064	5.0330
8	7.6517	7.3255	7.0197	6.7327	6.4632	6.2098	5.9713	5.7466	5.5348
9	8.5660	8.1622	7.7861	7.4353	7.1078	6.8017	6.5152	6.2469	5.9952
10	9.4713	8.9826	8.5302	8.1109	7.7217	7.3601	7.0236	6.7101	6.4177
11	10.3676	9.7868	9.2526	8.7605	8.3064	7.8869	7.4987	7.1390	6.8052
12	11.2551	10.5753	9.9540	9.3851	8.8633	8.3838	7.9427	7.5361	7.1607
13	12.1337	11.3484	10.6350	9.9856	9.3936	8.8527	8.3577	7.9038	7.4869
14	13.0037	12.1062	11.2961	10.5631	9.8986	9.2950	8.7455	8.2442	7.7862
15	13.8651	12.8493	11.9379	11.1184	10.3797	9.7122	9.1079	8.5595	8.0607
16	14.7179	13.5777	12.5611	11.6523	10.8378	10.1059	9.4466	8.8514	8.3126
17	15.5623	14.2919	13.1661	12.1657	11.2741	10.4773	9.7632	9.1216	8.5436
18	16.3983	14.9920	13.7535	12.6593	11.6896	10.8276	10.0591	9.3719	8.7556
19	17.2260	15.6785	14.3238	13.1339	12.0853	11.1581	10.3356	9.6036	8.9501
20	18.0456	16.3514	14.8775	13.5903	12.4622	11.4699	10.5940	9.8181	9.1285
25	22.0232	19.5235	17.4131	15.6221	14.0939	12.7834	11.6536	10.6748	9.8226
30	25.8077	22.3965	19.6004	17.2920	15.3725	13.7648	12.4090	11.2578	10.2737
40	32.8347	27.3555	23.1148	19.7928	17.1591	15.0463	13.3317	11.9246	10.7574
50	39.1961	31.4236	25.7298	21.4822	18.2559	15.7619	13.8007	12.2335	10.9617
60	44.9550	34.7609	27.6756	22.6235	18.9293	16.1614	14.0392	12.3766	11.0480

TABLE B–2—Continued

10%	12%	14%	15%	16%	18%	20%	24%	28%	32%
0.9091	0.8929	0.8772	0.8696	0.8621	0.8475	0.8333	0.8065	0.7813	0.7576
1.7355	1.6901	1.6467	1.6257	1.6052	1.5656	1.5278	1.4568	1.3916	1.3315
2.4869	2.4018	2.3216	2.2832	2.2459	2.1743	2.1065	1.9813	1.8684	1.7663
3.1699	3.0373	2.9137	2.8550	2.7982	2.6901	2.5887	2.4043	2.2410	2.0957
3.7908	3.6048	3.4331	3.3522	3.2743	3.1272	2.9906	2.7454	2.5320	2.3452
4.3553	4.1114	3.8887	3.7845	3.6847	3.4976	3.3255	3.0205	2.7594	2.5342
4.8684	4.5638	4.2883	4.1604	4.0386	3.8115	3.6046	3.2423	2.9370	2.6775
5.3349	4.9676	4.6389	4.4873	4.3436	4.0776	3.8372	3.4212	3.0758	2.7860
5.7590	5.3282	4.9464	4.7716	4.6065	4.3030	4.0310	3.5655	3.1842	2.8681
6.1446	5.6502	5.2161	5.0188	4.8332	4.4941	4.1925	3.6819	3.2689	2.9304
6.4951	5.9377	5.4527	5.2337	5.0286	4.6560	4.3271	3.7757	3.3351	2.9776
6.8137	6.1944	5.6603	5.4206	5.1971	4.7932	4.4392	3.8514	3.3868	3.0133
7.1034	6.4235	5.8424	5.5831	5.3423	4.9095	4.5327	3.9124	3.4272	3.0404
7.3667	6.6282	6.0021	5.7245	5.4675	5.0081	4.6106	3.9616	3.4587	3.0609
7.6061	6.8109	6.1422	5.8474	5.5755	5.0916	4.6755	4.0013	3.4834	3.0764
7.8237	6.9740	6.2651	5.9542	5.6685	5.1624	4.7296	4.0333	3.5026	3.0882
8.0216	7.1196	6.3729	6.0472	5.7487	5.2223	4.7746	4.0591	3.5177	3.0971
8.2014	7.2497	6.4674	6.1280	5.8178	5.2732	4.8122	4.0799	3.5294	3.1039
8.3649	7.3658	6.5504	6.1982	5.8775	5.3162	4.8435	4.0967	3.5386	3.1090
8.5136	7.4694	6.6231	6.2593	5.9288	5.3527	4.8696	4.1103	3.5458	3.1129
9.0770	7.8431	6.8729	6.4641	6.0971	5.4669	4.9476	4.1474	3.5640	3.1220
9.4269	8.0552	7.0027	6.5660	6.1772	5.5168	4.9789	4.1601	3.5693	3.1242
9.7791	8.2438	7.1050	6.6418	6.2335	5.5482	4.9966	4.1659	3.5712	3.1250
9.9148	8.3045	7.1327	6.6605	6.2463	5.5541	4.9995	4.1666	3.5714	3.1250
9.9672	8.3240	7.1401	6.6651	6.2492	5.5553	4.9999 '	4.1667	3.5714	3.1250

TABLE B–3

Monthly Installment to Amortize a $1 Loan

Years	6.0%	6.5%	7.0%	7.5%	8.0%	8.5%	9.0%	9.5%	10.0%
1	.086066	.086296	.086527	.086757	.086988	.087220	.087451	.087684	.087916
2	.044321	.044546	.044773	.045000	.045227	.045456	.045685	.045914	.046145
3	.030422	.030649	.030887	.031106	.031336	.031568	.031800	.032033	.032267
4	.023485	.023715	.023946	.024179	.024413	.024648	.024885	.025123	.025363
5	.019333	.019566	.019801	.020038	.020276	.020517	.020758	.021002	.021247
6	.016573	.016810	.017049	.017290	.017533	.017778	.018026	.018275	.018526
7	.014609	.014849	.015093	.015338	.015586	.015836	.016089	.016344	.016601
8	.013141	.013386	.013634	.013884	.014137	.014392	.014650	.014911	.015174
9	.012006	.012255	.012506	.012761	.013019	.013279	.013543	.013809	.014079
10	.011102	.011355	.011611	.011870	.012133	.012399	.012668	.012940	.013215
11	.010367	.010624	.010884	.011148	.011415	.011686	.011961	.012239	.012520
12	.009759	.010019	.010284	.010552	.010825	.011101	.011380	.011644	.011951
13	.009247	.009512	.009781	.010054	.010331	.010612	.010897	.011186	.011478
14	.008812	.009081	.009354	.009631	.009913	.010199	.010489	.010784	.011082
15	.008439	.008711	.008988	.009270	.009557	.009847	.010143	.010442	.010746
16	.008114	.008391	.008672	.008958	.009249	.009545	.009845	.010150	.010459
17	.007831	.008111	.008397	.008687	.008983	.009283	.009588	.009898	.010212
18	.007582	.007866	.008155	.008450	.008750	.009055	.009364	.009679	.009998
19	.007361	.007649	.007942	.008241	.008545	.008854	.009169	.009488	.009813
20	.007164	.007456	.007753	.008056	.008364	.008678	.008997	.009321	.009650
21	.006989	.007284	.007585	.007892	.008204	.008522	.008846	.009174	.009508
22	.006831	.007129	.007434	.007745	.008062	.008384	.008712	.009045	.009382
23	.006688	.006991	.007299	.007614	.007935	.008261	.008593	.008930	.009272
24	.006560	.006865	.007178	.007496	.007821	.008151	.008487	.008828	.009174
25	.006443	.006752	.007068	.007390	.007718	.008052	.008392	.008737	.009087
26	.006337	.006649	.006968	.007294	.007626	.007964	.008307	.008656	.009010
27	.006240	.006556	.006878	.007207	.007543	.007884	.008231	.008584	.008941
28	.006151	.006470	.006796	.007129	.007468	.007812	.008163	.008519	.008880
29	.006070	.006392	.006721	.007057	.007399	.007748	.008102	.008461	.008825
30	.005996	.006321	.006653	.006992	.007338	.007689	.008046	.008409	.008776

TABLE B–3—Continued

10.5%	11.0%	11.5%	12.0%	13.0%	14.0%	15.0%	16.0%	17.0%
.088149	.088382	.088615	.088849	.089317	.089787	.090258	.090731	.091205
.046376	.046608	.046840	.047073	.047542	.048013	.048487	.048963	.049442
.032502	.032739	.032976	.033214	.033694	.034178	.034665	.035157	.035653
.025603	.025846	.026089	.026334	.026827	.027326	.027831	.028340	.028855
.021494	.021742	.021993	.022244	.022753	.023268	.023790	.024318	.024853
.018779	.019034	.019291	.019550	.020074	.020606	.021145	.021692	.022246
.016861	.017122	.017386	.017653	.018192	.018740	.019297	.019862	.020436
.015440	.015708	.015979	.016253	.016807	.017372	.017945	.018529	.019121
.014351	.014626	.014904	.015184	.015754	.016334	.016924	.017525	.018136
.013494	.013775	.014060	.014347	.014931	.015527	.016133	.016751	.017380
.012804	.013092	.013384	.013678	.014276	.014887	.015509	.016143	.016788
.012241	.012536	.012833	.013134	.013746	.014371	.015009	.015658	.016319
.011775	.012075	.012379	.012687	.013312	.013951	.014603	.015267	.015943
.011384	.011691	.012001	.012314	.012953	.013605	.014270	.014948	.015638
.011054	.011366	.011682	.012002	.012652	.013317	.013996	.014687	.015390
.010772	.011090	.011412	.011737	.012400	.013077	.013768	.014471	.015186
.010531	.010854	.011181	.011512	.012186	.012875	.013577	.014292	.015018
.010322	.010650	.010983	.011320	.012004	.012704	.013417	.014142	.014879
.010141	.010475	.010812	.011154	.011849	.012559	.013282	.014017	.014764
.009984	.010322	.010664	.011011	.011716	.012435	.013168	.013913	.014668
.009846	.010189	.010536	.010887	.011601	.012330	.013071	.013824	.014588
.009725	.010072	.010424	.010779	.011502	.012239	.012989	.013750	.014521
.009619	.009970	.010326	.010686	.011417	.012162	.012919	.013687	.014465
.009525	.009880	.010240	.010604	.011343	.012095	.012859	.013634	.014418
.009442	.009801	.010165	.010532	.011278	.012038	.012808	.013589	.014378
.009368	.009731	.010098	.010470	.011222	.011988	.012765	.013551	.014345
.009303	.009670	.010040	.010414	.011174	.011945	.012727	.013518	.014317
.009245	.009615	.009989	.010366	.011131	.011908	.012695	.013491	.014293
.009193	.009566	.009943	.010324	.011094	.011876	.012668	.013467	.014273
.009147	.009523	.009903	.010286	.011062	.011849	.012644	.013448	.014257

GLOSSARY OF TERMS

absorption rates Rates at which the market will take up a product; the rate at which units will be purchased.

acceleration clause A clause that permits the mortgagee to declare the full amount of a debt due and payable if the mortgagor defaults on any of the agreed-upon terms.

accrued depreciation A loss in value due to physical deterioration, functional obsolescence, and economic or locational disadvantage.

adjusted basis The amount paid for property, plus all subsequent capital expenditures made to improve it, minus all tax deductions for depreciation or cost recovery allowances.

adverse possession Wrongful occupancy of real estate in a manner and for a time period described in state statutes. Title then vests in the adverse possessor by operation of law and is independent of any previously recorded title to the property.

all-inclusive mortgage See wraparound mortgage.

alternative minimum tax A provision that specifies the minimum amount of federal income tax for which all taxpayers are liable. After computing tax liability the regular way, taxpayers must perform the alternative computation. They are required to pay the greater of the regular or the alternative minimum tax.

amortization table A schedule of equal periodic payments necessary to repay a $1 loan, with interest, over a specified number of payment periods.

amortize To claim a receipt or expenditure, which occurs at the beginning of the period, as an annual income or expense item over an extended period of years.

anchor tenants Tenants who are expected to attract customers to a shopping center and thereby generate business for other merchants in the center.

annual mortgage constant The percentage of the original principal amount that must be paid annually in order to fully repay interest and principal over the term of the loan.

annuity   Any series of periodic payments received or paid at regular intervals.

articles of agreement   See installment sales contract.

assignment   Transfer of contractual rights from one contracting party (the assignor) to another person (the assignee) who is not a party to the contract.

assumption clause   A clause whereby mortgagors agree not to sell mortgaged property subject to the mortgage or to have a buyer assume an existing mortgage without prior approval of the mortgagee.

assumption fee   A fee charged by a lender as a condition for permitting assumption of mortgage indebtedness by a party other than the original mortgagor. This permits mortgagees to adjust their rates of return to the current market when interest rates have risen.

blanket mortgage   The pledge of two or more parcels of property as security for a single loan.

blind pool syndication   A form of limited partnership in which the promoter assembles a group of investors with the purpose of acquiring an undesignated asset of a specific type.

book value   The value at which assets are recorded on a firm's books of account (that is, its accounting records); usually cost minus accumulated depreciation or cost recovery allowances.

boot   Assets received as consideration in what would otherwise be an exchange of entirely like-kind assets. Receipt of boot may trigger tax liability in what would otherwise be a tax-deferred transaction.

breakeven ratio   The relationship between cash expenditure requirements and net operating income from an investment project. Sometimes called a *default ratio*.

capitalization rate   The relationship between net income from a real estate investment and the value of the investment. This relationship is usually expressed as a percentage.

capitalize   To add an amount to the tax basis of a property

cash-on-cash rate of return   The first year's expected after-tax cash flow divided by the initial cash outlay required to acquire the investment.

certified historic structure   Any structure that is either listed in the National Registry of Historic Places or located in a registered historic district and certified as being of historic significance to the district.

commitment letter   A letter to a prospective borrower, wherein a lender states terms and conditions under which it will provide the requested funds. A precise period is usually specified during which the commitment remains effective. Commitment letters generally state conditions under which the lender may revoke the commitment and set forth any further provisions upon which the commitment is contingent.

community shopping center   A shopping center that typically draws most of its customers from an area extending from 10 to 15 minutes in driving time. Community shopping centers usually feature a food store and a junior department store or a discount store as anchor tenants. Size may range from 50,000 to 100,000 square feet of retail space.

compound interest   Interest income attributable to previously accrued interest that has been left on deposit.

condominium   An ownership arrangement whereby title to specified portions of a property vests in individual users, and title to common area vests in all users jointly.

conduit   See tax conduit.

consideration   Under contract law, the impelling reason to enter into a contract. Something of value given in exchange for a promise.

constructive notice   A legal doctrine under which notice may be attributed even though a party may be completely ignorant of the facts. Recording statutes provide that recording a document in the public record constitutes constructive notice to the world.

consumer price index   An index of changes in the price of a representative "market basket" of consumer goods, relating the current price to that in a designated base year.

contract for deed   See installment sales contract

contract price   Total selling price minus any pre-existing mortgage to which a property will remain subject when sold under conditions permitting the transaction to be reported for tax computation purposes under the installment sales method. If the pre-existing mortgage exceeds the seller's adjusted basis in the property, the excess of the mortgage over the seller's basis must be added back to the contract price

cooperative An apartment the tenant purchases by buying stock in the corporation that owns the building rather than by simply buying the apartment.

cost recovery allowance An income tax rule that provides for recovery of capital expenditures on property having a finite useful life, acquired on or after January 1, 1981, and used in a trade or business or for production of income.

cost recovery assets Assets on which tax-deductible cost recovery allowances may be claimed.

cotenancy Real property title held in the name of two or more owners.

covenant Promises that property will, or will not, be used in some specified manner.

covenant against waste A restriction imposed by a mortgagee prohibiting the mortgagor from allowing the building to deteriorate during the period of the mortgage.

covenant of seizin A mortgage clause whereby the mortgagor warrants that he or she is the lawful owner of the property being mortgaged.

covenant of title A promise or assurance made by the grantor in connection with title transfer

debt amortization The process of gradually extinguishing a debt by a series of periodic payments to the creditor.

debt constant The percentage of the original principal amount that must be paid annually in order to fully repay interest and principal over the term of the loan. The constant can be expressed as an annual percentage or monthly percentage. Sometimes called a *debt-service constant.*

debt coverage ratio The relationship between a project's annual net operating income and the obligation to make principal and interest payments on borrowed funds. Debt coverage ratios are often employed to evaluate a lender's margin of safety regarding mortgage loans.

debt service Payments to a lender. Debt-service obligations may involve payment of interest only or both principal and interest so as to fully or partially amortize a debt over a specified term.

debt-service constant See debt constant.

debt-to-equity ratio The ratio between borrowed funds and equity funds.

deed   A legal document that conveys title in real property from one party to another. The document must be signed, witnessed, delivered, and accepted.

default   A mortgagor's failure to fulfill any of the agreed-upon terms in a security agreement.

default ratio   See breakeven ratio.

defeasance clause   Mortgage provisions intended to render nominal conveyance void upon satisfaction of the mortgagor's obligation.

deficiency judgment   A judgment against a debtor's personal assets beyond those assets owned on a defaulted debt instrument.

delivery   The legal act of transferring ownership of real estate.

depreciable property   Property upon which a tax- deductible depreciation allowance may be claimed.

depreciation   Decline in an asset's value or useful life because of wear, tear, action of the elements, or obsolescence.

depreciation allowance   A tax-deductible allowance to account for the decline in value or useful life of an asset because of wear, tear, obsolescence, or action of the elements

discount points   A reduction in net loan proceeds to make the effective interest rate equal the current market rate.

discount rate   A rate that measures return on investment after the recovery of invested capital

discounted cash-flow approach   An investment evaluation technique that incorporates adjustments for both volume and timing of anticipated future cash flows and is generally accepted as the most desirable approach to evaluating opportunities

discounting   Expressing anticipated future cash flows as present-worth equivalents.

earnest money   Money paid as evidence of good faith or actual intent to complete a transaction, usually forfeited by willful failure to complete the transaction.

easement   Nonpossessory interest that permits limited use of someone else's land. Conveys only a right to use the land.

effective gross income   Potential gross rental revenue, minus losses for vacancies and uncollectible accounts, plus income from related sources.

effective interest rates   Rates actually paid for the use of borrowed funds. Effective rates are a function of the amount borrowed and the amount and timing of the required repayment.

efficient markets   Markets in which all relevant information is immediately and fully reflected in market prices. Participants in efficient markets are unable to consistently achieve above-average market yields. The hypothesis that a market is completely efficient is referred to as the strong form of the efficiency hypothesis.

eminent domain   Authority vested in both federal and state governments allowing them to take private property for public use without the owner's consent.

encumbrances   A lien, charge, or claim against real property that diminishes the value of the property but does not prevent the passing of title.

end loan   A loan secured by a mortgage on a completed building, terminating a chain of loans to finance land acquisition and construction. Also called a *permanent loan* or a *takeout loan.*

end-loan commitment   An agreement by a lender to provide an end loan upon satisfaction of all contingencies specified by the lender.

equitable right of redemption   The legal right of a borrower, or the borrower's heirs or assigns, to redeem mortgaged property for a limited period of time after default. Also called *equity of redemption.*

equity of redemption   See equitable right of redemption.

equity REIT   A type of real estate investment trust that concentrates its resources on equity interests in real property.

equity yield rate   Annual equity cash flow divided by down payment.

escalator clause   Lease clause that requires tenants to pay all operating expenses above amounts specified in the lease.

escheat   The legal principle that property title reverts to the state when an intestate owner (one with no will) dies with no heirs.

escrow   The holding by a third party of something of value that is the subject of a contract between two other parties, until the contract has been consummated.

feasibility study   Estimate of the likelihood of achieving explicit project objectives through a proposed course of action, given a specific set of constraints and limited resources.

financial leverage   The impact of borrowed money on investment return. That is, the use of borrowed money to amplify consequences to equity investors

foreclosure by sale   Sale of mortgaged property at public auction as a consequence of default by the mortgagor. Foreclosure by sale extinguishes the equitable right of redemption.

foreclosure decree   A court order specifying an exact time period (a period determined by state laws) during which the equity of redemption will exist.

free and clear rate of return   See overall capitalization rate.

functional efficiency   A measure of how well a property performs its intended function.

functional obsolescence   The loss of functional efficiency due to defective or dated design. This reduces a building's competitive position relative to more functionally efficient structures and may eventually lead to abandonment or succession of use.

gap financing   See standby financing.

graduated-payment mortgage (GPM)   A mortgage that allows a borrower, in effect, to borrow additional money during the early years of the mortgage to reduce the monthly mortgage payment obligation during those early years. This additional loan is added to the mortgage and is repaid by increased debt-service obligation in the later years.

grantee   A person to whom a grant is made; the purchaser.

grantor   A person who conveys real estate by deed; the seller.

gross income multiplier   Evaluation technique that describes the relationship between most probable sales price and gross revenue. Sometimes called a *gross rent multiplier*.

gross rent multiplier   See gross income multiplier.

hedging   Taking an investment position that will pay off even if the investor's primary investment does not. Hedging reduces aggregate investor risk.

historic structure   See certified historic structure.

hurdle rate   The minimum acceptable yield on investment funds. Projects that are not expected to yield at least the investor's hurdle rate are rejected.

hybrid REIT   A real estate investment trust that mixes mortgage and equity instruments in its portfolio.

income multiplier analysis   A technique for expressing the relationship between price and either gross or net income.

incubator buildings Relatively small, multitenant structures in which new or small-but-growing firms rent space on an interim basis until growth generates a need for larger quarters.

information search costs The cost of generating relevant market information. High information search costs tend to reduce market efficiency.

initial tax basis The tax basis of a property at the time of acquisition. Usually, cost plus any additional outlays required to ensure good and defensible title.

installment sales contract Contract that sets forth terms and conditions under which a seller is obligated to render a deed of conveyance to the buyer at some future date. Also called a *land contract, contract for deed,* or *articles of agreement.*

installment sales method A method for reporting sales to the IRS whereby a portion of the resulting income tax liability may be deferred when some of the proceeds from the sale are not collected during the current taxable year.

interim financing Financing used during the construction phase, to be superseded by takeout financing after construction is completed.

internal rate of return A financial analysis technique that involves setting net present value at zero and finding a discount rate to satisfy the equality condition; that is, the discount rate that makes present value exactly equal to required initial cash outlay.

intrastate offering A security issue offered for sale solely within one state by an issuer resident in or a corporation incorporated and doing business in that state. A qualifying intrastate offering is exempt from requirements for federal registration.

investment interest limitation Provision of the Internal Revenue Code that places a dollar limit on the amount of investment interest that can be deducted in any one taxable year on loans used to finance investments.

investment tax credit A credit against income tax liability, earned as a consequence of investing in qualifying assets.

investment value The summation of the present value of the equity position plus the present value of the debt position. The present value of the equity position is calculated on an after-tax basis and considers the tax consequences to a specific investor.

joint tenancy An estate held jointly by two or more persons under the same title in which each has the same degree of interest and the same right of possession. Joint tenancy usually entails the right of the surviving tenant(s) to take title to a decedent's interest (right of survivorship).

junior mortgage   A mortgage that is legally subordinate to another (senior) mortgage.

land contract   See installment sales contract.

lease   Legal document conveying limited right to use a property. Document generally specifies all terms of lease as well as permitted use.

leasehold   Right of a tenant in leased property.

leasehold interest   A tenant's claim against a fee holder's property rights.

lessee   The holder of a leasehold interest in a property. Generally referred to as a *tenant*.

lessor   A property owner who transfers certain rights for a limited period to a tenant. Generally referred to as a *landlord*.

lien   Claim against a property that allows the proceeds from a forced sale of the property to be used to satisfy the debt.

like-kind exchange   Exchanges of assets deemed under Internal Revenue Code Section 1031 to be of like kind. Gains or losses on exchanges that involve only like-kind assets must be deferred until the newly acquired (substitute) asset is disposed of. Transactions that are only partially like-kind may result in total or partial recognition of gains or losses. Also frequently called *tax-free exchanges* or *Section 1031 exchanges*.

limited partner   See limited partnership.

limited partnership   An ownership arrangement involving one or more general partners and one or more limited partners. General partners assume full liability for debts of the partnership and exercise control over operations, while a limited partner's liability is limited to the extent of actual capital contribution to the partnership or additional liability voluntarily assumed.

linkages   Relationships requiring the movement of goods or people from one location to another.

liquidity   Ability to convert an asset to cash without incurring loss.

loan broker   Individual who places loans with primary lenders for a fee.

loan commitment   Obligation of a lender to provide specific funds at some future date. Terms may be specified, or they may be those prevailing on the date funds are advanced.

loan origination fee   A charge by a lender assessed at the time a loan commitment is made or at the time funds are advanced.

loan-to-value ratio   Relationship of debt funds to total project value, stated as a percentage.

locational advantages   Advantages garnered by an occupant caused solely by the locational desirability of a site.

locational benefits   The benefits derived from the use of real estate that are properly attributable to the desirability of the site location.

market value   The price at which a property can be acquired on the open market in an arm's-length transaction under all conditions requisite to a fair sale. The generally accepted definition presumes that both buyer and seller act prudently and knowledgeably and that the price is not affected by undue stimulus experienced by either party.

monthly constant   The monthly debt-service obligation expressed as a percentage of the amount borrowed.

mortgage   A document that pledges real estate as collateral for a loan.

mortgage-backed securities   Securities backed by real estate mortgages as collateral.

mortgage bankers   Individuals or firms that originate real estate loans. They may either hold such loans in their own investment portfolios or sell them in the secondary market.

mortgage commitment   Obligation on the part of a lender to provide funds at some future date. Loan terms may be either fixed or those that prevail at the time the funds are to be advanced.

mortgage correspondents   Individual mortgage bankers or brokers representing an institutional lender in a specified geographic location.

mortgage participation certificates   A bond backed by real estate as collateral. Bondholders participate in the proceeds of a group of mortgages that back the certificates.

mortgage REIT   A real estate investment trust that invests primarily in real estate loans secured by first mortgages.

mortgage warehousing   The process of accumulating a portfolio of real estate loans that are subsequently sold to investors.

mortgagee   Party to whom real estate is pledged under the terms of a mortgage. Typically the lender in a real estate transaction.

mortgagor   Party pledging real estate under the terms of a mortgage. Borrower who pledges real estate as collateral for a loan.

most probable selling price   A probabilistic estimate of the price at which a future property transaction will occur; a prediction of the transaction price for a property that is offered for sale under current market conditions for a reasonable length of time at terms of sale currently predominant for such properties.

neighborhood shopping centers   Shopping centers that serve a trade area from which customers can commute by automobile within roughly five to ten minutes. Anchor tenants are usually food stores and drug stores, which may occupy a combined total area between 35,000 and 50,000 square feet.

net cash flow   Net monetary benefits an individual or group of individuals receive as a reward for committing funds to an enterprise. Net cash flow before taxes ignores the tax effect of investments, and net cash flow after taxes accounts for the tax effects of investment.

net income multiplier   Property market value expressed as a multiple of its net operating income.

net lease   Lease arrangement under which tenants are required to pay all property operating costs.

net operating expenses   Total expenses associated with the operations of a real estate project.

net operating income   Effective gross revenue minus operating expenses.

net present value   Current capital value of all the benefits of an investment minus the required initial cash outlay.

nominal interest rates   Quoted cost of borrowing. Actual or effective interest rates may be substantially higher because of charges such as loan origination fees and the cost of maintaining required compensating balances.

normalized expenses   An appraisal term for the operating expenses of a property as they would occur in a typical year.

normalized net operating income The net income figure that would result when a typical year's operating expenses were subtracted from a typical year's effective gross income.

offering memorandum A document intended to fully disclose the nature of a private offering of a security.

operating expense ratio Operating expenses expressed as a percentage of gross income. Sometimes called simply *operating ratio*.

operating expenses Cash expenditures required to maintain property in sufficient condition to generate effective gross revenue.

operating ratio See operating expense ratio.

opportunity cost of capital Forgone opportunity to earn interest on funds committed to other investments.

option agreement An agreement giving one party the right to buy or sell an asset within a specified time period at a fixed or determinable price.

overall capitalization rate Net operating income divided by a property's market value. Also called the *free and clear rate of return*.

partial release A mortgage clause providing for segments of a property to be released after specified lump-sum payments on the loan. Typically used in subdivision and development financing.

partnership agreement Document that specifies the rights and responsibilities of individuals who join together to carry on a business for profit. May be oral, but is usually written.

passive activity Any trade or business is passive for a taxpayer who is not actively involved in operations on a regular, continuous, and substantial (year-round) basis.

passive activity income Income from passive trade or business activities. Income from passive activities can be used to offset losses from other passive activities. Any passive activity income not offset by losses is merged with taxable income from other sources.

passive activity losses Losses from passive trade or business activities. Passive activity losses can generally be offset against only passive activity income. Any remaining passive activity losses, with certain important exceptions, must be carried over and applied against future years' passive activity income, even though a taxpayer may have substantial taxable income from nonpassive sources during the year of the loss.

pass-through certificates Certificates backed by a pool of insured mortgages. Interest and principal collected is used to pay interest on the certificates as well as retire them.

payback period The amount of time required for an investor to recover the capital committed to a venture.

payee Individual to whom a promise has been made to repay a specified sum at some future date under the provisions of a promissory note.

percentage clause Lease provision that specifies rental based on some base rate plus a percentage of the tenant's gross sales.

percentage lease Lease that provides for rental payments based upon the tenant's gross sales.

permanent loan See end loan.

perpetuity A never-ending stream of payments or receipts.

personal property Ownership interests in all properties other than real property. Examples include securities, partnership interest in a business, and ownership of an automobile. Also called *personalty*.

personalty See personal property.

physical deterioration Term used by appraisers to describe any loss in value caused by physical wear.

plat Diagram of a subdivision showing the location of all streets, sites, and easements.

portfolio income Income from interest, dividends, rents, royalties, gain from disposition of investment property, passive activity income that is treated as portfolio income under the phase-in rules of the Tax Reform Act of 1986, and income from a trade or business in which the taxpayer does not materially participate (unless the activity is a passive activity under the passive loss rules).

potential gross income The maximum amount of revenue a property would produce if fully rented at market rates.

potential gross rent The amount of rental revenue a property would generate if there were no vacancies.

preliminary prospectus Memorandum providing full disclosure of all items pertinent to a public security offering. A preliminary prospectus must be submitted to and approved by the SEC prior to any advertising of the offering.

prepayment clause Typically a clause in a mortgage specifying penalties to be paid by the borrower in the event a loan is prepaid.

present value   The value today of anticipated future receipts or disbursements.

primary mortgage markets   Markets in which real estate loans originate.

principal   In finance, the amount upon which interest liability is computed.

private placement   Sale of a securities offering to a small group as opposed to a public offering, where sale is advertised to the general public. Sometimes called a *private offering*.

private placement memorandum   Prospectus for a private placement. Does not have to be submitted for SEC approval, but must provide full disclosure.

profitability index   Measure of present value per dollar of cash outlay, calculated by dividing the present value of expected future cash flows by the initial cash outlay.

promissory note   Agreement containing promise to pay a specified sum at some specific future date.

prospectus   A document that fully discloses the nature of a securities offering.

purchase-money mortgage   Mortgage given by a buyer to a seller to secure partial payment of the purchase price. A purchase-money mortgage is typically recorded when deed is passed, establishing its precedence over all other claims.

purchase option   The right to purchase a property within a specified time and at a predetermined price.

quiet title suit   Suit filed by an adverse possessor to gain title to property, or by any other claimant in an attempt to remove a cloud from the title.

quitclaim deed   A deed that purports to convey only those rights in a property that are possessed by the person making the conveyance, with no warrants that any such rights in fact exist.

real estate investment trusts (REITs)   Untaxed corporate entities organized to pool the resources of individuals for investment in real estate. Some REITs invest in mortgages while others take ownership positions.

Real Property Administrator (RPA)   Professional designation conferred on property managers by the Building Owners and Managers Association International. Designation is a sign of professional achievement for those who completely fulfill prescribed educational and experiential requirements.

recovery property   Property subject to the cost recovery allowance provisions first introduced into the tax system by the 1981 revision of the Internal Revenue Code.

red herring   Term sometimes used for a preliminary securities prospectus that must be submitted to and approved by the SEC before any advertising is undertaken for a public issue.

redlining   Term used to describe the unwillingness of certain financial institutions to provide real property financing in certain areas; derived from the practice of delineating areas with red lines on city maps.

regional shopping center   A shopping center that draws the majority of its customers from a trade area extending from 15 to 30 minutes in driving time from the center. It may encompass 200,000 to 400,000 square feet of retail space and usually features one or two major department stores as anchor tenants.

registered historic district   Any area listed in the National Registry of Historic Places. Also includes any area so designated by appropriate state or local statute, provided that the Secretary of the Interior certifies that the statute will substantially achieve its purpose of preservation and rehabilitation and that the district meets substantially all the requirements for listing in the National Registry.

renegotiable rate mortgage   Mortgage with an interest rate subject to redetermination at fixed intervals as specified in the body of the mortgage or the accompanying promissory note.

rent concessions   Agreements between landlord and tenant that reduce actual rental payments or receipts below those specified in a lease. A landlord might, for example, give one month's free occupancy, thereby reducing the effective rental rate over the entire occupancy period. Also simply called *concessions*.

rent escalator clauses   Lease provisions that require tenants to pay all operating expenses above amounts specified in their leases.

rent roll   A record of all tenants showing the rent paid by each.

reservation   Clause used in a deed to withhold some portion of the grantor's property rights.

restrictive covenant   Promise to refrain from using land or buildings for purposes specified in the clause creating the covenant.

right to rescind   Right of an individual to terminate an agreement, returning all parties to the legal position or relationship existing prior to the agreement.

risk-free discount rate Opportunity cost of capital based on riskless alternative investments.

secondary mortgage market A market in which existing mortgage notes are traded.

Section 1031 exchange See like-kind exchange.

seizin A covenant found in a warranty deed whereby the grantor warrants that he or she does in fact possess the rights or interest being transferred.

senior mortgage A mortgage that takes priority over all other mortgages.

specific asset syndication A type of syndication where the promoter gains control of a property and then assembles a group of investors.

spread The difference between interest earned on mortgage loans and interest paid to depositors by financial intermediaries.

standby financing An arrangement wherein a lender agrees to keep a certan amount of money available to a prospective borrower for a specified period of time.

standby loan commitment A binding option, sold for a nonreturnable standby fee by a lender to a borrower, providing that the lender will loan a specific amount on stated terms to a borrower at any time within a stated future period. The borrower may or may not exercise the option.

statutory right of redemption A statutory right granting a defaulting mortgagor an additional opportunity to recover foreclosed property. Limited in time by state statute.

strict foreclosure Foreclosure accomplished by transferring a defaulting mortgagor's title directly to the mortgagee.

subordination agreement A clause in a mortgage or lease stating that the right of the holder shall be secondary or subordinate to a subsequent encumbrance.

subscription agreement A document that specifies the relationship between limited partners and the sponsoring general partner in a limited partnership arrangement.

substitute basis The initial tax basis of property acquired in a like-kind exchange. The substitute basis reflects any deferred gain or loss on the property tendered in the exchange.

superregional shopping center A shopping center that draws customers from an extremely wide geographical area and supports very large concentrations of retail facilities. Superregional centers frequently feature as much as 500,000 to 750,000 square feet of retail space. They may have as many as four major department stores as anchor tenants.

syndicate A group of two or more people united for the purpose of making and operating an investment. A syndicate may operate as a corporation, a general partnership, or a limited partnership.

tax basis See initial tax basis.

tax conduit A partnership characteristic whereby tax-deductible losses pass through the partnership and are reported by each partner in accordance with his or her individual ownership interest in the partnership.

tax credits Direct offsets against a taxpayer's income tax liability, provided as tax incentives to induce actions thought to be in the best interests of the nation.

tax-deferred exchange See like-kind exchange.

tax-free exchange See like-kind exchange.

tax lien A lien placed on taxpayer's property by government for nonpayment of taxes.

tax preference item Tax deductions or exemptions that are added back to adjusted gross income for purposes of computing the alternative minimum tax liability.

tax stops Lease provisions that require tenants to pay all property taxes beyond some specified level.

title closing The meeting of parties to a sales contract at a designated place and time for the purpose of executing the contract.

title defect A possible legal difficulty that may limit the marketability of the title.

title insurance Insurance against losses resulting from the passage of legally invalid title, issued by a title insurance company after a title search by that company has established that legally valid title exists in the seller, who then is able to pass that title to the insured.

title search A circumspect review of all pertinent documents and records to determine if a seller has good title to the property.

trade area The geographic area from which a store or shopping center draws the majority of its patronage.

transaction costs Items such as brokerage fees, recording fees, transfer taxes, and attorney's fees, incurred in connection with a real estate transaction.

transaction price The price at which a transaction actually occurred; the outcome of a bargaining process between buyer and seller.

unfavorable financial leverage Use of borrowed funds when their cost exceeds the rate of return on assets being financed.

Uniform Limited Partnership Act A model law to govern creation and operation of limited partnership entities that has been enacted (in some cases, in substantially revised form) by every state except Louisiana.

variable rate mortgage A financing instrument that permits the lender to alter the interest rate, with a certain period of advanced notice, based on a specific base index.

vendee The purchaser of real estate under articles of agreement or a contract for deed.

vendor The seller of real estate under articles of agreement or a contract for deed.

voluntary conveyance Voluntary transfer by a defaulting mortgagor of the mortgaged property to the mortgagee, to avoid a foreclosure suit and a possible deficiency judgment.

warranty deed A deed that contains a clause warranting that title to real property is clear and the property is unencumbered.

wraparound lender Assumes responsibility for meeting debt-service obligations on the mortgage note that has been wrapped.

wraparound mortgage A mortgage subordinate to, but still including a balance due on a pre-existing mortgage note, in addition to any amount to be disbursed on the new note. Also called an *all-inclusive mortgage*.

INDEX